THE SANCTUARY.

AND THERE WAS SEEN IN HIS TEMPLE
THE ARK OF HIS TESTAMENT.

THE

SANCTUARY

AND THE

TWENTY-THREE HUNDRED DAYS

—— OF ——

DANIEL VIII, 14.

BY URIAH SMITH.

"Unto two thousand and three hundred days, then shall the sanctuary be cleansed."

STEAM PRESS
OF THE SEVENTH-DAY ADVENTIST PUBLISHING ASSOCIATION.
BATTLE CREEK, MICH.
1877.

PREFACE.

In introducing to the reader a work on the subject of the sanctuary, we have no occasion to make any apology for adding another to the multitude of books that have been written on this subject; for no such multitude of books on this question exists. Indeed, we know of but two works that have preceded this, each of them published under the auspices of the same denomination to which the writer of this belongs, and each of them advocating the same view that is here presented. The first of these was by Eld. J. N. Andrews, author of the History of the Sabbath, and other important works, and who, though the pioneer in the presentation of the subject, left no essential feature to be discovered by additional light. It was thought that the importance of this subject would warrant a work giving it a more extended examination and setting forth more fully the reasons upon which it rests. To this thought the present volume owes its existence.

That which is perhaps most calculated to excite our wonder in connection with this subject is the fact that a question so intimately connected with, and so essentially modifying, some of the most important subjects of the Bible, should have lain so long unnoticed. And this furnishes all the greater reason why, now that light is shining upon it, and its commanding position in the great temple of truth is discovered, the most earnest efforts should be made to bring it to the attention of the people.

This subject is intimately connected with the prophecies, and this may be one reason why it has not sooner come up for consideration; for it has been reserved to this present generation, living in "the time of the end," to behold the seal broken from the prophetic page and to see a wonderful increase of knowledge respecting its soul-inspiring utterances. But an understanding of the subject of the sanctuary is essential to the understanding of some of the most important of these prophetic records.

There is, it is said, in Rome a room the walls of which are covered with tracings which to the beholder, as he enters, appear but a mass of inextricable confusion. But as he reaches one certain point in the room, immediately all lines fall into place, all forms assume their due proportion, the laws of perspective assert their sway, and the room appears covered with harmonious and beautiful imagery.

The sanctuary occupies this true point of perspective in the prophetic apartment of the Sacred Scriptures. From it the unity and harmony of the prophetic lines can be seen as from no other standpoint.

It is interwoven also with subjects of the greatest practical importance; and we commend it to the reader as having a wider bearing and involving a greater number of important topics than any other subject to which our attention is called by the unfoldings of prophecy.

U. S.

July, 1877.

CONTENTS.

THE SANCTUARY.

Chapter One.

THE SUBJECT INTRODUCED.

THE Sanctuary—what is it? when is it? where is it? What are its uses, and why? What its relations, and how extensive? What part does it act in the great scheme of human redemption? What prominence is given to it on the inspired pages of the book of God's revelation to men? What bearing has it upon the interpretation of the prophecies? How is its past history calculated to interest, or how does its present work concern, us? What claims has it upon our attention? In what way are our dearest interests connected with it?

The traveler who visits those marked spots where nature has displayed her most marvelous works or her profoundest mysteries, avails himself of the aid of a guide, who has explored each perilous path, knows the way to wonders and beauties hidden from a stranger's eye, and understands what dangers beset the steps of the unwary. We have to some extent explored this remarkable subject, and would be glad to point out to him who has not made it his study some of the beauties we have discovered, though we may have been able to explore but a small proportion of the whole. Those who have acquainted themselves with what the Bible teaches upon this question, will understand the correctness of the following statements. To those who have not, we will offer abundant proof of their truthfulness, if they will go with us in this investigation.

Let us then say, by way of anticipation, that the sanctuary is a great central object in the plan of salvation. Next to our Lord himself and his work, it claims our attention, as the place where the wonderful process of a world's redemption is carried forward. There is no one subject which so fully as this unites together all parts of revelation into one harmonious whole. The spokes of a wheel, considered by themselves and apart, may be symmetrical and beautiful; but their uses are made apparent and their utility demonstrated only when, fixed together by a central hub and exterior fellies, they appear as component parts of a perfect wheel. In the great wheel of truth, the sanctuary occupies this central position. In it, the great truths of revelation find their focal point. From it, in every direction, they radiate. It unites the two great dispensations, the Mosaic and the Christian, and shows their relation to each other. It divides with no other subject the high honor of explaining the position and work of our Lord Jesus Christ. Like a brilliant lamp introduced into a darkened room, it illuminates the whole Mosaic economy. In the light of this subject, the books of Moses, with their detail of offerings and sacrifices, their minutiæ of rites and ceremonies, usually considered so void of interest and use, if not of meaning also, become animated with life and radiant with consistency and beauty.

It is a key to the interpretation of the most important prophecies which are having their fulfillment at the present time. We confidently assert that no person who either ignores this subject, or misapprehends it, can rightly interpret the prophecies for this time. While with this subject understood, it is almost as difficult to come to wrong conclusions as it is otherwise impossible to reach correct ones. These may seem like bold and rash assertions; but they are uttered only under the firmest conviction that they can be made good to the mind of every intelligent and candid reader.

Strange that a subject occupying so important a position in the divine economy should have been so long overlooked. Strange that so few even now are found to give it in any degree their attention, still less their study. In one movement only is it made a prominent feature. By one people only is it made a special subject, discussed in full, and dwelt upon with delight.

It has come up of necessity in the study of the prophecies. In one line it is the objective point to which the prophecy looks. When that point is reached, it thenceforth becomes, in that line, the principal object. To give it that place, is to furnish presumptive proof that the prophecy is understood and correctly handled. To leave it out, is to nullify the prophecy, and confess one's self lost and bewildered in its interpretation. That Seventh-day Adventists give it this place, not only in that line of prophecy where it so prominently appears, but in all others connected more or less remotely therewith, we offer as proof that they are the ones who now believe and teach in accordance with the true light of prophetic development.

Another important purpose which this subject

serves, in connection with a great question before the world at the present time, may receive a passing remark at this point. The present generation has seen a religious movement such as no other generation ever witnessed: a world-wide agitation of the question of Christ's immediate second coming, calling out hundreds of thousands of believers in the doctrine. Time has continued; and under the name of Millerism it now receives the flippant sneer of the careless multitude. But the fact that such a remarkable movement has been made, nevertheless remains; and its significance cannot be lost.

It must have been a mighty influence of some kind, which was sufficient to impress men simultaneously in almost every quarter of the globe to go forth and proclaim to their fellow-men the approaching advent of the Messiah. It must have been no small accumulation of evidence which could lead men of the best minds and highest culture to give the assent of their judgment to the validity of the proof and the truthfulness of the position. The concurrent testimony of all the Scriptures, and the corroborative evidence of the signs of the times, formed a fortress of truth of impregnable strength. The Advent body were a unit, and their testimony shook the world.

Suddenly their power was broken, their strength scattered, their ranks divided, and their testimony paralyzed. They passed the point of their expectation, and realized not their hope. That a mistake had been made somewhere, none could deny. From that point, the history of the majority of that once happy, united people has been marked by discord, division, confusion, speculation, new mistakes, fresh disappointments, disintegration and apostasy. The world, without careful scrutiny, looks complacently upon this result, and, relieved of its anxiety respecting the Lord's coming, is wont to regard all classes of Adventists as only the remnants of an exploded delusion.

But there is a remedy for this state of things, an explanation why a movement so evidently led at first by divine agency, has fallen into such misfortunes and weakness.

The sanctuary is the one subject which brings order out of all this chaos, points out the mistake, shows where and how it was made, reveals the rock on which so many have foundered, vindicates the past movement, and points out the path to further truth and final triumph.

To him, therefore, who feels any interest in the past Advent movement, this subject must be one of exceeding interest. And to him who feels nothing more than a curiosity to investigate the phenomena of one of the most remarkable religious movements of this or any other age, we believe it has features which will well repay the examination of at least a leisure hour.

We therefore call the attention of all to the subject of the sanctuary as one of great importance, interest, and profit.

It is a subject of great importance on account of the position it holds in the divine plan.

It is one of interest, so intimately is it connected with the work of our redemption.

Received, it will affect the life, to elevate and sanctify, and so be found at last to be one of infinite profit.

Chapter Two.

CONNECTION WITH PROPHECY.

IT has already been stated that in the fulfillment of one of the most important lines of prophecy given in the Bible, the sanctuary becomes the principal object presented to our view. The prophecy referred to is that found in the 8th chapter of Daniel. As we travel down over the line of that prophecy, made plain and smooth to our feet, like the level, well-beaten path of a public thoroughfare, suddenly we find suspended over and across the way a banner with this remarkable inscription:—

"UNTO TWO THOUSAND AND THREE HUNDRED DAYS; THEN SHALL THE SANCTUARY BE CLEANSED." Verse 14.

Raising the inquiry, why and by whom these words were spoken, we find they were called out by a conversation between two of the angels of God. And the question raised by one was answered by the other, not to the speaker, but to the prophet Daniel. The question was, "How long shall be the vision concerning the daily sacrifice and the transgression of desolation, to give both the sanctuary and the host to be trodden under foot?" And in answer, the angel turning to Daniel said, "Unto two thousand and three hundred days; then shall the sanctuary be cleansed."

The question is one which is calculated to enlist our whole attention. It is one of deepest interest; for it pertains to the time when the heel of oppression shall be forever lifted from the host, the people of God, and opposing powers shall no longer be able to pervert his worship.

The time was when the words here spoken, "Unto two thousand and three hundred days, then shall the sanctuary be cleansed," were household words with every happy believer in the Lord's soon coming. They were emblazoned on the shield of every soldier in the Advent ranks. They were joyfully uttered from many lips as the watchword of their most ardent desires and their brightest hopes. But the times, in this respect, are strangely altered. Over a portion of the Advent body a mysterious silence now reigns concerning this positive and prominent promise. Lips which were once its joyful heralds seem now to be sealed to its utterance. It seems by some to be studiously ignored, avoided, and set aside. But ignored and set aside it cannot be. The glowing prophecy, of which it forms so conspicuous a part, and which must enter into every Advent theory, forbids that it should be passed by unnoticed. There are some things in the regions of prophetic truth, as well as in the political world, which are the occasion of "irrepressible conflict;" and this is one of them. Men may not think to avoid it by giving their attention to other themes, and passing it by in silence. In every theory, deserving the name of theory, which professes to show the present age of the world, and the nearness of the great consummation, it imperatively demands a place and an explanation. It is the embarrassing specter which, with unvarying constancy, confronts every theory which would endeavor, with ill-concealed dread of its just claims, to turn aside from the strait path to avoid its presence. And it is well that it should be so; for it claims no more than it deserves; it presents no demands which the lover of truth ought not promptly and willingly to grant.

What, therefore, has been the cause of this change? Why are not these words dwelt upon by all, as formerly, with frequency and pleasure? To this question but one answer can be given. The expectations based upon this scripture have once been disappointed; and the different methods adopted by different individuals to account for that disappointment, determine their views of the sanctuary and 2300 days.

The fact has already been alluded to, that, previous to the autumn of 1844, the Advent people were a unit. Zealous for the great doctrine of the soon coming of their Redeemer, clothed with the blessing and power of God, devoted, harmonious, united, they presented a spectacle which made the saints rejoice and the world tremble. But since the tenth day of the seventh month, Oct. 22, Jewish time of that year, dissension and division have been to a mournful degree inscribed upon their history, and the paths they have taken have been various and divergent. The cause of this division must be found in some question involved, in some point at issue, in the events of that memorable day.

The expectation then entertained was, that at that point of time the Lord would come. Arguments had been produced, invulnerable to all the attacks of opposers, and entirely satisfactory to all lovers of the Advent doctrine at that time, that the 2300 days would end in 1844. Making this fact a starting-point, an argument was easily constructed as follows:—

The prophecy asserts that the sanctuary shall

then be cleansed. The sanctuary is the earth, or at least some portion of the earth. Its cleansing is to be by fire. But the renovation of the earth by fire is to take place only at the second coming of the Lord. Therefore the Lord will come at the termination of the 2300 days. The point of time at length came; but the Lord did not. No cleansing of the earth by fire took place; and believers were still left here upon the earth, having then not only their own disappointment to bear, which was grievous and keen, but also the flood of obloquy and reproach which the world poured upon them. What was the matter? Where had the mistake been made? What was the cause of the disappointment?

On this point different views are entertained, and different opinions advanced. Before examining these, let it be remembered that God cannot be the author of the confusion that has existed since that time in some branches of the Advent body. All the various theories that have since sprung up, cannot every one be true. And yet every Adventist will admit that the truth of God at the present day must be found in connection with the Advent doctrine. Every Adventist will admit that if God designs, previous to the coming of the Lord, to warn the world of that event, the great Advent movement of 1840–1844, in so far as it tended to arouse a slumbering world to the fact that we are living in the time of the end, and to warn them of the nearness of the close of probation, and the consummation of all things, was in the order and purpose of God. He must therefore still have a people on the earth as a result of that movement; he must still have a truth among men bearing some relation to that great work; and there must be some correct explanation of the great disappointment connected with that movement.

The theory of the time, as held in 1844, consisted of two main propositions: 1. That the 2300 days would end in 1844. 2. That the earth was the sanctuary then to be cleansed. So, based upon these two propositions, two answers are given to the question why those who looked for their Lord at that time were disappointed. The first is, that the reckoning of the time was wrong. The second is, that the view taken of the sanctuary was wrong. More fully expressed, the matter stands thus: One class answers, We were disappointed because the 2300 days did not then expire, and consequently the time had not come for the earth to be cleansed with fire; the other class answers, We were disappointed because, though the days did then terminate, as we believed they would, neither the earth nor any part of the earth is the sanctuary which was then to be cleansed.

Either of these answers would be sufficient to explain the disappointment; and both have been offered by different ones. But it will be seen that they are at perfect antipodes to each other; and it remains to determine which is the correct one.

We inquire, then, Is it correct to say that the time was wrongly calculated, and that the 2300 did not end in 1844? Previous to 1844, the Advent people had unanimously held that Dan. 9 was a key to chapter 8, and that the seventy weeks of Dan. 9:24–27, afforded a clue to the explanation of the 2300 days of chapter 8. Immediately on the passing of the time, a large class denied that the 2300 days did end in 1844; but they were not agreed in regard to the manner of sustaining their new position, and two methods have been resorted to, as follows:—

The first is to deny the connection between Dan. 8 and 9, between the seventy weeks and the 2300 days. This class claim that the seventy weeks of Dan. 9 are no part of the 2300 days of Dan. 8, and that, consequently, the date of the former does in nowise determine the date of the latter. They acknowledge that the date assigned by all Adventists previous to 1844, for the commencement of the seventy weeks, namely B. C. 457, cannot be disproved; but as they are no part of the 2300 days, they furnish no clue to the commencement of that period. Where the 2300 days did commence, or what event marked their beginning, they cannot tell. This much only, on this point, they profess to know, that is, they did not end in 1844, because the earth is the sanctuary, and the earth was not then burned.

Those who resort to the second method to show that the 2300 days did not end in 1844, acknowledge the validity of the arguments by which the seventy weeks are shown to be a part of the 2300 days, as held by all Adventists up to 1844, but deny that the date of their commencement was rightly placed in B. C. 457. Commencing at that point, they would end in 1844; but this class, like the one first mentioned, contend that they could not then have ended, and for the very same reason, namely, because the earth is the sanctuary, and earth was not then burned.

From this general survey of the subject, one

would be led to conclude that there was something all-potent in the theory that the earth is the sanctuary. From what it has done, we should suppose it had been able to intrench itself behind infallible evidence. It has led the majority of those who were in the past Advent movement, while divided on many other points, to agree on this, that the 2300 days did not end in 1844. It has led them to make a full surrender of positions which were once acknowledged to be the ground and pillar of the Advent faith; positions which able men were led to take when their hearts were glowing with a newly found and life-giving truth, and their intellects quickened by the out-pouring of the Spirit and power of God; positions which passed unscathed through the most fiery ordeal of scrutiny and opposition to which, perhaps, it has been the lot of any truth in any age to be subjected; positions which stood the test when the world was aroused to the subject of the Advent as never before nor since, when opposition was called forth in all its strength, and the highest worldly wisdom played its heaviest batteries against the unpopular movement. The reason which would lead men to abandon positions like these should be infinitely weighty; but these positions have all been surrendered to the solitary view, which has thus been set up paramount to them all, that the earth is the sanctuary. Where is the mighty array of evidence by which this is sustained? All that has been, or can be, produced, it will not be difficult to find, as we proceed.

We therefore invite the reader to a brief review of the argument respecting the reckoning of the time, and then to an exhaustive search for some vestige of proof that the earth, or any part of it, is the sanctuary. The objects of inquiry are not complicated, the issue is plain, and we may hope to reach conclusions which are clear and satisfactory.

Chapter Three.

EXPOSITION OF DAN. 8.

THE preceding chapter closed with the inquiry upon our hands, Did the 2300 days end in 1844? The answer to this question involves an answer to two other questions already noticed; namely, 1. Are the seventy weeks of Dan. 9 a part of the 2300 days of Dan. 8? and, 2. Are they rightly dated from B. C. 457? To determine these points, it will be necessary to look briefly at the prophecy of Dan. 8, in which the mention of the 2300 days is found. Beginning with the second verse of that chapter, several objects presented themselves in succession before the eye of the prophet.

Scene first. The first object he beheld was a ram standing before the river, having two horns, one higher than the other. He saw this ram pushing westward, northward, and southward, with such vigor that no beast could stand before him, and he did according to his will, and became "great."

Scene second. A rough he-goat, with a notable horn between his eyes, came from the west with such rapidity that he seemed not to touch the ground. And he dashed into the ram, overthrew him, broke his horns, and trampled him into the ground. The he-goat waxed "very great."

But while he was defiantly prancing about in the plenitude of his power, suddenly the great horn between his eyes was broken, and in its place as suddenly sprang forth four notable horns toward the four winds of heaven.

Scene third. Out of one of these four horns of the goat the prophet then saw a little horn protruding. And lo, it grew with marvelous rapidity. It took a turn toward the south, and toward the east, and toward the pleasant land. It sprang upward to the host of heaven, and, encircling some of the stars, brought them to the ground and stamped upon them. It even reared itself against the Prince of the host, took away the daily, cast down the place of his sanctuary, gathered to itself an overwhelming host by reason of transgression, cast down the truth to the ground, and practiced and prospered. The little horn waxed "exceeding great."

Scene fourth. Other objects now come into the field of vision. Heaven does not look with indifference upon all the transactions indicated by the symbols and their work thus far introduced, especially as such work affects the people of God. Angels regard it, and consult about it. Two of them held converse respecting it in the hearing of the prophet. "How long," said one to the other, "shall be the vision concerning the daily sacrifice, and the transgression of desolation, to give both the sanctuary and the host to be trodden under foot?" Then turning to Daniel, as in addressing him he would address the people of God, who are more especially interested in the response, the angel made answer: "Unto two thousand and three hundred days; then shall the sanctuary be cleansed."

This is the entire matter of the vision, and fills the chapter to the 15th verse. It was now necessary that it should be explained; and Daniel immediately heard

AN EXPLANATION COMMANDED.

"And it came to pass, when I, even I Daniel, had seen the vision, and sought for the meaning, then, behold, there stood before me as the appearance of a man. And I heard a man's voice between the banks of Ulai, which called, and said, Gabriel, make this man to understand the vision. So he came near where I stood; and when he came, I was afraid, and fell upon my face; but he said unto me, Understand, O son of man; for at the time of the end shall be the vision. Now as he was speaking with me, I was in a deep sleep on my face toward the ground; but he touched me, and set me upright. And he said, Behold, I will make thee know what shall be in the last end of the indignation; for at the time appointed the end shall be." Verses 15–19.

It is impossible to read this language without perceiving the interest which angels take in the purposes of God concerning the human family. They are all ministering spirits, says Paul, ministering to those who shall be heirs of salvation; and Peter testifies that they desire to look into the things which God has before revealed by his prophets concerning the glory that should accrue to Christ in his future eternal kingdom on account of his intervention in behalf of the human family. So when John, in his vision of the opening of the seven seals, began to weep much through fear that no one would be found in Heaven or earth to open the seals, and that the important truths would forever remain hidden, one of the elders came to him and told him to weep not, for the Lion of the tribe of Judah would open the book. To return to Daniel,

Gabriel, true to the commission here laid upon him, proceeded at once to enter upon his duty and to give the explanation he was enjoined to make.

SYMBOL OF THE RAM EXPLAINED.

"The ram which thou sawest having two horns are the kings of Media and Persia." Verse 20.

This is plain language. It cannot be misunderstood. This being the first symbol, we know at what point the vision commences. It does not begin with the empire of Babylon, as do the visions of the second and seventh chapters, for the Babylonian empire being very near its close in the third year of Belshazzar, when the vision was given, the view commences with the incoming Medo-Persian empire. The two horns of the ram denote the union of these two powers, the Medes and the Persians, in one government.

The Medo-Persian supremacy commenced at the overthrow of Babylon by Cyrus, B. C. 538, and extended to the battle of Arbela, B. C. 331, two hundred and seven years. So long a time is covered by the first symbol. In the explanation of the next symbol we have the power that overthrew the Persian empire, and consequently succeeded to its place.

SYMBOL OF THE GOAT EXPLAINED.

"And the rough goat is the king of Grecia; and the great horn that is between his eyes is the first king. Now that being broken, whereas four stood up for it, four kingdoms shall stand up out of the nation, but not in his power." Verses 21, 22.

This also is plain and unequivocal language. The power that was to succeed the Persian in the empire of the world, according to the prophecy, was the Grecian. It was fulfilled two hundred and thirty-one years after the vision was given, when, at the battle of Arbela, Oct. 1, B. C. 331, Alexander the Great utterly routed the forces of Darius Codomannus, and became absolute lord of the empire to the utmost extent ever possessed by any of the Persian kings.

The great horn between his eyes was the first king. This was Alexander the Great. That horn was broken. Eight years after the battle of Arbela, Alexander died in a drunken debauch at the age of 33, Nov. 12, B. C. 323.

In the place of this first horn, four came up toward the four winds of heaven. These, the angel said, signified four kingdoms to arise out of the nation. After the death of Alexander much confusion arose among his followers respecting the succession. It was finally agreed, after a seven days' contest, that his natural brother, Philip

Aridæus, should be declared king. By him and Alexander's sons, Alexander Ægus and Hercules, the name and show of the Macedonian empire were for a time kept up. But these were all soon murdered; and the regal family being then extinct, the chief commanders of the army, who had gone into different parts of the empire as governors of the provinces, assumed the title of kings. They thereupon fell to leaguing and warring with each other to such a degree that within the short space of fifteen years from Alexander's death the number was reduced to just four, as the prophecy had declared. These kingdoms thus originated about 308 B. C. They were Macedonia, Thrace, Syria, and Egypt, ruled respectively by Cassander, Lysimachus, Seleucus, and Ptolemy. The kingdom of the goat dates from B. C. 331 to the time when a succeeding power appears upon the scene, B. C. 161, as we shall hereafter see. A period of 170 years is thus covered by this symbol.

In the foregoing illustration of the four horns of the goat, the little horn which came from one of them is represented as just protruding from the Macedonian horn. We here present a larger illustration of that little horn, as it waxed exceeding great.

SYMBOL OF THE LITTLE HORN EXPLAINED.

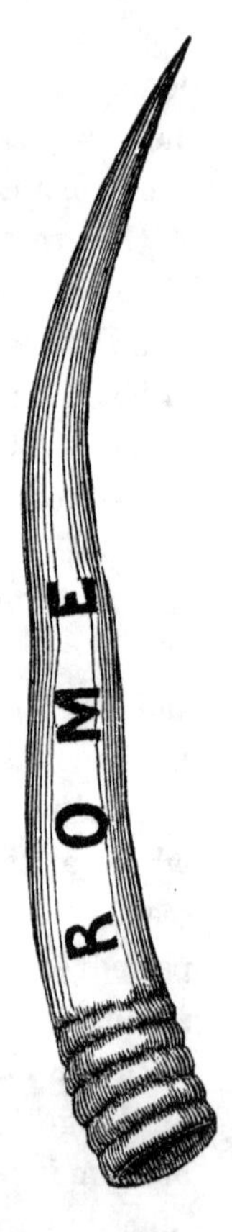

"And in the latter time of their kingdom, when the transgressors are come to the full, a king of fierce countenance, and understanding dark sentences, shall stand up. And his power shall be mighty, but not by his own power; and he shall destroy wonderfully, and shall prosper, and practice, and shall destroy the mighty and the holy people. And through his policy also he shall cause craft to prosper in his hand; and he shall magnify himself in his heart, and by peace shall destroy many: he shall also stand up against the Prince of princes; but he shall be broken without hand." Verses 23–25.

This little horn is unquestionably a symbol of the power that succeeded Grecia in the dominion of the world. And this, according to the prophecies of Dan. 2 and 7, was Rome. Some special reasons must be given if we are to take the ground that this prophecy does not run parallel with the others, and from the time of its beginning bring to view the same universal kingdoms.

The view is however taken by some that this prophecy is not parallel with Dan. 2 and 7, and that the little horn of this chapter does not symbolize Rome; but the good reasons upon which such a view ought to rest are not forthcoming. Romanists, to avoid the application of this part of the prophecy to the Roman power, pagan and papal, endeavor to shift the application from Rome to Antiochus Epiphanes. And this lead of the papists has been followed by the majority of those who oppose the Advent faith. We will now show that this view cannot be correct, but that the reasons fixing this upon Rome are more clear and numerous than those even which determine the application of the other symbols.

The little horn of Dan. 8 does not symbolize Antiochus Epiphanes, but it does symbolize Rome. To prove this is easy. If people would only treat interpretations of prophecy as they treat bank-bills, that is, compare them with the detector to see if they are genuine, there would be no trouble. Our only wonder is that any one could ever have supposed the application to Antiochus to be genuine.

We say, then, that the little horn of Dan. 8 does not symbolize Antiochus, but does symbolize Rome, because,

1. This horn came out of one of the four horns of the goat. Verse 9. It was therefore another horn separate and distinct from any of the four. One of these four horns, as we have seen, was the kingdom of Syria, founded by Seleucus, from whom sprung the famous line of kings known in history as the Seleucidæ. Of these there were twenty-six, in order as follows:—

1. Seleucus Nicator. 2. Antiochus Soter. 3. Antiochus Theus. 4. Seleucus Callinicus. 5. Seleucus Ceraunus. 6. Antiochus the Great. 7. Seleucus Philopater. 8. *Antiochus Epiphanes.* 9. Antiochus Eupator. 10. Demetrius Soter. 11. Alexander Bala. 12. Demetrius Nicator. 13. Antiochus Theos. 14. Antiochus Sidetes. 15. Zebia. 16. Seleucus, son of Nicator. 17. Antiochus Grypus. 18. Antiochus the Cyzicenian. 19. Seleucus, the son of Grypus. 20. Antiochus Eusebes. 21. Antiochus, second son of Grypus. 22. Philip, third son of Grypus. 23. Demetrius Eucheres. 24. Antiochus Dionysius. 25. Tigranes. 26. Antiochus Asiat-

icus, who was the last of the Seleucidæ, and who, after an insignificant reign of four years, was driven from his dominions by Pompey, the Roman, B. C. 65.

It will thus be seen that Antiochus Epiphanes was simply one of the twenty-six kings who constituted the Syrian horn of the goat. He was for the time being that horn; hence he could not be at the same time a separate and independent power, or another remarkable horn, as the little horn was.

Rome *was* such a separate horn, and, from the stand-point of this prophecy, came out of one of the horns of the goat, thus answering exactly to the prophetic description. In the year 161 B. C., Rome became connected with the Jews by the famous Jewish League, 1 Mac. 8; Josephus' Antiq., b. xii., chap. x., sec. 6; Prideaux, vol. ii., p. 166. Nations are noticed in prophecy when they become connected with God's people. Right here the conquering legions of the Roman power came into the prophet's view. But just seven years before this, B. C. 168, Rome had conquered Macedonia (one of the four horns of the goat), adding it to its empire. And as if coming from that horn, the prophet beholds it from that point pursuing its triumphant career. It is therefore spoken of as coming forth from that horn.

2. Were we to apply the little horn to any one of these twenty-six Syrian kings, it should be to the most illustrious and powerful one of them all. But this was not Antiochus Epiphanes. For historians inform us that his name, Epiphanes, the illustrious, was changed to Epimanes, the fool, on account of his vile and extravagant folly.

The little horn cannot apply to Antiochus, but must signify the Roman power, because,

3. This little horn, in comparison with the preceding kingdoms, Media and Persia, waxed "exceeding great." There is in the prophecy a regularly increasing gradation of power: great, very great, exceeding great. Applying the little horn to Antiochus, the following result is presented: 1. "Great," Persia. True. 2. "Very great," Grecia. True. 3. "Exceeding great," Antiochus. Nonsense.

The Persian empire is simply called "great," though it ruled "from India even unto Ethiopia, over an hundred and twenty and seven provinces." Grecia, still more extensive and powerful, is called "very great." Then comes the power in question, which is called "*exceeding great.*" Was Antiochus great in comparison with Alexander, who conquered the world? or with the Romans, who conquered vastly more than all of Alexander's dominions? The kingdom of Antiochus was only a portion of the empire ruled by the goat. Is a part more than the whole? Of the relation between Antiochus and the Romans, the Religious Encyclopedia says: "Finding his resources exhausted, he [Antiochus] resolved to go into Persia to levy tributes and collect large sums which he had *agreed to pay to the Romans.*"

Can any king be said to have waxed exceeding great, when he left his kingdom no larger than he found it? But Sir Isaac Newton testifies that Antiochus did not enlarge his dominions. He made some temporary conquests in Egypt, but immediately relinquished them when the Romans took the part of Ptolemy and *commanded* him to give them up.

It surely cannot take any one long to decide which was the greater power, the one which evacuated Egypt or the one which commanded that evacuation; the one compelled to pay tribute, or the one to whom he was compelled to pay it. One was Antiochus; the other was Rome. With Rome as the third member of the series, we have this result: 1. "Great," Persia. True. 2. "Very great," Grecia. True. 3. "Exceeding great," Rome. More emphatically true than either or both the others.

4. The little horn was to stand up against the Prince of princes, by which title, without doubt, our Lord is meant. But Antiochus died 164 years before Christ was born. There was a power, however, which did stand up against the Saviour. Rome was then in the zenith of its glory. And Rome, in the person of Herod, endeavored to destroy the infant Jesus. Subsequently, when Pilate was its mouth-piece in Judea, it nailed him to the cross.

The same work is attributed to the great red dragon of Rev. 12, a symbol referring so evidently to Rome that none care to dispute the application.

Antiochus answers not one specification of the prophecy; and here we may therefore dismiss him. But, for a more full elucidation of the prophecy, we may further say of Rome :—

5. This horn was "little" at first. So was Rome, but it "waxed," or grew, "exceeding great" in three several directions. What better terms could be used to describe the course of that power which from a small beginning rose to be the mistress of the world?

6. It gathered dominion toward the south. Egypt was made a province of the Roman empire B. C. 30, and continued such for over six centuries.

7. It marched its conquering legions toward the east. Rome subjugated Syria B. C. 63, and made it a province of the empire.

8. It set its face toward the pleasant land. Judea is so called in many scriptures. Ps. 106: 24; Zech. 7:14; etc. First by a league of assistance and friendship the Romans took under their influence the holy land and people. They subsequently made Judea a Roman province, and finally destroyed the city of Jerusalem, burned their beautiful temple with fire, and scattered the Jews over the face of the whole earth to be gathered no more till time shall end.

9. It waxed great even to the host of heaven. These terms, used in a symbolic sense in reference to earthly scenes, must denote persons of illustrious character or exalted position. The great red dragon, Rev. 12:4, Pagan Rome, is said to have cast down a third part of the stars of heaven to the ground. This is the same power, and we think the same work, referring to its acts of oppressing the Jews and deposing their rulers.

10. By him the daily (not daily sacrifice, as our translators have supplied, but daily desolation, which is paganism) was taken away, and the transgression of desolation, the papacy, was set

up. Chap. 11:31. Rome, and Rome alone, did this. While Rome was ruler, the religion of the empire was changed from paganism to that corrupted form of Christianity known as the papacy. And the place where paganism had long had its sanctuary, Rome with its Pantheon, or temple of all the gods, was cast down, or degraded to the second rank, by the removal of the seat of government to Constantinople, in A. D. 330. So in Rev. 13:2, the dragon, Pagan Rome, gave to the beast, Papal Rome, his seat, the city of Rome, and great authority.

11. An host was given him against the daily. The barbarians that subverted the Roman empire became converts to that nominal Christianity before which they were thus brought face to face, and were soon transformed into willing instruments whereby their former religion, paganism, was dethroned. No other power has in any respect fulfilled this prophecy.

12. In the interpretation, verse 23, it is called a king of fierce countenance and understanding dark sentences. Such was emphatically Rome, with its warlike paraphernalia, and its strange language which the Jews did not understand. Moses uses similar language, referring, as all agree, to the Romans. Deut. 28:49, 50.

13. It was to stand up in the latter time of their kingdom, when the dominion of the four horns of the goat was drawing to an end. There Rome appeared.

14. It was to destroy wonderfully. Hear all opposing powers, which it so rudely overthrew, testify, Thus did Rome.

15. Rome has destroyed the mighty and holy people, the people of God, more than all other powers combined. A many-tongued voice from the blood of more than fifty millions of martyrs, goes up to testify against it.

16. And it has "practiced,"—practiced its deceptions upon the people, and its schemes of cunning among the nations, to gain its own ends, and aggrandize its power.

17. And it has "prospered." It has made war with the saints, and worn them out and prevailed against them.

18. It has run its allotted career, and is to be "broken without hand." Verse 25. How clear a reference to the stone cut out without hand which is to smite the image upon its feet and dash it to pieces. So the papacy is soon to perish in the consuming glories of the second coming of our Lord.

Thus Rome fulfills all the specifications of

the prophecy. No other kingdom meets even one. Rome is the power in question. No other can be.

In view of all these facts, if any one still affirms that Antiochus was the little horn, or if he even hesitates to admit its application to Rome, all we can do is to take such person by the hand, and exclaim, with the deepest commiseration for his unfortunate condition, "*Non compos mentis.* Farewell."

Chapter Four.

THE YEAR-DAY PRINCIPLE.

FROM the exposition of the symbols thus far given we have the field of vision laid clearly out before us. The first symbol, Persia, covers a period of 207 years; the second, Grecia, 170 years; the third, which we have seen to be Rome in both its phases, pagan and papal, from B. C. 161 to its division into ten parts, in 483, A. D., continued 644 years; and if we come down to the close of papal supremacy in 1798, we have the long period of 1959 years; and if we come still forward to our own time, for this power is not yet broken without hand, we have the surprising period of 2033 years covered by this symbol.

Putting these periods together, we have from the commencement of Persian supremacy, B. C. 538, to the division of Rome, 483 A.D., 1021 years; to the temporary overthrow of Papal Rome, 1798 A. D., 2336 years; to our own time, 2410. So vast is the sweep of this vision, which was given to the beloved Daniel.

This fact has an important bearing upon the subject of time, which we are now prepared to consider. One point alone remains unexplained in Daniel 8, and that is the sanctuary and 2300 days of verse 14. On this we now inquire:—

1. Does the word "days," which in the margin is rendered "evening morning," mean days as commonly understood by that term?

2. Have we the correct reading, 2300?

3. Are the days literal or symbolic? and can we tell how long a period they denote?

On the first of these inquiries, we present the following testimony from Dr. Hales:—

"The earliest measure of time on record is the *Day*. In that most ancient and venerable account of the creation, by Moses, the process is marked by the operations of each day. The *evening* and the *morning* were the first *day*, etc. Gen. 1:5, etc. Here the word 'day' denotes the civil or calendar day of 24 hours, including 'the evening,' or natural night, and 'the morning,' or natural day; while the sun is either below or above the horizon of any place, in the course of the earth's diurnal rotation between two successive appulses of the same meridian to the sun; corresponding, therefore, to a *solar day* in astronomy. It is remarkable that the 'evening,' or natural *night*, precedes the 'morning,' or natural *day*, in the Mosaic account. Hence the Hebrew compound, ערב בקר, '*evening morning*,' is used by the prophet Daniel to denote a civil day, in his famous chronological prophecy of the 2300 days, Dan. 8 : 14."—*Sacred Chronology*, vol. i. p. 10.

Again he says, when speaking on this text in vol. ii. p. 512, note, "The evening morning was a civil or calendar day."

The first question then is sufficiently answered, the word days (evening morning) in Dan. 8 : 14, is such as is used to designate days as commonly understood, and hence is correctly translated.

On the second inquiry, Is 2300 the correct reading? we quote again from the same author:—

"There is no number in the Bible whose genuineness is better ascertained than that of the 2300 days. It is found in all the printed Hebrew editions, in all the MSS. of *Kennicott* and *De Rossi's* collations, and in all the *ancient versions*, except the Vatican copy of the Septuagint, which reads 2400, followed by *Symmachus;* and some copies noticed by Jerome, 2200; both evidently literal errors, in excess and defect, which compensate each other and confirm the mean, 2300." *Id.*, vol. ii. p. 512.

These points being thus established, that the expression is the proper one to denote a civil day, and that the reading, 2300, is correct, we next inquire, Are these days literal, or symbolic? If they are literal, they give us (dividing by 365) six and one-third years, as the extent of the whole period. If they are symbolic, each day signifying a year, they bring to view a period 2300 years in length. Which of these two views is the more consistent with the rest of the prophecy?

The question was, "How long the vision?" The question, certainly, covers almost the whole, if not the whole, duration of the vision; and that, as we have seen, extends over a period of over 2400 years. Now if, in reply, the angel singled out a period only six years and one-third in length, there is no correspondence either between this answer and the vision in connection with which it was given, or between the answer and the question which directly called it forth. These days, if taken literally, would be far from covering the duration of any one of the kingdoms of the prophecy taken singly, how much less of them all taken together.

This is symbolic prophecy; it would be natural therefore to conclude that the time introduced would be of a like nature. Twenty-three hundred literal days would not be out of proportion to the lives of the beasts shown in the vision; and as these short-lived beasts are symbols, representing long-lived kingdoms; so the days are symbols representing the years of their continuance.

The Bible observes this rule of chronological proportion in a general way. In Eze. 16, the Jewish nation is symbolized under the figure of a youthful woman, the youthful age of the woman, and the comparatively short period of growth to womanhood, representing the youthful period of the nation, and the years during which it was coming to maturity. See Elliott's "Horæ Apocalypticæ," vol. iii. p. 241.

But more than this, the Bible gives the exact proportion between literal and symbolic time. Ezekiel, during the self-same Babylonish captivity in which Daniel's prophecies were delivered, symbolizes *years* by *days*. He was commanded to make known to his fellow-exiles by the river Chebar, near the Euphrates, the fate of Jerusalem, with her last king Zedekiah, and also God's reason for it. For this purpose he was to lie prostrate with his face toward the city, on his left side three hundred and ninety days for Israel, and on his right side forty days for Judah, restricted all the while to a famine diet, like the Jews he represented shut up in the siege. And God said, "I have appointed thee *each day for a year.*" Eze. 4 : 6.

In this representation Ezekiel himself became a symbol. He was acting a symbolic part, an individual representing a nation, the *days* in which he was acting his part symbolizing the actual *years* of the punishment of those whom he represented.

Another instance, not so evidently symbolic in its nature, but equally definite in showing how God uses short periods of time to represent longer ones, and the proportion to be observed between them, is found in Num. 14 : 34: "Forty days, each day for a year."

It is objected against this principle of interpretation that it is novel, not having been known in the church from the days of Daniel to those of Wyckliffe, and, secondly, that those who adopt the year-day principle are in confusion among themselves respecting their interpretations of prophecy.

The first of these objections is shown by Mr. Elliott not to be well founded; as this principle of interpretation, though not the exact application of this prophecy, was adopted by Augustine, Tichonius, Primasius, Andreas, the venerable

Bede, Ambrosius, Ansbertus, Berengaud, Bruno Astensis, etc.

As to the second objection, there certainly is no more confusion among year-day interpreters than among those who take the day-day view; and it is not strange that there should have been discordant views in days past, since the prophecy was closed up and sealed till the time of the end; but the intimation is given that then the seal would be broken, the wise understand, and knowledge be increased on these things. And right here the year-day principle has been brought out and especially defended as a key to the interpretation of the prophecies.

But that which demonstrates beyond question the correctness of the year-day principle, is the fact that we, living down in the last years of prophetic fulfillment, are now able to trace out in history the accomplishment of these predictions; and we find that the seventy weeks of Dan. 9, the 1260, 1290, and 1335 days of Dan. 7 and 12, and Rev. 12 and 13, and the five months, and hour, day, month, and year of Rev. 9, have all been exactly fulfilled a day for a year.

The 2300 days of Dan. 8:14, are therefore 2300 literal years. Where do they begin? and where do they end?

Chapter Five.

DAN. 8 EXPLAINED BY DAN. 9.

HAVING now seen that the 2300 days of Dan. 8 are symbolic, and denote 2300 literal years, the inquiry is resumed, When do they commence, and when terminate? The symbols of the ram, goat, and little horn, were clearly explained in chapter 8. Gabriel was commanded to make him understand the entire vision. But at the conclusion of the chapter, Daniel says, "I was astonished at the vision, but none understood it."

So far therefore as the record of the 8th chapter is concerned, Gabriel had not then fulfilled his mission. The point left unexplained was the 2300 days. Why did not Gabriel continue his instructions till this point also was made clear? Because Daniel had heard all he could endure, and fainted and was sick certain days. But Gabriel must somewhere explain this matter of the time, or prove disobedient to his instructions, and thus become a fallen angel. But he did not thus become apostate; for more than five hundred years after this, we find him still in divine employ, sent on a sacred mission to Zacharias and to Mary. Gabriel has therefore somewhere given Daniel further instruction on that part of the vision which remained unexplained, namely, the 2300 days. We are to look for this, of course, in the subsequent records of Daniel's prophecy.

Fifteen years elapse, and the record of chapter 9 opens. We have now reached the year 538 B. C. A mighty revolution has just taken place. The empire of the world has changed hands. Babylon lies prostrate and bleeding in the dust. The proud oppressor of God's people is brought low. Medo-Persia now wields the scepter. Daniel beholds in all this the hand of God, and the fulfillment of prophecy. He understood by the writings of Jeremiah that Jerusalem should lie desolate for seventy years, and that the termination of that period would be marked by the punishment of the king of Babylon. Jer. 25 : 12. He has seen the punishment of Babylon, and concludes that the day of deliverance for his people is at hand. The seventy years did actually terminate two years later, in the first year of Cyrus, B. C. 536, and their expiration was marked by the decree of Cyrus for the rebuilding of the temple.

Daniel therefore sets his heart to seek the

Lord, and to pray to him for the fulfillment of his word. Then follows the wonderful prayer of Dan. 9 : 4–19. In the course of his prayer he said, "O our God, hear the prayer of thy servant, and his supplications, and cause thy face to shine upon thy sanctuary that is desolate."

We remember, as Daniel doubtless did, that the 2300 days ended with a promise respecting the sanctuary. And it is evident from this expression that Daniel had in some way connected the end of the 2300 days with the end of the seventy years of Jewish captivity. In this it was necessary that he now be set right.

Again the prophet is rapt in vision; and a heavenly messenger appears upon the scene. We ask the reader to consider carefully who this is. We last beheld Daniel in converse with Gabriel. The angel was explaining to him the things he had seen, in compliance with the mandate of One qualified to command even so high an angel as Gabriel, "Make this man to understand the vision." He had explained all but the time, when Daniel's powers gave way, the prophet fainted, and he was obliged to desist. Thus the 8th chapter leaves us, Gabriel departing Heavenward, his work unfinished, and Daniel, though sufficiently recovered to attend to the king's business, wondering at the vision but not understanding it. This vision of the 9th chapter is the very next vision, so far as we have any account, which the prophet had. Again he is honored with the presence of a heavenly guest. And who is it? "*Gabriel,*" exclaims the prophet; and that there may be no doubt as to his identity, Daniel adds, "whom I had seen in the vision at the beginning." Thus our minds are carried directly back to the vision of chapter 8, and the prophet declares that the very same angel he had seen at that time was with him again.

The vision of chapter 9 therefore opens as the vision of chapter 8 closed, Daniel and Gabriel in communication with each other. And there is no intervening vision to cut off the connection between these two scenes. And here we behold two of the manifold links that bind these chapters together: the same vision called up, and the same angel introduced whom we there beheld.

Gabriel speaks; and his first words confirm this view: "O Daniel, I am now come forth to give thee skill and understanding." As if he had said, O Daniel, when last I was with you, explaining the vision you had seen, I was obliged to leave my explanation midway, because you could endure no more; hence you did not understand it; but I was commissioned to make you understand it; and therefore I am now come forth to give you the understanding which I could not then impart.

Gabriel continues; and every word he utters strengthens this conclusion: "At the beginning of thy supplications the commandment came forth; and I am come to show thee; for thou art greatly beloved; therefore understand the matter, and *consider the vision.*"

It would be useless for any one to deny that a previous vision is here referred to; and it would be equally useless for him to deny that that is the vision of chapter 8.

Now we will introduce a test to settle beyond a peradventure the truthfulness or falsity of the position here taken. *If* chapter 9 is connected with chapter 8; *if* the vision of chapter 9 is the sequel of that of chapter 8; *if* the expression used by Gabriel in chapter 9, "consider the vision," refers to the vision of chapter 8; and *if* he has now come to complete the instruction which he there omitted,—it is certain that he will commence with the very subject which he was obliged to leave unexplained in that vision, namely, the subject of the time. If he does this, the connection between these two chapters, for which we here contend, is established. If he does not, it is perhaps still an open question.

And what does he say? "*Seventy weeks are determined* upon thy people and upon thy holy city." He does therefore commence with the subject of time. But how do we know that this time has any connection with the time of chapter 8? Because he says of it that it is "determined;" and the word determined here signifies "cut off." But there is no period of time from which they could be said to be cut off, except the 2300 days of chapter 8. Thus are the expressions relating to the time connected together; and Gabriel undertakes an explanation of the 2300 days by dividing it into two periods, the first of seventy weeks or 490 days, and the remainder of 1810 days, and then explaining the shorter, which is a key to the whole.

Proof that the word "determined" signifies "cut off," and testimony from eminent writers who have acknowledged the connection between Dan. 8 and 9, we consider of sufficient importance to be set apart in a chapter by themselves.

Chapter Six.

"DETERMINED," DAN. 9:24, MEANS "CUT OFF."

FIRST WITNESS. "'Seventy weeks are *determined*,' literally, '*cut off*.' Hebraists all admit that the word determined, in our English version, does signify '*cut off*.' *Not one* has disputed it."—*Josiah Litch, Midnight Cry*, vol. iv. No. 25.

Second witness. "Seventy weeks have been cut off upon thy people and upon thy holy city, to finish the transgression, and to make an end of sin-offerings, and to make atonement for iniquity, and to bring in everlasting righteousness, and to seal the vision and prophecy, and to anoint the Most Holy." Dan. 9:24.—*Whiting's Translation.*

Third witness. Gesenius, the standard Hebrew lexicographer, thus defines this word in his Hebrew lexicon: "*Nechtak:* Properly, to cut off; tropically, to divide; and so to determine, to decree."

Fourth witness. The Chaldeo-Rabbinic Dictionary of Stockius, defines the word *nechtak* as follows: "*Scidit, abscidit, conscidit, incidit, ex-*

cidit—to cut, to cut away, to cut in pieces, to cut or engrave, to cut off."

Fifth witness. Mercerus, in his "Thesaurus," furnishes a specimen of Rabbinical usage in the phrase, *chatikah shel basar,* "a piece of flesh," or "a cut of flesh." He translates the word as it occurs in Dan. 9:24, by "*præcisa est,*" was cut off.

Sixth witness. Arias Montanus in a literal version of the text translates it "*decisa est,*" was cut off; in the marginal reading, which is grammatically correct, the rendering is in the plural, "*decisæ sunt,*" were cut off.

Seventh witness. In the Latin version of Junius and Tremellius, *nechtak* (the passive of *chathak*) is rendered "*decisæ sunt,*" were cut off.

Eighth witness. Theodotion's Greek version of Daniel (which is the version used in the Vatican copy of the Septuagint, as being the most faithful), renders it by συνετμήθησαν, *sunetmethesan,* were cut off; and the Venetian copy by τετμηνται, *tetmeentai,* have been cut.

Ninth witness. In the Vulgate the phrase is, "*abbreviatæ sunt,*" have been shortened.

"Thus Chaldaic and Rabbinical authority, and that of the earliest versions, the Septuagint and Vulgate, give the single signification of *cutting off* to this verb."

Tenth witness. Hengstenberg, who enters into a critical examination of the text, says: "But the very use of the word, which does not elsewhere occur, while others, much more frequently used, were at hand if Daniel had wished to express the idea of determination, and of which he has elsewhere, and even in this portion, availed himself, seems to argue that the word stands from regard to its original meaning, and represents the seventy weeks in contrast with a determination of time (*en platei*) as a period cut off from subsequent duration, and accurately limited."--*Christology of the Old Testament,* vol. ii. p. 301. Washington, 1839.

This translation is further vindicated by Prof. N. N. Whiting, from whom a quotation has already been given, in the following language: "As the period of 2300 days is first given, and verses 21 and 23, compared with Dan. 8:16, show that the ninth chapter furnishes an explanation of the vision in which Gabriel appeared to Daniel, and of the 'matter'—(the commencement of the 2300 days)—the *literal* (or rather, to speak properly, the *only*) signification demanded by the subject matter, is that of '*cut off.*'"—*Midnight Cry,* vol. iv. No. 17.

No further nor better evidence could be required on this point. Beyond question the seventy weeks are cut off from some other period; and just as evidently that other period is the 2300 days of chapter 8. Should it be asked why our translators rendered the word "determined" when it so obviously signifies "cut off," a sufficient answer would be that they doubtless overlooked the connection between the 8th and 9th chapters; and considering it improper to speak of a period of time as cut off, when nothing was given from which it could be cut off, they gave the word its tropical instead of its literal meaning.

In connection with this point, we promised testimony from prominent writers on the prophecies who have acknowledged the connection between Dan. 8 and 9. In perusing them the reader will be able to decide which class have proved recreant to the original Advent faith, we who adhere still more tenaciously than ever to these views, or those who, without any assignable reason, repudiate and reject them. We commence with an extract from an article in the *Advent Shield*, which reads:—

"We call attention to one fact which shows that there is a necessary 'connection' between the seventy weeks of the ninth chapter, and something else which precedes or follows it, called '*the vision.*' It is found in the 24th verse: 'Seventy weeks are determined [or cut off] upon thy people . . . to seal up the vision,' etc. Now there are but two significations to the phrase 'seal up.' They are, first, 'to make secret,' and, secondly, 'to make sure.' We care not now in which of these significations the phrase is supposed to be used. That is not the point now before us. Let the signification be what it may, it shows that the prediction of the seventy weeks necessarily relates to something else beyond itself, called 'the vision,' in reference to which it performs this work, 'to seal up.' To talk of its sealing up itself is as much of an absurdity as to suppose that Josephus was so much afraid of the Romans that he refrained from telling the world that he thought the fourth kingdom of Daniel was 'the kingdom of the Greeks.' It is no more proper to say that the ninth chapter of Daniel 'is complete in itself,' than it would be to say that a map which was designed to show the relation of Massachusetts to the United States, referred to nothing but Massachusetts. It is no more complete in itself than a bond given in security for a note, or some other document to which it refers, is complete in itself; and we doubt if there is a school-boy of fourteen in the land, of ordinary capacity, who would not on reading the ninth chapter, with an understanding of the clause before us, decide that it referred to something distinct from itself, called the vision. What vision it is, there is no difficulty in determining. It naturally and obviously refers to the vision which was not fully explained to Daniel, and to which Gabriel calls his attention in the preceding verse—*the vision of the eighth chapter*. Daniel tells us that Gabriel was commanded to make him understand that vision (8:16). This was not fully done at that interview connected with the vision; he is therefore sent to give Daniel the needed 'skill and understanding,' to explain its 'meaning' by communicating to him the prediction of the seventy weeks."—*Advent Shield*, 1844.

"We claim that the ninth of Daniel is an appendix to the eighth, and that the seventy weeks and the 2300 days or years commence together. *Our opponents deny this.*"—*Signs of the Times*, 1843.

"The grand principle involved in the interpretation of the 2300 days of Dan. 8:14, is that the seventy weeks of Dan. 9:24, are the first 490 days of the 2300 of the eighth chapter."—*Advent Shield*, p. 49.

"If the connection between the seventy weeks of Dan. 9, and the 2300 days of Dan. 8, does not exist, the whole system is shaken to its foundation; if it does exist, as we suppose, *the system must stand.*"—*Harmony of Prophetic Chronology,* p. 33.

Says the learned Dr. Hales, in commenting upon the seventy weeks, "This chronological prophecy was evidently designed to explain the foregoing vision, especially in its chronological part of the 2300 days."

What more need be said? The arguments which show the seventy weeks to be a part of the 2300 days, are all invulnerable. We may consider this question decided, and hereafter appeal to this decision as authoritative.

Chapter Seven.

THE SEVENTY WEEKS.

IT has now been proved, 1. That there is the clearest connection between the 8th and 9th chapters of Daniel. 2. That the seventy weeks are consequently a part of the 2300 days. 3. That these weeks are cut off from those days. 4. That the seventy weeks are the first 490 days of the 2300 days. 5. That, consequently, where the seventy weeks begin, there the 2300 days begin.

Respecting the time, therefore, we have now only to inquire further, From what point are the seventy weeks to be reckoned? The data which the Bible furnishes on this point are found in the further instruction which the angel gave to Daniel in chapter 9. After informing him that seventy weeks were cut off from the 2300 days, and allotted to his people and the city of Jerusalem, he proceeds immediately to tell him in the following language where they begin, and what events would mark their termination:—

"Know therefore and understand, that from

the going forth of the commandment to restore and to build Jerusalem unto the Messiah the Prince shall be seven weeks, and threescore and two weeks; the street shall be built again, and the wall, even in troublous times. And after threescore and two weeks shall Messiah be cut off, but not for himself; and the people of the prince that shall come shall destroy the city and the sanctuary; and the end thereof shall be with a flood, and unto the end of the war desolations are determined. And he shall confirm the covenant with many for one week; and in the midst of the week he shall cause the sacrifice and the oblation to cease, and for the overspreading of abominations he shall make it desolate, even until the consummation, and that determined shall be poured upon the desolate." Dan. 9:25–27.

From this testimony respecting the seventy weeks we learn, 1. That a commandment to restore and build Jerusalem marks their beginning. 2. That seven weeks, or forty-nine years, were allotted to the work of restoration. 3. That sixty-nine weeks, or 483 years, would span the interval to the time when the Messiah the Prince should appear upon the earth, or when our Lord should commence his public ministry here among men. 4. That during the last or seventieth week, the Messiah should confirm the covenant (the new covenant) with many. 5. That in the midst or middle of that last week, he should be cut off, and cause the sacrifice and oblation to cease; expressions which must be considered as referring to his crucifixion, and the effect which his thus offering himself upon the cross would have upon the Jewish sacrifices and ceremonies, in causing them virtually to cease. When the seventy weeks, therefore, are correctly located, we shall find the seventieth week falling at such a time that the commencement of Christ's ministry will stand at the beginning, and his crucifixion, three and a half years later, in the middle, of that last week. The whole question might therefore be left to an argument on the date of the crucifixion of Christ, since this has as much bearing upon the point at issue as even the commandment to restore and build Jerusalem, from which this period is to be dated.

But it is not difficult to find the commandment to restore Jerusalem, and to ascertain that it went forth at the precise time to render the prophecy harmonious in all its parts.

There are four events which have by different ones at different times been regarded as the commandment to restore and build Jerusalem. These are, 1. The decree of Cyrus for the rebuilding of the house of God, B. C. 536. Ez. 1 : 1–4. 2. The decree of Darius for the prosecution of that work, which had been hindered, B. C. 519. Ez. 6 : 6–12. 3. The decree of Artaxerxes Longimanus to Ezra, B. C. 457. Ez. 7. And 4. The commission to Nehemiah, from the same king in his twentieth year, B. C. 444. Neh. 2.

1. Respecting this last, we find no feature about it necessary to constitute it a Persian decree. It was essential that such decree should be put in writing, and signed by the king. Nehemiah had nothing of the kind. His commission was only verbal. If it be said that the letters granted him constituted a decree, then the decree was issued not to Nehemiah, but to the governors beyond the river; and moreover these would constitute a plurality of decrees, not one decree, as the prophecy contemplates.

2. The occasion of Nehemiah's petition to the king for permission to go up to Jerusalem was the report which certain ones, returning, had brought from thence, that those in the province were in great affliction and reproach, that the wall of Jerusalem also was broken down, and the gates thereof burned with fire. Neh. 1.

What wall and gates were those that were broken down and burned with fire? Evidently some which had been built by the Jews who had returned to Jerusalem under one, or all, of the preceding decrees, of Cyrus, Darius, and Artaxerxes; for it cannot for a moment be supposed that the utter destruction of the city by Nebuchadnezzar, one hundred and forty-four years previous to that time, would have been reported to Nehemiah as a matter of news, or that he would have considered it, as he evidently did, a fresh misfortune, calling for a fresh expression of his grief. A decree, therefore, authorizing the building of these, had gone forth previous to the grant to Nehemiah.

3. Should any contend that the commission to Nehemiah must be the decree in question, because the object of his request was that he might build the city, it is sufficient to reply as above, that gates and walls had been built previous to his going up; besides, the work of building which he went to perform was accomplished in fifty-two days; whereas the prophecy allows for the building of the city, seven weeks, or forty-nine years.

4. There was nothing granted to Nehemiah not embraced in preceding decrees, while those

decrees had already granted vastly more privileges than his commission.

5. Reckoning from the commission to Nehemiah, B. C. 444, the dates throughout are entirely disarranged; for from that point the troublous times which were to attend the building of the street and wall did not last seven weeks, or forty-nine years. Reckoning from that date, the sixty-nine weeks, or 483 years, which were to extend only to the Messiah the Prince, bring us to A. D. 39–40; but Jesus was baptized of John in Jordan, and the voice of his Father was heard from Heaven declaring him his Son, in A. D. 27, thirteen years before. According to this calculation, the midst of the last, or seventieth, week, which was to be marked by the crucifixion, is placed in A. D. 44; but the crucifixion took place in A. D. 31, thirteen years previous. And lastly, the seventy weeks, or 490 years, dating from the 20th of Artaxerxes, extend to A. D. 47, with absolutely nothing to mark their termination. Hence, if that be the year, and the grant to Nehemiah the event, from which to reckon, the prophecy has proved a failure. But such a conclusion is simply an overwhelming proof that that theory which dates the seventy weeks from the commission to Nehemiah in the 20th of Artaxerxes, is an utter failure.

We may therefore dismiss this commission, and this date, from consideration. The question now lies between the decrees of Cyrus, Darius, and Artaxerxes. Which one, if only one, and how many, if more than one, of these did it take to make that decree to which the prophecy refers as the starting-point of the seventy weeks?

As already noticed, we must look to one, or all, of the decrees issued by Cyrus, Darius, and Artaxerxes, for the commandment to restore and build Jerusalem. And the selection must be determined largely by a consideration of how much is embraced in the prophecy respecting the restoration of this city.

The promise embraced the restoration as well as the rebuilding of Jerusalem. To restore and build, is more than simply to build. The rebuilding of its demolished palaces, the re-opening of its deserted streets, the re-erection of its leveled walls, and the setting up again of its broken gates, would not alone meet the provisions of the prophecy. There must be the forms and privileges of religious worship, the regulations of society, judges to interpret, and officers to execute, the laws, and the re-establishment of that civil polity which made Jerusalem what she was before her fall.

The Decree of Cyrus. The decree of Cyrus, standing nearest to the prophecy respecting the commandment to restore and build Jerusalem, naturally first engages our attention.

Some have claimed that this decree of Cyrus must be the commandment in question, because God by the prophet Isaiah speaks of Cyrus as the one who should say to Jerusalem, "Thou shalt be built." Isa. 44 : 28. But there are three conclusive objections to this view: 1. It is not Cyrus who, in the prophecy of Isaiah, says to Jerusalem, "Thou shalt be built;" but the Lord is the one who says this. See verses 26 and 27. 2. The decree of Cyrus pertained simply to the temple at Jerusalem. See Ez. 1 : 2. It did not even make provision for the building of the city, much less those other provisions, which, as we have seen, must have been included in the prophecy. 3. From the date of this decree, B. C. 536, the sixty-nine weeks, or 483 years which were to extend to the Messiah the Prince, fall fifty-three years short of reaching even to the birth of Christ. An effort has consequently been made by those who take the decree of Cyrus to be the commandment in question, to change the date of that decree, placing it at a point late enough to harmonize with the prophecy respecting the Messiah. But this cannot be done, as we shall hereafter see.

By these remarks we do not design in the least to rob the decree of Cyrus of any measure of its importance. It occupies a prominent place in connection with the history of Jerusalem's restoration. The work which Cyrus did was given him of the Lord to do. He was called by name over a hundred years before his birth, and his work, in a measure at least, pointed out. And that which his decree granted was one of the first steps, and a very necessary step, in the work of restoration; but its provisions were too limited to meet the specifications of the prophecy. Some things, to be sure, would follow as a necessary consequence, such as the building of houses for the workmen, the opening of worship, and the carrying on of some necessary traffic. But the decree did not provide for them.

The Decree of Darius. The decree of Darius stands next in order. It was occasioned by the following circumstances: The next year after the Jews had commenced the work under the decree of Cyrus, the enemies of the Jews made request that they be permitted to join them in the work. This the Jews refused, whereupon their enemies set themselves to work to trouble them in their building and to frustrate them in their purpose, "all the days of Cyrus, ... even until the reign of Darius, king of Persia." Ez. 4.

Seven years after issuing his decree, Cyrus died, and was succeeded by Cambyses, called in Ez. 4 : 6, Ahasuerus, who reigned seven years and five months, and who was in turn succeeded by Smerdis the Magian, called in Ez. 4 : 7, Artaxerxes, from whom the enemies of the Jews obtained an edict prohibiting the further prosecution of the work at Jerusalem. Ez. 4 : 21–24. But the land being smitten with barrenness, the prophets Haggai and Zechariah, having made known to the Jews the cause of this calamity, exhorted them to resume the work of building the house of God, which they accordingly commenced again B. C. 520.

Again their enemies endeavored to hinder and stop them, and appealing to Darius who had now come to the Persian throne, he caused search to be made among the chronicles of the kingdom, and finding the decree of Cyrus, re-affirmed it, with some provisions of his own; and thus the work went forward prosperously again.

Here was a second decree. It was, however, only seventeen years from the decree of Cyrus, and therefore does not meet the prophecy any better than the former, in the matter of dates. And further, it was but a re-affirmation of the decree of Cyrus, and was therefore too limited in its provisions to constitute the commandment to restore and build Jerusalem. But it was a second step in the work, and, adding somewhat to the decree of Cyrus, was some advancement toward the end in view.

The Decree of Artaxerxes Longimanus. Third and last stands the decree of Artaxerxes Longimanus, as recorded in Ez. 7. This Artaxerxes was the Ahasuerus of the book of Esther, which will account for the remarkable favor he showed to the Jewish people. The decree which he issued was given to Ezra at the earnest solicitation of that man of God; for it is said that the king granted Ezra "all his request."

A mere perusal of this decree shows its full and ample provisions. It is drawn up in a formal manner. It is expressly called "a decree." It is written, not in Hebrew, but in Chaldaic or Eastern Aramaic. "Thus," says Prof. Whiting, "we are furnished with the original document, by virtue of which Ezra was authorized to 'restore and build Jerusalem;' or, in other words, by which he was clothed with power, not merely to erect walls or houses, but to regulate the affairs of his countrymen in general, to 'set magistrates and judges which may judge all the people beyond the river.' He was commissioned to enforce the observance of the laws of his God, and to punish those who transgressed with death, banishment, confiscation, or imprisonment. See verses 23–27."

No such ample powers as this decree conferred upon Ezra can be found in any previous or subsequent act of this kind. This, in connection with those which had been given before, contained all the provision that could possibly be made for any people who were still to be held tributary to the Persian throne. And we have in Ez. 6:14, a remarkable declaration showing that all three of these decrees are taken as the commandment to restore and build Jerusalem: "And they builded, and finished it, according to the commandment of the God of Israel, and according to THE COMMANDMENT of Cyrus, and Darius, and Artaxerxes king of Persia." Here the decrees of these three several kings, are called "*the* commandment," singular number, according to which the work in Jerusalem was finished. When therefore this last decree went forth from Artaxerxes, enlarging and completing all the provisions that had been made before, then the work was finished; and with the provisions of that decree carried out, the commandment "*went forth*" in the sense of the prophecy.

We have now to determine when this decree went forth, and then test its agreement with the remainder of the prophecy.

Having ascertained that the decree for the restoration and building of Jerusalem was the authority granted to the Jews to restore their temple, their worship, their city, and their civil state, by the three-fold decree of the Persian kings, Cyrus, Darius, and Artaxerxes, and that it was completed, and went forth, when the last touch of authority granted to Ezra by Artaxerxes Longimanus was put into operation by Ezra, in carrying out the work which it gave him liberty to perform, the question next arises,

In what year was this?

Ezra says that it was in the seventh year of that king. Ez. 7:7, 8.

What year before Christ was the seventh year of Artaxerxes Longimanus?

The following testimony is a concise and conclusive answer to this important question:—

"The Bible gives the data for a complete system of chronology, extending from the creation to the birth of Cyrus, a clearly ascertained date.

From this period downward we have the undisputed Canon of Ptolemy, and the undoubted era of Nabonassar, extending below our vulgar era. At the point where inspired chronology leaves us, this Canon of undoubted accuracy commences. And thus the whole arch is spanned. It is by the Canon of Ptolemy that the great prophetical period of seventy weeks is fixed. This Canon places the seventh year of Artaxerxes in the year B. C. 457; and the accuracy of the Canon is demonstrated by the concurrent agreement of more than twenty eclipses. The seventy weeks date from the going forth of a decree respecting the restoration of Jerusalem. There were no decrees between the seventh and twentieth years of Artaxerxes. Four hundred and ninety years, beginning with the seventh, must commence in B. C. 457, and end in A. D. 34. Commencing in the twentieth, they must commence in B. C. 444, and end in A. D. 47. As no event occurred in A. D. 47 to mark their termination, we cannot reckon from the twentieth; we must, therefore, look to the seventh of Artaxerxes. This date we cannot change from B. C. 457 without first demonstrating the inaccuracy of Ptolemy's Canon. To do this, it would be necessary to show that the large number of eclipses by which its accuracy has been repeatedly demonstrated, have not been correctly computed; and such a result would unsettle every chronological date, and leave the settlement of epochs and the adjustment of eras entirely at the mercy of every dreamer, so that chronology would be of no more value than mere guess-work. As the seventy weeks must terminate in A. D. 34, unless the seventh of Artaxerxes is wrongly fixed, and as that cannot be changed without some evidence to that effect, we inquire, What evidence marked that termination? The time when the apostles turned to the Gentiles harmonizes with that date better than any other which has been named. And the crucifixion, in A. D. 31, in the midst of the last week, is sustained by a mass of testimony which cannot be easily invalidated."—*Advent Herald*, March 2, 1850.

Again the *Herald* says;—

"There are certain chronological points which have been *settled* as *fixed;* and before the seventy weeks can be made to terminate at a later period, those must be unsettled, by being shown to have been fixed on *wrong principles;* and a new date must be assigned for their commencement based on *better principles.* Now, that the commencement of the reign of Artaxerxes Longimanus was B. C. 464–3, is demonstrated by the agreement of above twenty eclipses, which have been repeatedly calculated, and have invariably been found to fall in the times specified. Before it can be shown that the commencement of his reign is wrongly fixed, it must first be shown that those eclipses have been wrongly calculated. This no one has done, or will ever venture to do. Consequently, the commencement of his reign cannot be removed from that point."—*Advent Herald,* Feb. 15, 1857.

It will thus be seen that the date of the seventh year of Artaxerxes rests very largely upon the records of history respecting eclipses, and the testimony of astronomy as to the time when those eclipses occurred. Of the accuracy with which the dates of eclipses may be settled, Prof. Mitchell eloquently says:—

"Go back three thousand years—stand upon that mighty watch-tower, the temple of Belus, in old Babylon—and look out. The sun is sinking in eclipse, and great is the dismay of the terror-stricken inhabitants. We have the fact and circumstances recorded. But how shall we prove that record correct? The astronomer unravels the devious movements of the sun, the earth, and the moon, through the whole period of three thousand years; with the power of intellect, he goes backward through the cycles of thirty long centuries, and announces that at such an hour and such a day—as the Chaldean has written—that eclipse did take place."

Respecting the authority of the Canon of Ptolemy, Prideaux, vol. i. p. 242, thus speaks:—

"But Ptolemy's Canon being fixed by the eclipses, the truth of it may at any time be demonstrated by astronomical calculations, and no one hath ever calculated those eclipses but hath found them fall right in the times where placed; and therefore this being the surest guide which we have in the chronology, and it being also verified by its agreement everywhere with the Holy Scriptures, it is not, for the authority of any other human writing whatsoever, to be receded from."

Thus positively do we find the date for which we seek. The seventh of Artaxerxes was B. C. 457, and there the seventy weeks commenced.

Chapter Eight.

INTERMEDIATE AND CLOSING DATES OF THE SEVENTY WEEKS.

FROM the seventh of Artaxerxes Longimanus, B. C. 457, the point from which we have found that the seventy weeks are to be dated, we drop the plummet down through following years to ascertain whether, measuring our lines according to the prophecy, we strike the other events which the prediction brings to our view.

The first line is forty-nine years in length; for, says the prophecy, there shall be seven weeks (49 symbolic days, or 49 literal years), during which the street and wall shall be built in troublous times. Dan. 9:25. This brings us to the time when the work of building was completed; and this was finished in the last act of reformation under Nehemiah, in the fifteenth year of Darius Nothus.

Forty-nine years from B. C. 457 bring us to B. C. 408.

The fifteenth year of Darius Nothus was B. C. 408.—*Prideaux, Bliss, Hales.*

Thus at our first testing-point, the event answers to the prophecy, as the shadow answers to the face in the mirror.

Three other events remain by which to test the application of this prophecy: 1. Sixty-nine weeks, or 483 years, were to extend to the Messiah the Prince; 2. Sixty-nine and one-half weeks, or 486½ years, were to extend to the cutting off of the Messiah; and 3. The seventy weeks, 490 years, were to extend to that point when the Jews should no longer be the peculiar people of God. If, reckoning from B. C. 457, we find the measurements to reach the events specified, the correctness of the application will be assured beyond the least shadow of uncertainty.

The word Messiah means "the anointed;" and the expression "to the Messiah the Prince," must point to the time when Christ was manifested to the world as the anointed of God. This was not at his birth, as some have imagined, but at his baptism, as is proved by Acts 10:38; 4:27; Luke 4:18, etc.

We have therefore to inquire (1) at what point, according to the foregoing dates, the baptism of Christ should have occurred; (2) at what point it did occur; (3) to ascertain the length of Christ's ministry; (4) the date of the crucifixion; and (5) the time when the blessings of the gospel ceased to be especially offered to the Jews.

1. From some point in the year B. C. 457, the period of sixty-nine weeks or 483 years to the Messiah the Prince would carry us to a corresponding point in the year A. D. 27. This is the answer to the first point of inquiry; and if the first date is correct, here we should find the baptism of the Saviour.

2. When Christ entered upon his mission, immediately after his baptism, he came into Galilee preaching the gospel of the kingdom of God, and saying, "*The time is fulfilled.*" Mark 1:14, 15. This must mark the fulfillment of some definite period, or it would not be asserted that "the time is fulfilled." The time here fulfilled can be none other than that given in Dan. 9:25: "Unto the Messiah the Prince shall be seven weeks, and threescore and two weeks," 483 years. We are therefore correct in saying that this is the period that reaches to his baptism. Can we now ascertain in what year his baptism occurred?

Christ was six months younger than John the Baptist, and is generally considered to have entered upon his ministry six months later; both of them commencing their work, according to the law of the priesthood, when they were thirty years of age. Of Christ, Luke says expressly that at the time of his baptism he began to be about thirty years of age. Luke 3 : 23. Now John entered upon his ministry, as Luke informs us (3 : 1), in the fifteenth year of Tiberius Cæsar. Tiberius was the successor of Augustus, who reigned to A. D. 14. The date of Augustus' death is indisputably fixed by means of the great lunar eclipse soon after, Sept. 27, which served to quell the mutiny of the Pannonian legions, and to induce them to swear fidelity to Tiberius, as recorded by Tacitus, Anal. 1 : 28, and Dio. lib. 57, p. 604. But the reign of Tiberius is to be reckoned, according to Prideaux, Dr. Hales, Lardner, and others, from his elevation to the throne to reign jointly with Augustus his step-father, in August, A. D. 12, two years before the death of the latter. The fifteenth year of Tiberius would therefore be from August, A. D. 26, to August, A. D. 27. If John commenced in the spring in the latter portion of the fifteenth year of Tiberius, it would bring the commencement of Christ's ministry in the autumn of A. D. 27, the very point where the 483 years of Dan. 9 expire.

3. The length of Christ's ministry. This may be quite accurately determined by enumerating the passovers which he attended. There were but four of these as recorded in John 2 : 13; 5 : 1; 6 : 4; and 13 : 1. At the last of these he was

crucified. This would make the duration of his ministry three years and a half. Thus, if he commenced in the autumn of A. D. 27, he would preach six months before his first passover in the spring of 28. His second passover would be in the spring of 29, his third in the spring of 30, and his fourth in the spring of 31, when he was crucified.

This would correspond exactly to the prophecy; for he was to confirm the covenant with many for one week, seven years, and in the midst, or middle, of the week, he was to be cut off, and cause the sacrifice and oblation to cease. This he did when he expired upon the cross, three and one-half years from the commencement of his ministry; and during the remainder of the week he confirmed the covenant through his apostles. Heb. 2:3. Dr. Hales, vol. i. p. 94, quotes Eusebius, A. D. 300, as saying: "It is recorded in history, that the whole time of our Saviour's teaching and working miracles was *three years and a half*, which is the *half of a week* [of years]. This John the evangelist will represent to those who critically attend to his gospel."

4. The date which this gives us for the crucifixion, A. D. 31, is confirmed by abundance of tes-

timony. The crucifixion was attended by a preternatural darkening of the sun, for the space of three hours. Matt. 27 : 45. "A total eclipse of the moon may occasion a privation of her light for an hour and a half, during her total immersion in the shadow; whereas a total eclipse of the sun can never last in any particular place above *four minutes,* when the moon is nearest to the earth and her shadow thickest."—*Hales,* vol. i. p. 69.

This darkness was observed at Heliopolis in Egypt, by Dionysius the Areopagite, afterward the illustrious convert of Paul at Athens, Acts 17 : 34, who in a letter to the martyr Polycarp describes his own astonishment at the phenomenon, and that of his companion, the sophist Apollophanes. "These, O good Dionysius," exclaimed Apollophanes, "are the vicissitudes of divine events." To which Dionysius answered, "Either the Deity suffers or he sympathizes with the sufferer." And that sufferer, according to tradition, recorded by Michael Syncellus of Jerusalem, he declared to be, "the unknown God, for whose sufferings all nature was darkened and convulsed."—*Id.,* vol. iii. p. 230.

"Hence it appears that the darkness which 'overspread the whole land of Judea' at the time of our Lord's crucifixion was preternatural, 'from the sixth until the ninth hour,' or from noon till three in the afternoon, in its *duration*, as also in its *time*, about full moon, when the moon could not possibly eclipse the sun. The *time it happened*, and the *fact itself*, are recorded in a curious and valuable passage of a Roman Consul, Aurelius Cassiodorius Senator, about A. D. 514. 'In the consulate of Tiberius Cæsar Aug. v. and Ælius Sejanus (U. C. 784, A. D. 31), our Lord Jesus Christ suffered, on the 8th of the Calends of April (25th of March): when there happened such an eclipse of the sun as was never before nor since.' In this year and in this day agree also the Council of Cæsarea, A. D. 196 or 198; the Alexandrian Chronicle, Maximus Monachus, Nicephorus Constantinus, Cedrenus; and in this year, but on different days, concur Eusebius, Epiphanius, followed by Kepler, Bucher, Patinus, and Petavius, some reckoning it the 10th of the Calends of April, others the 13th."—*Id.*, vol. i. pp. 69, 70.

The common Bible chronology placing the crucifixion in A. D. 33, was, according to Dr. Hales, assumed on no earlier authority than that of Roger Bacon, in the 13th century, who, finding by computation that the paschal full moon fell on Friday in the year 33, was led by that circumstance to suppose that that must have been the year of the crucifixion. But this very circumstance Dr. H. claims as proof that that was not the year; for the true paschal full moon should come not on the day of the crucifixion, but the day before, when Christ ate the passover with his disciples.—*Id.*, p. 100.

We have thus thirteen creditable authorities locating the crucifixion in the spring of A. D. 31. And all the evidence on this point tends also to establish the date of Christ's baptism in the autumn of A. D. 27; for, according to the prophecy, the Messiah was to be cut off after three years and a half from the time of his manifestation; and, according to the evangelists, his ministry continued just that length of time, three years and a half. If, therefore, he was crucified in the spring of A. D. 31, he was baptized and commenced to preach three and a half years before, in the autumn of A. D. 27.

And right at that point the sixty-nine weeks ended, reckoned from B. C. 457, and in A. D. 31 we reached the middle of the last or seventieth week, where the Messiah was to be cut off, and cause the sacrifice and oblation (the Jewish sacrifices and offerings) to cease by the offering of himself, as the great antitype of them all, upon the cross.

So far, we find the most striking and indisputable harmony. We now go forward three and a half years to the terminal point of this grand prophetic period of seventy weeks, and inquire what then occurred. On this point we quote again from the learned Dr. Hales:—

"Eusebius dates the first half of the passion week of years as beginning with our Lord's baptism, and ending with his crucifixion. The same period precisely is recorded by Peter, as including the duration of our Lord's personal ministry: 'All the time that the Lord Jesus went in and out among us, beginning from the baptism of [or by] John, until the day that he was taken up from us,' at his ascension, which was only 43 days after the crucifixion. Acts 1:21, 22. And the remaining half of the passion week ended with the martyrdom of Stephen, in the seventh or last year of the week. For it is remarkable that the year after, A. D. 35, began a new era in the church, namely, the conversion of Saul, or Paul, the apostle, by the personal appearance of Christ to him on the road to Damascus, when he received his mission to the *Gentiles*, after the *Jewish* Sanhedrim had formally rejected Christ

by persecuting his disciples. Acts 9 : 1–18."
—Vol. i. p. 100.

Thus at precisely the right point we find events which fitly mark the termination of that period which was allotted to Jerusalem and the Jews: Stephen is martyred, Paul is raised up an apostle to the Gentiles, the Jews formally reject Christ and the gospel in the persons of the first disciples, and the apostles turn from the Jews to other nations. Surely a fulfillment of prophecy so plain cannot be questioned.

And with these facts all established by the clearest evidence, and the dates of the prophecy all thus harmonized, we have in our hands the key which will draw every bolt, and give us free entrance into all departments of the larger prophecy and longer period of the 2300 days.

From this point, the way is short and clear to the end of the argument respecting the time.

If we have a period of ten years, in reference to the location of which we wish to inform our friends, we need not tell them where the whole period terminates to convey to them the desired information. It would be sufficient to say, We will tell you all about the first five years of that period, where they begin and end, with intermediate dates and events. Then they could easily ascertain the termination of the whole period. After the first five years, five more would remain, and adding them to the date where the five terminated, they would have the true date of the termination of the ten.

Just this course inspiration has followed with the 2300 days. It is as if the angel had said to Daniel, I have not come to give you the year in which the 2300 days will end; but a portion of this period belongs to your people and your holy city Jerusalem; and this period, comprising seventy weeks which are the first 490 years of the 2300, I will tell you all about, giving you the time when they will commence, and the chief events which will mark intermediate dates, and finally their termination. And the angel well knew that he who had interest enough to inquire, could then easily find the termination of the whole period.

Thus four hundred and ninety years taken from twenty-three hundred, leave eighteen hundred and ten. Briefly expressed in figures it stands thus: $2300-490=1810$. And this number, eighteen hundred and ten, added to the date where the four hundred and ninety terminated, will give us the termination of the period of twenty-three hundred. But we have found that the four hundred and ninety ended in the autumn of A. D. 34. This gives us the following numerical statement: A. D. 34, autumn, +1810= A. D. 1844, autumn. In the autumn of A. D. 1844, we thus have the termination of the longest and most important prophetic period revealed in the Bible.

But some may fall into perplexity over the calculation of this period from another standpoint, and query how, if the 2300 days commenced B. C. 457, they can extend to A. D. 1844, since if we take 457 from 2300 we have only 1843 remaining. Did they not therefore terminate in 1843? So Adventists reasoned previous to that year; and this is the reason why that year was first set for the coming of the Lord. But further thought showed that they must extend into the following year. For it would take 457 *full* years before Christ, and 1843 *full* years after Christ, to make 2300. Therefore if the days commenced with the very *first* day of 457 B. C. they would not terminate till the very *last* day of 1843. But we have evidence to show that they did not commence with the first day of 457 B. C., but that some portion of that year had elapsed before we are to begin to reckon.

It is evident from the wording of the prophecy that the actual commencement of the work at Jerusalem marks the commencement of the seventy weeks, inasmuch as the first seven weeks are allotted to the building of the city, which we could hardly begin to reckon, consistently, before the work of building was actually begun. But Ezra did not arrive at Jerusalem till the fifth month of the seventh year of Artaxerxes (B. C. 457). Ez. 7 : 8. And after he had reached the city the large company that went up with him were to be provided with homes, and arrangements made for their living, etc., before they would be ready to take hold of the work of rebuilding the wall and the city proper. Two months would certainly be short enough time to allow for this work, which would bring us to the seventh month, or the autumn of the year. Now whatever portion of the year B. C. 457 had elapsed before the 2300 years began, just that portion of a year we must add to 1843 A. D. to make out the 2300 full years; for if only 456 years and a fraction are to be reckoned before Christ, we must have 1843 and a fraction after Christ to make out the number. For taking 456 years and five months from 2300 years, we have remaining 1843 years and seven months, which seven months carry us so far into the year 1844. Thus are we brought again to the autumn of 1844, as the point where the 2300 days terminated.

The same argument will apply to the date of Christ's baptism. How do we make that date to be A. D. 27, when 457 years before Christ and only 26 after Christ make out the 483 years which were to reach to Messiah the Prince? In the same way as above presented. For if any portion of B. C. 457 had elapsed before we should begin to reckon, a corresponding portion of A. D. 27 must be taken to fill out the specified number of full years. And the events associated with this, in the prophecy of the seventy weeks, are such as to show conclusively that the days terminated in the autumn of the year. At the beginning of the seventieth week the Messiah was to be manifested, that is, commence his ministry as the Anointed One. In the midst, or middle, of that week, which would be three years and six months from its commencement, he was to be cut off. This cutting off can refer to nothing else but his crucifixion. But his crucifixion, in whatever year it may have occurred, was in the spring; for it was at the passover. Then, as we go back from the crucifixion of Christ three years and six months to find the commencement of his ministry, we are brought to the autumn; and as we go forward from the crucifixion three years and six months, to the end of the seventieth week, we are again brought to the autumn. But, as has already been shown, A. D. 31 has been established beyond dispute as the year of the crucifixion; and as this was the middle of the seventieth week, the last half of the week, three and a half years more, brings us to the autumn of A. D. 34. But if the first 490 years ended in the autumn of A. D. 34, the remaining 1810 years just as conclusively ended in the autumn of A. D. 1844.

We are thus particular upon this point, because this is *the* important one of all the prophetic periods; and it is desirable that all points in the argument should be clearly understood.

And what were some of the circumstances which rendered 1844 a memorable date in the history of the church and the world? We then reached, if we may so speak, the climax of the world's great prophetic era. Within the forty-six years preceding, five of the seven prominent prophetic periods of the Bible had terminated.

1. The 1290 years had ended in 1798.

2. The 1260 years had ended in the same

year, and marked the commencement of the "time of the end."

3. The 391 years and 15 days of Rev. 9, had ended Aug. 11, 1840, and marked the fall of the Ottoman empire as an independent government; for since that time it has existed only by the sufferance of the so-called Christian powers of Europe.

4. The 1335 years had expired in 1843, and marked the manifestation of such a "blessing" as the disciples at Christ's first advent were themselves permitted to enjoy. Dan. 12:12; Matt. 13:16, 17.

5. And now in 1844, the great period of 2300 years was finished, which marked the commencement of the work of the cleansing of the sanctuary.

God has never left his church without faithful watchmen, and in such an important epoch as the one we are considering, we cannot suppose that they would be asleep. And they were not asleep. A warning message to the world, which commenced some years before, had now swelled into a mighty cry. A movement such as the world had never before witnessed, now reached the height of its power. The impending second advent of the Son of God was the burden of the proclamation. Sublimer theme never engaged the attention of man. In different parts of the world, men simultaneously called of God to this work were heralding it abroad. It went to every missionary station on the globe. Treasure was poured out like water in its promulgation. An army of able and devoted men appeared, who freely gave their time, talent, and strength to its vindication. The spirit of revival everywhere followed the proclamation of the message. God was in the movement; and Christendom was shaken from center to circumference.

What did all this mean? It meant that the first division of this three-fold warning which was to precede the coming of Christ was going forth. Rev. 14:6–12. It meant that the mighty angel standing on the sea and on the land had uttered his solemn oath that time (prophetic) should be no more; Rev. 10:6; for the time had come for the longest and latest prophetic period to meet its termination.

A grievous disappointment was experienced in that movement, and a mistake had somewhere been made, yet it becomes us not hastily nor rashly to decide in regard to the nature of that work. As was asked respecting the baptism of John, we ask respecting this movement: Was it of Heaven or of men? And the same difficulties are involved in the answer: If it was of Heaven, we cannot give it up; but how then can we account for the mistake connected with it, without compromising its heavenly origin? But if it was of men, how shall we solve the still harder problem of accounting for the presence and power of God that so manifestly attended it?

Now if in 1840, 1843, and 1844, the last prophetic periods did end, that fact would be a sufficient reason why God's hand should be in the movement based upon that fulfillment of his word, even though we might have adopted wrong views in reference to the event to occur, as did the disciples of our Lord, when in fulfillment of his word, they escorted him into Jerusalem, as their immediately expected King, shouting, "Hosanna to the Son of David. Blessed is he that cometh in the name of the Lord." Matt. 21: 4–9.

With this view, therefore, that the prophetic periods did expire, but the mistake was in relation to the event, we are not obliged to repudiate and throw away that great work. We can give it its place in prophecy, and gratefully acknowledge the wonderful work of God connected with it.

But if we take the ground that the prophetic

U OF M

periods did not then expire, the whole work falls to the ground as wholly false and unscriptural. For if the termination of the prophetic periods is yet future, another like movement is to transpire, and the one we have had was a counterfeit and a fraud. Then we must attribute to fanaticism that work which gave every evidence of being wrought by the Spirit of God, and admit that in this important age, marked as the time of the end, when the world is to be warned of coming Judgment, the most devoted and intelligent students of prophecy, and the most consecrated servants of Christ, were left to enter upon a false movement, and make an unpardonable mistake, which was calculated to destroy the confidence of the world in all prophetic investigation. But such a conclusion cannot for a moment be entertained by any candid and consistent mind. Hence we must look for the mistake, not in the prophetic periods, the evidence for which, as we have seen, remains unshaken, but in the views then entertained of the event to take place at their termination.

We need not pursue this line of thought to any greater length. The evidence is now before the reader that the calculation of the time was correct; that Dan. 9 is an explanation of Dan. 8;

M 10 U

that the seventy weeks are a part of the 2300 days; that they are correctly dated from B. C. 457, and that, consequently, the 2300 days terminated in 1844. With the utmost assurance, we therefore say that those who endeavor to account for the disappointment of 1844 on the supposition that the mistake was made in the time, and not in the sanctuary question, are entirely wrong.

Chapter Nine.

THE ORIGINAL ADVENT FAITH.

SEVENTH-DAY ADVENTISTS are sometimes charged with being a mere offshoot from the Advent body, followers of side issues and newly created hobbies. We claim, and shall show, that we are the only ones who adhere to the original principles of interpretation on which the whole Advent movement was founded, and that we are the only ones who are following out that movement to its logical results and conclusions.

The reader has seen something of the strength of the argument by which the original application of the prophetic periods is sustained. Those who have attempted to re-adjust those periods, in order to extend them to some future point of time when Palestine or the earth should be purified by fire, have found themselves in an extremely embarrassing position. Their own confessions have proved this; and the reader will be interested to see some of them.

Josiah Litch, a prominent writer and laborer in the early stage of the Advent movement, spoke as follows in the *Advent Herald* of Dec. 28, 1850:—

"Chronologically, *the period* [2300 days] *is at an end,* according to the best light to be obtained on the subject; and where the discrepancy is, I am unable to decide. But of this we shall know more in due time.

'God is his own interpreter,
And he will make it plain.'"

The *Advent Herald,* seeing the utter inconsistency of denying the termination of the 2300 days in the past, while at the same time it was setting forth unanswerable arguments in vindication of the original date for the commencement of the period, as it long continued to do, in connection with the seventy weeks, it at last *denied* the *connection* between the seventy weeks and the 2300 days, and thus cut this latter period adrift upon the prophetic sea. This appears from the following queries by a correspondent, and the answers of the then editor of the *Herald,* inclosed in brackets, which appeared in the *Herald* of May 22, 1852:—

"In your 'chronology' the cross is placed in A. D. 31. What are the principal objections which bear against its being placed in A. D. 39?

[Ans. 1. The absence of any evidence placing it there. 2. The contradiction of the wonderful astronomical, chronological, and historical co-incidences, which show beyond the shadow of controversy that the seventh of Artaxerxes was in B. C. 457–8, that the birth of Christ was B. C. 4–5, that the thirtieth year of Christ was 483 years from the seventh of Artaxerxes, that the crucifixion was in A. D. 31, and that that was the point of time in the last week, when the sacrifice and oblation should cease.]

"If the seventy weeks of Dan. 9 do not commence in the twentieth of Artaxerxes, how can the 2300 days begin at the same time with them, and yet terminate in the future? [Ans. They cannot.] Must we not henceforth consider that they have different starting-points? [Ans. Yes.]"

To understand how serious a departure this was from the "original Advent faith," the reader should bear in mind the following statements which under the significant heading of "Points of Difference between Us and our Opponents," once formed a standing notice in the Advent papers:—

"We claim that the 9th of Daniel is an appendix to the 8th, and that the seventy weeks and the 2300 days or years commence together. *Our opponents deny this.*" See *Signs of the Times,* 1843.

Who now deny this? All who call themselves Adventists, so far as we know, except the Seventh-day Adventists. And in what position do they place themselves by this denial? In the position of those who were originally the *opponents* of the Advent faith. Gone over to the side of their opponents, and yet claiming to be the adherents of the original Advent faith!

The declaration above quoted is as good for us to-day as it was for the *Signs of the Times* in 1843. It still flies from our mast-head.

"*We claim that the 9th of Daniel is an appendix to the 8th, and that the seventy weeks and 2300 days or years commence together.* OUR *opponents* [*apostatized Adventists*] DENY THIS."

Who, then, are the original Adventists?

Again, to show the importance which was formerly attached to this matter, we quote from the *Advent Shield,* p. 49, art., "The Rise and Progress of Adventism":—

"The grand principle involved in the interpretation of the 2300 days of Dan. 8:14, is, that the seventy weeks of Dan. 9:24, are the first 490 days of the 2300 of the 8th chapter."

Those who have yielded this point have therefore given up the "grand principle involved in the interpretation of the 2300 days." If to do this, and go over to the position of "our [their] opponents," is not a serious defection from the original Advent faith, we greatly err.

The following well-founded opinion was expressed by Apollos Hale in 1846:—

"The second point to be settled, in explaining the text [Dan. 9:24], is to show what vision it is which the seventy weeks are said to seal. And it should be understood this involves one of the great questions which constitute the main pillars of our system of interpretation, so far as prophetic times are concerned. If the connection between the seventy weeks of Dan. 9, and the 2300 days of Dan. 8, does not exist, the whole system is shaken to its foundation; if it does exist, as we suppose, the system must stand."—*Harmony of Prophetic Chronology*, p. 33.

Mark this language. The connection between Daniel 8 and 9 constitutes one of the "*main pillars*" of our system of interpretation. If it does not exist, the whole system is shaken to its foundation. If it does exist, the system must stand. We rejoice in the fact to-day that this connection does exist, and the system stands.

And now, what are the reasons offered for

taking a position which denies one of the main pillars of this system of interpretation, and shakes it to its very foundation? Simply this:—

"We have no new light respecting the connection between the seventy weeks and 2300 days. The *only* argument against their connection is, the passing of the time. Why that has passed, is a mystery to us, which we wait to have revealed."—*Advent Herald*, Sept. 7, 1850.

The same paper, in its issue of Feb. 22, 1851, further said:—

"Before 1843, we became satisfied of the validity of the arguments sustaining their connection and simultaneous commencement. There has nothing transpired to weaken the force of those arguments but the passing of the time we expected for their termination. We now have no other fact to advance against their connection; and, therefore, can only wait for the mystery of the passing of time to be explained. But of the commencement and termination of the seventy weeks, we are satisfied that they cannot be removed from the position which Protestants have always assigned them."

Before such a matter-of-course surrender was made of the strongest evidence and clearest proofs that can be drawn from the word of God on any subject, we submit to the reader if it would not have been more logical to inquire whether there might not possibly be some mistake in the view that the earth is the sanctuary, and that the cleansing of the sanctuary is to be by fire at the second coming of Christ; whether the days may not have ended, and the work to which they brought us, whatever it is, be now in process of fulfillment. S. D. Adventists, before rejecting the past movement, raised this inquiry, and the result has repaid our researches a thousand-fold, as will hereafter appear.

And how do those who disconnect the seventy weeks and 2300 days dispose of this latter period? for something must be done with it. They attempt to date it from the point at which Daniel saw the ram pushing westward and northward and southward so that no beast might stand before him; and that pushing they make to be the decree issued against the Jews, as recorded in the book of Esther. As the result of the pushing in the prophecy, no beast could stand before him. This view therefore makes the Jews to be the beasts. But how did this matter come out? A counter decree was issued; fear of the Jews fell upon all the people; many joined themselves to them; and when the day of slaughter came, no man could withstand the Jews. Esth. 9:2. They smote all their enemies. Verse 5. Seventy and five thousand Persians fell before them; and it was to them a day of triumph and joy. This, forsooth, was the ram pushing and doing according to his will, and becoming "great," so that none could deliver out of his hand! To such absurdities are men driven in trying to avoid the plain and evident conclusions to be derived from God's word. That men should seriously argue in this manner is one of those strange phenomena that sometimes appear in the workings of the human mind.

But even dating from this point, and recklessly changing the date of it as some have done to as late a year as B. C. 426, the time has now run out. Every limit to which the 2300 days can be extended is passed by. Time has thus demonstrated that these days have ended. All we now ask of any one is to accede to unquestionable facts, and admit that these days are in the past.

But if time has demonstrated that these days are in the past, it has also demonstrated that the earth is not the sanctuary, the very point claimed by those who offer this fact as the explanation of our disappointment in 1844; for no change has come over the earth except, physically, increasing signs of infirmity and old age, and, morally, a deeper plunge into wickedness and sin, on the part of its fast-degenerating sons and daughters. The former view, that the earth is the sanctuary, being thus demonstrated to be incorrect, the inquiry, What is the Sanctuary? is now fairly in hand, and peremptorily demands an answer.

Chapter Ten.

WHAT IS THE SANCTUARY?

THIS is exclusively a Bible question. With the testimony of the Bible only, then, have we to do. The object of our inquiry can only be, What does the Bible reveal to us respecting the sanctuary? And we shall find its testimony neither brief nor obscure on this important subject. The word occurs in the inspired Scriptures one hundred and forty-six times; and more times than this does it offer us instruction by prediction, definition, or historic record, concerning this wonderful object.

Perhaps no language can better introduce this subject than that of the apostle Paul in his letter to the Hebrews. In chapter 8, he speaks of the two covenants, the first and the second, the old and the new, under the latter of which we now live. In chapter 9, he shows that both these covenants have a sanctuary, as follows:—

"Then verily the first covenant had also ordinances of divine service, and a worldly *sanctuary.* For there was a tabernacle made; the first, wherein was the candlestick, and the table, and the show-bread; which is called the sanctuary. And after the second vail, the tabernacle which is called the holiest of all; which had the golden censer, and the ark of the covenant overlaid round about with gold, wherein was the golden pot that had manna, and Aaron's rod that budded, and the tables of the covenant; and over it the cherubims of glory shadowing the mercy-seat," etc. Verses 1–5.

Let this language of the apostle be carefully considered. It both introduces and settles one great division of this question. It tells us definitely what, for a time, constituted the sanctuary of the Lord. During the period covered by the first covenant, while the tabernacle, ordained as thus plainly described, was in existence, there can be, in the face of these words of Paul, no controversy as to what constituted the sanctuary. Turning to the records of those times, we find a more definite mention of this singular structure, which, from its bearings and relations in the temple of divine truth, deserves to be examined with absorbing interest.

Go back to the time when Israel, crowned with deliverance, stood on the shore of the Red Sea, while the Egyptians were perishing at their feet in the returning and angry waters. Listen to that song of triumph which Moses sings, and mark this language, "The Lord is my strength and song, and he is become my salvation; he is my God, and I will prepare him an habitation." Ex. 15 : 2. In this we receive the first intimation of that building that was afterward to be erected by the direction of the Lord, that he might dwell among his people. In Ex. 15 : 17, the word sanctuary occurs for the first time in the Bible.

Pursuing the sacred record, we find in the twenty-fifth chapter of Exodus, and onward, more definite information respecting the sanctuary. Here we read the commission which God gave to Moses for the erection of this building. In the third month after their departure from Egypt, the children of Israel came to the wilderness of Sinai. Moses was then summoned up into the mount, to an audience with his Maker. Forty days and nights were consumed in that memorable interview. During this time Moses was shown the pattern of the sanctuary, and all the sacred vessels, and received full instructions in relation thereto.

A particular description of the tabernacle, as erected by Moses, is minutely set forth in Exodus, chapters 25–31. It was a structure of extraordinary magnificence, and was erected after the following plan: Its walls on the north, west, and south sides were formed of upright boards set in sockets of silver. These boards were of shittim wood, each board being ten cubits in length and one cubit and a half in breadth. As there were twenty of these boards on each side, the tabernacle was thirty cubits in length. The best critics assure us that the shorter cubit of eighteen inches was the one now in use by the Jews, as it was not till after their return from the captivity that they occasionally used the Babylonian cubit of twenty-one inches. This would give us forty-five feet in English measurement as the length of the structure. Josephus gives ten cubits, or fifteen feet, as its width. This is more difficult to determine from the Scripture record. Six boards are mentioned as provided for closing the west end. These we are to suppose were of the same dimensions as the others, which would give us nine cubits. Then two more boards are spoken of "for the corners of the tabernacle in the two sides." Supposing these to have been each half a cubit in width, this would give the tenth cubit, and would preserve uniformity and consistency in the construction.

These boards were joined together in a manner to be easily taken apart. The two sockets which received the contiguous tenons of two boards as they stood up side by side may themselves have been joined together, which would have secured the lower ends of the boards firmly in place; while to strengthen the sides, five bars of shittim wood were provided to run through rings of gold secured to the boards. The middle bar was to reach from end to end. Both bars and boards were heavily overlaid with purest gold. So far, therefore, as this part of the structure is concerned, it presented the appearance of solid gold.

The space inclosed by these golden boards, forty-five feet in length, and fifteen in width, was divided into two apartments by a magnificent vail of blue and purple and scarlet and fine-twined linen, of cunning work, adorned with figures of cherubim, and suspended from four pillars of shittim wood overlaid with gold and set in sockets of silver. In what proportion the sanctuary was thus divided we are not informed; but it was undoubtedly the same as that afterward observed in the temple, 1 Kings 6, in which two-thirds of the space was allotted to the first apartment, and the remaining one-third to the second. On this calculation, the first apartment, called the holy place, was thirty feet by fifteen, the length being just twice as much as the width, and fifteen feet high, the length of the boards being ten cubits; while the second apartment, called the most holy, was a perfect cube, being fifteen feet in all its dimensions.

The roof of the tabernacle was formed by four sets of curtains. The dimensions of two of these are very fully given in Ex. 26:1, and onward. The innermost curtains of fine-twined linen were ten in number, each four cubits wide and twenty-eight in length. These were of various colors, and ornamented with cherubim of cunning work. Five of these were sewed together so as to form larger curtains, each twenty cubits by twenty-eight; and these two when used were joined together by fifty gold buckles or clasps. This being the first curtain thrown over, would form a surpassingly beautiful ceiling for both apartments.

Above this were placed curtains of goats' hair, each four cubits wide, and thirty cubits long, but eleven in number. These were also sewed together, six into one curtain, and five into the other, and when used were likewise joined together by fifty gold buckles.

Over these was placed a third covering of rams' skins with the wool on, dyed red, and a fourth covering of badgers' skins is also specified. The number of these coverings, and the material of which the two latter were composed, would suggest thorough protection against either the sun or rain. It is thought that the design could not be to provide against rain, as rain but rarely falls in the wilderness of Sinai, where the children of Israel now were. But we must remember that the sanctuary was to retain its present form after its entrance into the promised land, where provision would have to be made against heavy dews and abundant rains; and the tabernacle did remain as now constructed for over five hundred years, till the days of Solomon.

It has been a question how these coverings were applied to the tabernacle. If they were thrown straight over there would be a depression or sagging in the center, and water would certainly work through, and snow would form such a weight as to tear the curtains to pieces. Besides, applied in this way, the curtain of goats' hair, being thirty cubits long, would hang over the walls of the tabernacle ten cubits, or in other words, reach the ground on both sides; whereas it seems to have been designed, according to Ex. 26:13, to hang down only one cubit on each side.

In view of these difficulties and objections, Smith, in his unabridged Bible Dictionary, art., Temple, argues that the sacred tent must have been raised in the center, or have had a ridge, as all tents have had from the days of Moses to the present time; and that only the inner curtain of fine linen wrought with cherubim was drawn straight across over the walls of the tabernacle, while the other coverings were raised in the form of a tent inclosing and protecting the inner structure. These views are illustrated with a diagram and perspective view, which make it appear extremely probable that the coverings were arranged in this manner.

Around the tabernacle was a larger space called the court, Ex. 27:9–18, consisting of a double square fifty cubits, or seventy-five feet, wide, by one hundred cubits, or one hundred and fifty feet, long. This was inclosed by hangings, or canvas screens of fine-twined linen, suspended from pillars of brass five cubits in height, provided with sockets of brass and hooks and fillets of silver. These posts or pillars were set five cubits apart, and the inclosure was continuous except on the eastern side where an entrance was provided twenty cubits in width, closed with curtains of fine-twined linen, wrought with needle-work, and of the most gorgeous colors. It will be noticed that all the important dimensions of the court and the tabernacle were five cubits or some multiple of five cubits. Everything was constructed with regard to beauty and of such material as would impress every beholder with a sense of the importance of these objects, and the purity and sacredness of the worship connected therewith.

Around the tabernacle and its court, the tribes of the children of Israel were to pitch their tents in four great bodies, Zebulon, Judah, and Issachar, under the standard of Judah on the east; Gad, Reuben, and Simeon, under the standard of Reuben on the south; Benjamin, Ephraim, and Manasseh, under the standard of Ephraim on the west; and Naphtali, Dan, and Asher, under the standard of Dan on the north. Numbers 2. The grand encampment thus consisted of 186,400 men on the east, 151,450 on the south, 108,100 on the west, and 157,600 on the north. Besides these, the tribe of Levi was divided into three parts according to his three sons, Gershon, Kohath, and Merari, who were to locate in more immediate proximity to the tabernacle, the Kohathites, 2,750 strong, on the south side, the Gershonites, numbering 2,650, on the west, and the Merarites, 3,200, on the north. But on the east side of the tabernacle, Moses and Aaron and his sons were to encamp, and "keep the charge of the sanctuary." Num. 3:38.

Could we roll the wheels of time backward thirty-three hundred and twenty-eight years, and from some commanding height in Horeb look down upon the broad valley covered with Israel's moving multitudes, and white with their canvas dwellings, the priests in goodly array busy with their service, the smoke of sacrifice and the odor of incense ascending, and over all the glory of God hovering in a pillar of cloud by day and of fire by night, we should doubtless say, as Balaam did when the Spirit of God came upon him, and he heard the words of God and saw the vision of the Almighty, "How goodly are thy tents, O Jacob, and thy tabernacles, O Israel!" Here was then the connecting link between earth and Heaven. Here was that people whom God had chosen to keep alive the knowledge of himself and of his truth in the world, moving on under his guidance to the promised land, prefiguring that vaster multitude which shall one day go up from all lands to the possession of the heavenly Canaan. Here was his organized worship with its solemn and impressive forms set before the world; and of that worship, the tabernacle, this new-made sanctuary, was the life and the center.

Let us draw near and look at the furniture of

this wonderful building. As we enter the court we find standing nearest the door the altar of burnt-offering. This was five cubits square and three cubits high. As its name implies, it was used for the many burnt-offerings to be presented by that people. It was overlaid with brass, and all its instruments were made of brass.

Between this altar and the tabernacle, which was placed in the western square of the court, stood the laver, in which the priests were to wash both their hands and their feet when they went into the tabernacle of the congregation, or when they approached the altar to offer a burnt-offering unto the Lord. This also was made of brass.

The entrance to the tabernacle was closed by a curtain or vail like the one which divided between the holy place and the most holy place. In material, workmanship, and uses, these two vails were exactly alike. The curtain at the door may be called the *first* vail, as the curtain leading into the most holy is called the *second* vail. Heb. 9 : 3. These vails are described in Ex. 26 : 31–37, where in verse 36 the word rendered "hanging," which was at the door, is in the Septuagint the same word which is rendered "vail" in verse 33, which divided between the holy and the most holy.

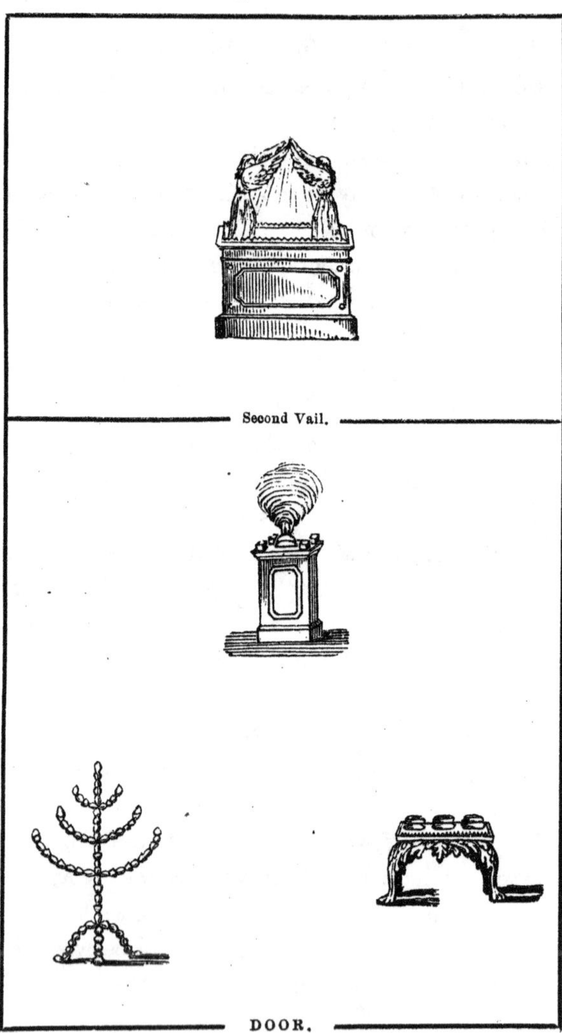

PLAN OF THE SANCTUARY.

In the holy place were three objects worthy of notice: a candlestick, a table of show-bread, and an altar of incense. The candlestick was made with a standard and seven branches, beaten out of one solid piece of gold about the weight of a talent. According to the Rabbis, says Smith's Dictionary, its height was five feet, and the breadth or distance between the exterior branches, three and one-half feet. It is estimated to have been worth 5,076 pounds sterling, or $25,380, exclusive of workmanship. The seven lamps supported by the seven branches of the candlestick were obviously for the purpose of giving light in the holy place; but whether they were kept burning by day as well as by night has been a matter of some discussion; and a difference of opinion is still entertained. As no light could penetrate through the thick coverings thrown over the sanctuary, there would be as much need of the light of the lamps by day as by night, unless the curtain which constituted the door of the tabernacle was drawn one side, which can hardly be supposed. It seems most consistent to believe that the lamps, like the fire on the altar, were to burn without cessation. The replenishing and trimming of the lamps would necessitate the removal of only one at a time from the candlestick. Thus each in turn could be trimmed while the others were burning. The position of the candlestick was on the south side of the holy place.

On the north side of the holy place, opposite the candlestick, stood the table of show-bread. It was about three feet in length, one and a half in width, and two feet and three inches in height. Like some of the other furniture, it was made of the fine shittim wood, or acacia, of that country, and was overlaid with pure gold, with a crown of gold running around its upper outer edge. On it the show-bread was always kept before the Lord, being changed by the priests every Sabbath. There were twelve loaves, representing the twelve tribes of the children of Israel, and when the fresh loaves were placed upon the table on the Sabbath, the old were not to be removed from the sanctuary, but were to be eaten by the priests in the holy place.

The third object in the holy place was the altar of incense, which stood in the center laterally, and nearer to the inner vail. It was a foot and a half square, and three feet in height, made like the table of shittim wood, or acacia, and overlaid with gold. It was for the purpose of burning incense before the Lord at morning and evening when the high priest dressed and trimmed the lamps of the sanctuary. Ex. 30: 1–8.

In the most holy place there were likewise three things worthy of notice: the golden censer, the ark, and the mercy-seat.

First, the censer. This was an instrument held in the hand of the priest, and used for burning incense from place to place. According to various authors there were different kinds, sometimes suspended by chains, or borne by a handle, some of silver, some of gold, but particularly one of fine gold which was used only on the day of atonement, and was probably always kept, when not in use, in the most holy place, and hence is spoken of as pertaining to that apartment.

Second, the ark. This was a coffer or chest of precious wood overlaid within and without with the purest gold, two cubits and a half, or three feet nine inches, in length, and a cubit and a half, or two feet and three inches, in width and height. In this ark were sacredly deposited the two tables of stone containing God's ten commandments. It was made expressly for this purpose, and hence was called the ark of the covenant, and the ark of the testament, the ten commandments being God's covenant, and the basis of the mutual covenant called in the New Testament the first or old covenant, which was made between God and Israel. The ark, with the mercy-seat, was the most sacred object connected with that system of worship.

Third, the mercy-seat. This was simply the cover or lid of the ark; but it was a magnificent and costly piece of workmanship. It was beaten out of one solid piece of gold of the same length and width as the ark, and two cherubim were made, one standing on each end, beaten out of the same piece of gold. These cherubim were made looking reverently down upon the mercy-seat, and covering it with their wings, which were spread aloft and touched each other midway, above it.

A correct view of the mercy-seat would correct what seems to be a very common misapprehension in relation to the position and work of the high priest. We often hear the expression that Christ is still upon the mercy-seat. There is no mercy-seat but the cover of the ark; and Christ is our great High Priest; but the high priest never took his seat upon the ark. The mercy-seat was not the seat of the high priest. It would have been entirely out of place for the high priest to sit down upon the ark. But the cover of that ark was called the mercy-seat because there mercy had its seat. Beneath it was the law, and upon it was sprinkled the blood of sacrifice which satisfied the claims of the law, and let the sinner free. Hence, here was the focal point where mercy appeared. As the psalmist expresses it, here "mercy and truth met together, and righteousness and peace kissed each other." Ps. 85 : 10.

It was in this consecrated spot, between the cherubim over the mercy-seat, that the holy shekinah of God's presence was manifested, and from whence he usually communicated with his people.

For the construction of all this wonderful work God called certain ones, and qualified them by putting his Spirit upon them. The sanctuary was not therefore merely the work of men; it was the inspiration of Heaven manifested in works of art.

How impressive must have been the scene presented by the interior of this building. There were its walls, having all the appearance of massive and solid gold, and reflecting in a thousand directions the light of the seven lamps of the golden candlestick; there were the table of show-bread and the altar of incense, glittering in its light like burnished gold; and there was the curtain that formed the gorgeous ceiling, with its mystic figures of cherubim in blue, and purple, and scarlet, adding its beauty to the brilliant scene. While in, beyond the second vail, was the glorious shekinah, or visible manifestation of God's glory, into the awful presence of which, except the high priest's entrance once every year, no man could venture and live.

In the second year after Israel had departed from Egypt, in the first month, on the first day of the month, the tabernacle was reared up. And Moses spread abroad the tent over the tabernacle, and he put the testimony (the tables of the ten commandments) into the ark, and the mercy-seat upon it, and brought it into the tabernacle, and set up the vail; he placed the table of show-bread and the golden candlestick in the first apartment, and lighted the lamps before the Lord; he put the golden altar of incense before the vail, and burnt sweet incense thereon; and on the altar, before the door of the tabernacle, he offered the burnt-offering and the meat-offering as the Lord commanded. Then a cloud covered the tent of the congregation, and the glory of the Lord filled the tabernacle. Ex. 40. God had now taken possession of his dwelling-place, in the midst of his people.

We have now before us the sanctuary as Moses erected it in the wilderness of Sinai 1490 years before Christ. With its ark of the covenant, its mercy-seat, and its glorious shekinah, it constituted the heart and center of Israel's religious worship under that typical system.

The children of Israel being at this time in the period of their wanderings, the sanctuary as first given to them was adapted to their condition. It was, as we have seen, so constructed that it could be easily taken down and borne with them in their journeys, and immediately erected wherever the divine presence, which accompanied them in a cloud by day and a pillar of fire by night, should direct them to pitch their camp. Num. 9 : 15–23.

The Levites were consecrated to the service of the sanctuary, and were commanded to bear it, and all its sacred vessels, when the camp set forward. Thus it was with them during the forty years in which they journeyed in the wilderness. During this time, this building which God claimed as his dwelling-place, and where his service was performed, is fifty-six times called the sanctuary, in the following instances: Ex. 25:8; 30:13, 24; 36:1, 3, 4, 6; 38:24–27; Lev. 4:6; 5:15; 10:4; 12:4; 16:33; 19:30; 20:3; 21:12 (twice), 23 (plural); 26:2; 27:3, 25; Num. 3:28, 31, 32, 38, 47, 50; 4:12, 15 (twice), 16; 7:9, 13, 19, 25, 31, 37, 43, 49, 55, 61, 67, 73, 79, 85, 86; 8:19; 10:21; 18:1, 3, 5, 16; 19:20.

Chapter Eleven.

POINTS OF HISTORY.

THE object we now have before us, the tabernacle built by Moses, is one of exceeding interest. Its erection marks one of the most important epochs in the religious history of the world. Like the full-orbed moon, shining with a light borrowed from a central sun, a new dispensation was now rising upon the world to reflect the glory of the coming ministration of the Messiah. A people long schooled in the furnace of Egyptian servitude, were now brought forth amid such displays of God's consuming judgment and overwhelming power as were fitting to his purpose and to that occasion. Such a migration of an entire nation from one land to another the world had never seen. With that people God purposed to maintain henceforth a visible symbol of his presence; and this purpose called for the erection of a suitable dwelling-place. Of this, he gave to Moses a pattern throughout, and calling Bezaleel and Aholiab, endowed them with heavenly wisdom for their sacred work.

This marvelous structure, the tabernacle, was the result, with its gold-plated walls, its gold-covered furniture, its wonderfully embroidered curtains, its holy places, and its solemn service.

In the center of that vast camp of more than three millions of souls, that tabernacle was set up, and over it stood in towering majesty the pillar of cloud, a shade and refreshment by day, but glowing like a blaze of fire, the light and glory of the camp by night, to govern and guide and guard that living multitude.

In and around this tabernacle, the Lord met with his people. There he told Moses he would commune with him. Ex. 25 : 22. There the Spirit came upon the seventy elders and they prophesied. Num. 11 : 24, 25. Thither Aaron and Miriam are called out, when they rebel against the servant of the Lord. Num. 12 : 4. There the glory of the Lord appears after the unfaithfulness of the twelve spies, Num. 14 : 10, and the rebellion of Korah and his company, 16 : 19, 42, and the sin of Meribah, 20 : 6. Thither, when there was no sin to punish, but a difficulty to be met, the daughters of Zelophehad came to bring their cause before the Lord. Num. 27 : 2. And there, when the death of Moses drew near, the solemn charge was given to his successor. Deut. 31 : 14.

For all these reasons, this structure is an object of surpassing interest, and entitled to our careful consideration; but chiefly for this, because Paul says plainly that this was *the sanctuary* of that first covenant which immediately preceded and ushered in the present. It will be worth our while, therefore, to notice further the important place it held in that dispensation by looking at some of the chief features of its history.

According to the commonly received chronology, the sanctuary made its entrance into the promised land on the 10th day of the first month, B. C. 1451. Up to this time, neither the children of Israel nor the sanctuary had had any long-continued abiding-place. But now, as the former enter upon their promised inheritance, the latter begins to be more permanently located.

The first encampment, after the passage of the Jordan, was in Gilgal. Josh. 4 : 19. Here it abode seven years, and was then removed to Shiloh, according to God's promise that he would choose the place of its location. Josh. 9:27; 18:1. Shiloh was about fifteen miles north from Jerusalem, and nearly in the center of the whole land. Here, according to our Bible chronology, it remained from B. C. 1444, to B. C. 1141, a period of 303 years. But Paul makes the time still longer; for he says that after the dividing of the land by lot, God gave them judges about the space of four hundred and fifty years until Samuel the prophet. And it was not till after the call of Samuel the prophet that the ark was removed from its place by the infatuated and backslidden Israelites, and in the disastrous campaign which it was meant to redeem, fell into the hands of the Philistines.

This instructive episode in the history of the sanctuary demands a passing notice. In the long period of the continuance of the sanctuary at Shiloh, Israel had greatly apostatized from God. In the yearly feast and solemn dances, Judges 21:19, 21, the religion of Israel had sunk far toward the orgies of heathenism. Troops of women, shameless as those of Midian, assembling at the tabernacle as the worshipers of Jehovah, became the concubines of his priests. 1 Sam. 2:22, margin. "A state of things which was rapidly assimilating the worship of Jehovah to that of Ashtaroth, or Mylitta, needed to be broken up." So God forsook his habitation, and raised up the Philistines to chastise his rebellious subjects into the right way again.

Israel, unmindful of their only source of

strength, went boldly out to meet the enemy, but, as any one might have foreseen, were routed before them. And now they were left to pursue a course which would show both to themselves and others how low they had fallen. They doubtless had learned how in former times their fathers had been beaten by their enemies when they took not the ark with them to battle, as in the case with the Canaanites, Num. 14:44, 45, and how they had succeeded with it around the walls of Jericho, and resolved that the ark should be brought forth, vainly supposing that that alone would preserve them, when the God of the ark had departed from them. Therefore in an evil hour the ark of the covenant of the Lord of hosts was carried forth by its adulterous priests into the midst of a sinful and God-forsaken army. But God was not long in teaching them by sad experience that the ark was no safeguard against their enemies when their transgressions had cut them off from his strength. Smitten again before their enemies with great slaughter, they fled every man to his tent, the ark was taken, and the two sons of Eli, Hophni and Phinehas, were slain.

Eli, the aged high priest, well-meaning but weak, so weak that he would suffer his sons to make themselves vile and restrain them not, so weak that he had permitted the ark to go forth under all these forbidding circumstances to battle, sat upon a seat by the wayside, anxiously waiting the result of the engagement; for "his heart trembled for the ark of God." A messenger soon returned in hot haste from the army, and in four brief sentences made known to him the sum of their misfortunes: 1. "Israel is fled before the Philistines." 2. "There hath been also a great slaughter among the people." 3. "*Thy two sons also, Hophni and Phinehas, are dead.*" Did not this bring the climax of his grief? No. All this, sad as it was, he bore with comparative composure; for there was another object which held a higher place in his heart, and for which he was more solicitous even than for these; and that was the precious ark of God; was the ark safe? The dregs of this tale of bitterness were yet to come: 4. "AND THE ARK OF GOD IS TAKEN." And when this terrible report from the ark broke upon his ears, "he fell from off the seat backward by the side of the gate, and his neck brake, and he died." The ark of God was more deeply enshrined in the affections of this venerable but misguided man, than even the welfare of Israel or the fate of his two sons. In his anxiety for that he had overlooked all other calamities, but when his hopes in regard to that were crushed, and his worst fears realized, he could no longer endure the weight of such accumulated disasters. Nature yielded, and he found his own grave by the side of his sons whom he had failed to rule, a failure by which he himself had helped to precipitate this dire calamity upon all the country.

So dark was the cloud which Israel's wickedness had raised to obscure the sun of their prosperity. They were now dishonored in the sight of the heathen. The name of the Lord would be blasphemed. The loss of the ark showed that God had departed from them; and the destruction of their nation and the ruin of their religion must have been to them no distant prospects. The language in which they embodied the burden of their woe was this: "The glory is departed from Israel; for the ark of God is taken." And when, in after years, the Lord would make the people understand the utter destruction he threatened against Jerusalem for still unchecked wickedness, he had only to say, I will do to this house as I have done to Shiloh, and make this city a curse to all the nations of the earth. Jer. 7:14; 26:6.

How long the tabernacle remained in Shiloh after the capture of the ark, we are not informed. But it does not appear that God's glory or the ark of his covenant ever returned to that building. The tabernacle next appears in the sacred record about seventy-nine years later, in the days of Saul, when we find it at Nob, 1 Sam. 21; Matt. 12:3, 4, a place about twelve miles west by north from Jerusalem. We again find it, twenty years later still, in the days of David and Solomon, at Gibeon. 1 Chron. 16:39; 2 Chron. 1:3. This was about eight miles north from Jerusalem. Here it remained thirty-eight years, till the building of the temple.

But where, during all this time, was the ark of the covenant of the Lord? We left it at the battle of Ebenezer, where it was captured by the Philistines, and the lament went up that the glory had departed from Israel, for the ark of God was taken. Being essential to the tabernacle, we must follow it until we find them together again.

The ark was retained in the land of the Philistines seven months. At Ashdod their god, Dagon, fell on two successive days before it, the second time his head and hands being severed, and nothing being left but the stump or fishy part of the old idol. The priests of Dagon hurried it off to Gath; and from thence it was taken to Ekron; and both these cities were sorely smitten on account of its presence. "So," says the record, "they sent and gathered together all the lords of the Philistines, and said, Send away the ark of the God of Israel, and let it go again to his own place, that it slay us not, and our people." 1 Sam. 5.

The providence of God was equally conspicuous in its return to the Israelitish people. To test the matter whether their calamities had been inflicted upon them by the hand of the God of Israel on account of the presence of the ark among them or not, the Philistines proposed that the ark with the golden trespass-offerings should be put on a new cart, and that two cows, their calves being shut up at home, should be attached to the cart, and left to take their own course. If they went up toward the coasts of Israel, to Beth-shemesh, they would know that God had inflicted their evils upon them. But if the cows, according to their nature, should only seek their own home, they would know that it was only chance that had happened unto them.

It was done as they proposed; "and the kine took the straight way to the way of Beth-shemesh and went along the highway, lowing as they went." Then the Philistines knew that something more than chance was seen in the events that had befallen them; and, filled with astonishment, they followed on behind it, even unto the border of Beth-shemesh.

"And they of Beth-shemesh were reaping their wheat harvest in the valley; and they lifted up their eyes and saw the ark, and rejoiced to see it." 1 Sam. 6:13. But for presuming to look into the ark, without any occasion, and contrary to God's order that not only was no one to look into it, but only the Levites were to touch it, the men of Beth-shemesh were smitten. How many? Our common version reads "fifty thousand and threescore and ten men." But it is not probable that a small place like Beth-shemesh would have so many inhabitants, and by no means probable that so many would be engaged in wheat harvest even if we take into the account all the region round about. Josephus omits the fifty thousand altogether, retaining only the seventy. He says (Antiq. Jud., lib. vi. cap. i. sec. 4), "But the displeasure and wrath of God pursued them so that seventy men of the village of Beth-shemesh, approaching the ark, which they were not worthy to touch (not being priests), were struck with lightning." Dr. Clarke argues that the whole difficulty may be explained by supposing that in transcribing, a single letter was accidentally omitted, "the particle of comparison, כ *ke,* like, as, or equal to, before the word חמשים *chamishshim:* thus כחמשים *kechamishshim.* The passage would then read: 'And he smote of the people seventy men, *equal to* fifty thousand men;' that is, they were elders or governors of the people." And this, Dr. C. argues, would account for the reading of Josephus, "who in his recital would naturally leave out such an explanation of the worth of the seventy men, as his Roman readers could not easily comprehend such comparisons."

From Beth-shemesh the ark was removed to Kirjath-jearim, to the house of Abinadab, where it abode twenty years. It was during this period that all Israel lamented after the Lord. 1 Sam. 7:2. Then David gathered together all the chosen men of Israel and went to bring up the ark from Kirjath-jearim to Jerusalem, the city of David, to the tent which he had there pitched for it. 2 Sam. 6:1, 2; 1 Chron., chapter 13. But on account of Uzzah's putting forth his hand to steady it, and being slain for his rashness, he not being a priest, and hence having no right to touch it, David was afraid, and would not remove the ark of the Lord unto him into the city of David, but carried it aside into the house of Obed-edom, the Gittite. There the ark continued three months; and the Lord blessed Obed-edom and all his household. "And it was told King David, saying, The Lord hath blessed the house of Obed-edom, and all that pertaineth unto him, because of the ark of God. So David went and brought up the ark of God from the house of Obed-edom into the city of David with gladness." 2 Sam. 6: 9–12; 1 Chron., chapters 15 and 16. Here it remained in the tent which David had pitched for it, till the erection of the temple, where we are soon to find the ark and the sanctuary together again, and the worship of God resumed in greater impressiveness and glory.

Chapter Twelve.

THE TEMPLE.

IT now pleased God that the sanctuary should take a more permanent form. All necessity for a movable structure, to be temporarily located in different places, had ceased to exist. The period of Israel's journeyings had long gone by. The period of the Judges, during which the affairs of Israel were often uncertain and the times troublous, though exceeding in duration more than four times the length of the existence of our own government, was at length ended. The tribes of Israel were consolidated into a new and powerful kingdom. Under David, the Hebrew scepter established its broadest sway.

At length God gave him rest from all his enemies round about. 2 Sam. 7 and 8. Then came the house of God into his mind, and to the prophet Nathan he thus spoke: "See now, I dwell in an house of cedar, but the ark of God dwelleth within curtains." This doubtless refers to the tent which he had pitched for it in the city ot David, of which the words of Uriah the Hittite, 2 Sam. 11 : 11, may also probably be understood.

The prophet approved of what was implied in the language of David, that he purposed to prepare a suitable structure for the permanent abiding-place of the ark of God, and he said, "Do all that is in thine heart; for God is with thee." But the Lord the same night reversed the decision of the prophet, saying to the king that he could not build a house for him to dwell in; for he had been a man of war and had shed much blood. This was an important and a holy work. In this house the olive branch of peace was to be held out by Heaven to a rebellious world, and none but those whose lives had been passed in peace could be employed in its erection.

THE TEMPLE, LIKE THE TABERNACLE, BUILT AFTER A PATTERN.

Nevertheless to David was given, by the Spirit of God, an accurate pattern of the temple, and all things pertaining thereto, just as Moses had received the pattern of the tabernacle in the wilderness of Sinai. This we find in 1 Chron. 28 : 11, and onward; and in verse 19, David says, "All this the Lord made me understand in writing by his hand upon me, even all the works of this pattern."

Besides thus receiving the pattern, it was permitted him to make also abundant preparation for the coming building. Its erection was committed to his son Solomon, and to him and the princes, David gave the following solemn charge concerning this work: "Now set your heart and your soul to seek the Lord your God; arise therefore, and build ye the sanctuary of the Lord God, to bring the ark of the covenant of the Lord, and the holy vessels of God, into the house that is to be built to the name of the Lord." 1 Chron. 22:19.

Again: 1 Chron. 28:10: "Take heed now; for the Lord hath chosen thee to build an house for the sanctuary; be strong, and do it."

Mark, it was the *sanctuary* for which provision was thus carefully being made, the *sanctuary*, of which David had seen the pattern, for which he had made ready his material, and concerning which he gave this solemn charge.

The pattern is now furnished, and the material prepared. Where was the sanctuary located? The spot chosen was most significant. It was none other than the threshing-floor of Ornan the Jebusite, 1 Chron. 21:14–18, where the angel of the Lord appeared to David, upon Mount Moriah, 2 Chron. 3:1, which was near to Mount Zion. Upon this spot Isaac had been offered eight hundred and sixty years before, and a lamb had been provided in his place. Gen. 22 : 1–14.

All questions being thus decided and all preparations made, the work commences. The sacred writer thus marks this important event: "And it came to pass in the four hundred and eightieth year after the children of Israel were come out of the land of Egypt, in the fourth year of Solomon's reign over Israel, in the month Zif, which is the second month, that he began to build the house of the Lord." 1 Kings 6 : 1.

A question of chronology here demands solution. Paul, in Acts 13 : 18–22, gives a far different reckoning of the time from the exodus to the building of the temple. He allows to the wilderness forty years, the time given to the destruction of the seven nations of Canaan, usually computed as six years (see Bliss' Sacred Chronology), to the Judges 450 years, to the reign of Saul forty years, to that of David forty years, and to Solomon's fourth year, three years, making in all 579 years, and bringing the building of the temple in the 580th year from the exodus, instead of the 480th as in 1 Kings 6. It is not necessary to give the long and elaborate opinions of critics upon this matter. There being a difference of just one hundred years goes far to show that a mistake of just that measure of time has somewhere been made. This could not be made in the text of the Judges, nor in the discourse of Paul, where the period is drawn out in items, so easily as in 1 Kings 6, where it is expressed in a single statement. Hence it is the opinion of chronologers that the reading in Kings is not genuine; that the building of the temple was commenced in the fourth year of Solomon, as here and elsewhere stated, but that this was the 580th year from the exode, instead of one hundred years earlier. See this question discussed at length in "Barrett's Synopsis of Criticism," vol. ii. part 2.

The intimate connection of the temple with its prototype, the tabernacle, is shown in the general arrangement and furniture of the building. Like the tabernacle, it had its holy, and most holy, place. But these, in all their dimensions—length, breadth, and height—were exactly double those of the tabernacle. Thus the most holy place was twenty cubits each way, instead of ten, and the holy place twenty by forty cubits, instead of ten by twenty.

Besides these apartments there was a porch of ten cubits at the entrance, and surrounding chambers for the use of the priests, besides various courts and covered porches surrounding the whole. Altogether it covered a large area, and presented an imposing and magnificent appearance. Rising from its commanding height like a mountain of marble and gold, it stood before the world a monument of splendor more gorgeous and wonderful than men had ever looked upon before. The carving of the walls of the house with figures of cherubim, the overlaying of it with pure gold within and without, the doors of olive-trees adorned with carved work and overlaid with gold fitted to the carvings, with other innumerable and costly ornaments and embellishments, were accomplished at an expense, says Dr. Clarke, which it is impossible to estimate.

Two gigantic cherubim, of olive wood overlaid with gold, each ten cubits high, were prepared for the most holy place, and put in position on either side of the spot upon which the ark was to rest. "And they stretched forth the wings of the cherubim, so that the wing of the one touched the one wall, and the wing of the other cherub touched the other wall, and their wings touched one another in the midst of the house."

Many of the vessels of the sanctuary were also

enlarged and multiplied for the temple service. Ten golden candlesticks shed their light in the holy place, and ten tables held the consecrated bread which was placed each Sabbath before the Lord. 2 Chron. 4 : 7, 8.

At the expiration of seven years and six months from the commencement of the work, the building was completed, though the dedication did not take place till the following year, the twelfth of Solomon's reign. Having all things prepared for this joyful occasion, Solomon assembled the elders of Israel, and all the heads of the tribes, the chief of the fathers of the children of Israel, that they might bring up the ark of the covenant of the Lord out of the city of David, to its new abode. 1 Kings 8. And King Solomon, and all the congregation of Israel that there assembled unto him, were with him before the ark, sacrificing sheep and oxen, that could not be told nor numbered for multitude. What a procession was that!

They also brought up the tabernacle. The original tabernacle was left at Gibeon thirty-eight years before; and it is generally supposed that David had erected a new one for the ark when he brought it to his city. Which of these was brought into the temple? Some think both; but Dr. Clarke suggests what seems the more probable view, that the original tabernacle was brought up from Gibeon, to be preserved in the temple as a relic, and the temporary one erected by David was destroyed.

What was in the ark? 1 Kings 8:9, states explicitly that there was nothing there save the tables of stone. Paul is supposed to say, in Heb. 9:4, that it contained also the golden pot of manna and Aaron's rod. That these were originally laid up before the testimony is evident from Ex. 16:33, 34; Num. 17:10; but we find no record that they were put into the ark with the tables of the law. Paul, in Heb. 9:3, speaks of the *tabernacle* which is called the holiest of all; and the word wherein, in verse 4, is simply the relative pronoun, "in which," which may refer to the tabernacle as its antecedent, instead of the ark. With this view, Paul's language would simply affirm that in the most holy, or second apartment, were placed the golden censer, the pot of manna, Aaron's rod, the ark, and the tables of the covenant; the tables, though contained in the ark, being mentioned separately from the ark by way of emphasis.

But even if Paul means that the pot of manna and Aaron's rod were in the ark with the tables of the commandments, it can easily be reconciled with 1 Kings 8:9; for Paul evidently speaks of the sanctuary as it was in the time of Moses; whereas the writer in Kings speaks of it as it was in the time of Solomon, about five hundred years later; and it would follow that at some time during this long period of five hundred years, the manna and rod had been removed from the ark, which might easily have occurred, so that in the days of Solomon there was nothing in it save the tables alone.

A passage similar to this in Hebrews is found in 1 Kings 8:21, which reads, "And I have set there a place for the ark, wherein is the covenant of the Lord, which he made with our fathers, when he brought them out of the land of Egypt." In this passage, the word, wherein, refers to the place, not to the ark. In the ark was God's covenant which he *commanded*, the ten commandments. The covenant which *he made with* the children of Israel, which was a mutual agreement between himself and them, was written in a book, and placed in the side of the ark. Deut. 31:26.

And this leads us to consider what is meant by this expression, "In the side of the ark." Prideaux has explained it so fully in his "Connexion," vol. i. p. 152, that we can do no better than to give his words:—

"As to the book, or volume of the law, it being commanded to be put *mitssad, i. e., on the side* of the ark, those who interpret that word of the inside, place it within the ark, and those who interpret it of the outside, place it on the outside of it in a case or coffer made on purpose for it, and laid on the right side; meaning by the right side, that end of it which was on the right hand. And the last seem to be in the right as to this matter; for, first, The same word, *mitssad,* is made use of, where it is said that the Philistines sent back the ark with an offering of jewels, of gold put in a coffer *by the side of it.* And there it is certain that word must be understood of the outside, and not of the inside. Secondly, The ark was not of capacity enough to hold the volume of the whole law of Moses, with the other things placed therein. Thirdly, The end of laying up the original volume of the law in the temple was, that it might be reserved there as the authentic copy, by which all others were to be corrected and set right; and, therefore, to answer this end, it must have been placed so as that access might be had thereto on all occasions requiring it; which could not have been done, if it had been put within the ark, and shut up there by the cover of the mercy-seat over it, which was not to be removed. And, fourthly, When Hilkiah the high priest, in the time of Josiah, found the copy of the law in the temple, there is nothing said of the ark; neither is it there spoken of as taken from thence, but as found elsewhere in the temple. And, therefore, putting all this together, it seems plain that the volume of the law was not laid within the ark, but had a particular coffer or repository of its own, in which it was placed on the side of it. And the word *mitssad*, which answers to the Latin *a latere*, cannot truly bear any other meaning in the Hebrew language. And therefore the Chaldee paraphrase, which goes under the name of Jonathan Ben Uzziel, in paraphrasing on these words of Deuteronomy—'Take this book of the law, and put it in the side of the ark of the covenant,' renders it thus, 'Take the book of the law, and place it in a case or coffer, on the right side of the ark of the covenant of the Lord your God.'"

The ark was brought into its position in the most holy place between the wings of the cherubim, and thus again became connected with the sanctuary after a separation of 136 years. God approved of all that had been done to suitably prepare for his worship as adapted to that time, and as he had taken possession of the first tabernacle, Ex. 40 : 34, so now he takes possession of this: "And it came to pass, when the priests were come out of the holy place, that the cloud filled the house of the Lord, so that the priests could not stand to minister because of the cloud; for the glory of the Lord had filled the house of the Lord." 1 Kings 8 : 10, 11.

That was a day of joy in Israel. The thousands of offerings consuming upon the altars, the clouds of incense that rose above the temple, the sounds of the instruments of music, and the voice of the singers, the inimitable prayer of Solomon, the wisest of men, the glory of the new temple, the vast concourse of people, and above all, the crowning visitation of the shekinah, or visible glory of God, as he took possession of his dwelling, all conspired to render this

THE MOST IMPOSING RELIGIOUS SERVICE EVER PERFORMED IN THIS WORLD, EITHER BEFORE OR SINCE THAT TIME.*

Twenty-two thousand oxen and one hundred and twenty thousand sheep constituted Solo-

* So Philip Smith calls it in his "History of this World," vol. i. p. 173.

mon's peace-offering. Besides this there were his meat-offerings, his burnt-offerings, and his drink-offerings, besides the offerings of the assembled multitudes. Fourteen days the king and all Israel kept a feast unto the Lord, and then the people returned to their homes, blessing the king, and glad of heart for all the goodness of the Lord.

During Israel's sojourn in the wilderness, the tabernacle, as we have seen, was fifty-six times called the sanctuary. From its entrance into the holy land, till its incorporation into the temple, it is nineteen times more called the sanctuary in the following passages:—

Josh. 24:26; 1 Chron. 9:29; 22:19; 24:5; 28:10; 2 Chron. 20:8; Ps. 20:2; 28:2, margin; 29:2, margin; 63:2; 68:24; 73:17; 77:13; 78:54, 69; 96:6, 9, margin; 134:2; 150:1.

Chapter Thirteen.

DESTRUCTION OF THE TEMPLE.

WITH the dedication of Solomon's temple, the earthly sanctuary reached the summit of its glory. Its sacred vessels were perfect and complete. It contained the very ark which was made by Moses, under the express direction of Heaven; and that ark contained the very tables of stone which had been written by Jehovah himself. The temple building was a structure of unsurpassed magnificence and glory, and there was nothing to hinder the Levitical worship from going forward in all its perfection.

It would be pleasant long to contemplate both the temple and the sanctuary in this prosperous condition; but the dark specter of sin, with its inevitable train of judgments and calamities, soon appears upon the scene.

The temple was dedicated B. C. 1005. Thirty-four years after this, B. C. 971, Shishak, king of Egypt, having declared war with Rehoboam, took Jerusalem and carried away the treasures of the temple. 1 Kings 14:25, 26; 2 Chron. 12:9. But when the king humbled himself, thus turning from the sins which had brought down the judgments of God upon him, God turned from his wrath against him. Verse 12.

Jehoash commenced the work of repairs B. C. 856. 2 Kings 12 : 4, 5. Ahaz, king of Judah, becoming involved in war with the kings of Israel and Damascus, robbed the temple to pay Tiglath-pileser, king of Assyria, whom he had summoned to his aid; 2 Chron. 28 : 21, 22; B. C. 740. Hezekiah, his son, in a measure repaired this loss, but was himself finally compelled to take all the riches of the temple to purchase peace from Sennacherib, who had come against him. 2 Kings 18 : 14–16.

Manasseh, son and successor of Hezekiah, profaned the temple of the Lord by setting up altars to all the host of heaven, even in the courts of the Lord, 2 Kings 21 : 4–7, for which God delivered him into the hands of the king of Babylon. He was loaded with chains and carried beyond the Euphrates, 2 Chron. 33 : 11, B. C. 677. But, humbling himself and repenting of his sins, he was sent back to his own dominions, and labored to repair the profanations he had committed upon the house of the Lord. Verses 14–16.

Josiah, king of Judah, labored zealously to

repair the edifices of the temple. 2 Kings 22: 4–6. He commanded the Levites to put the ark of the Lord, in the sanctuary, in its proper place, and that they should no more bear it about, as they probably had done during the administrations of the wicked kings who had reigned before him. 2 Chron. 35:3.

But these were only slight profanations and calamities, compared with the storm of destruction, the projected shadow of which was now beginning to darken that devoted land. The nation had sunk to so low a depth of sin that God could no longer dwell among them. Zephaniah complains that her prophets were light and treacherous persons, that her priests had polluted the sanctuary and done violence to the law. Zeph. 3:4. By the prophet Ezekiel, 23:38, 39, the Lord lay the same things to their charge, and adds (24:21), "Behold, I will profane my sanctuary." Therefore,

GOD AGAIN FORSAKES HIS SANCTUARY.

It is never without warning that God visits his people in judgment. The long record of his dealings with them presents no exception to this rule. In this case the warning had been given in these words:—

"But go ye now unto my place which was in Shiloh, where I set my name at the first, and see what I did to it for the wickedness of my people Israel. And now, because ye have done all these works, saith the Lord, and I spake unto you rising up early and speaking, but ye heard not; and I called you, but ye answered not; therefore will I do unto this house, which is called by my name, wherein ye trust, and unto the place which I gave to you and to your fathers, as I have done to Shiloh." Jer. 7:12–14; 26:1–7.

What had God done to Shiloh? David answers: "When God heard this, he was wroth, and greatly abhorred Israel, so that he forsook the tabernacle of Shiloh, the tent which he placed among men, and delivered his strength into captivity, and his glory into the enemy's hand." Ps. 78:59–61. To do the same to the temple would be to forsake it, and give it into the hands of the enemy.

The manner in which the people received this warning set the seal to God's purpose in this respect. "They mocked the messengers of God, and despised his words, and misused his prophets, until the wrath of the Lord arose against his people, till there was no remedy." 2 Chron. 36:16.

Nebuchadnezzar king of Babylon, the first

universal empire, the head of gold of the great symbolic image of Dan. 2, was the instrument God selected to carry out his purpose. In the year B. C. 606, Jerusalem was taken, the temple plundered, a part of the sacred vessels removed and placed in the temple of Belus in Babylon; multitudes of the people were transported into the land of their captors, the sons of the royal family, and the nobility of the nation were made eunuchs and slaves in the palace of the king of Babylon; the whole land was made tributary, the king Jehoiakim became a vassal to the king of Babylon, and the predicted seventy years' captivity commenced. 2 Chron. 36:6, 7.

The evil behaviour of Jehoiachin, son of Jehoiakim, brought Nebuchadnezzar against Jerusalem the second time, B. C. 599, when he made still further ravages on the house of the Lord, and its sacred vessels. Verse 10.

And lastly, the wicked course of Zedekiah, Jehoiachin's successor on the throne of Judah, drew upon Jerusalem that terrible destruction which for a while blotted it from the face of the earth. Zedekiah foolishly defied the power of the king who had already twice taken Jerusalem. Nebuchadnezzar was thus brought a third time against the doomed city, determined this time to quell forever its rebellious spirit. After a siege of about one year the city fell. All the vessels that could be found in the house of the Lord, were taken out, and all the riches were secured that could be found in every house in the city. The temple and the whole city were then set on fire. The walls, fortress, and towers were overthrown, and every building in the city was leveled to the ground, till, excepting only the piles of unconsumable rubbish, the site of Jerusalem was as bare as if no human foot had ever trod thereon.

As God had done to the sanctuary at Shiloh, he had now done to the sanctuary at Jerusalem, but with tenfold heavier judgment. In the light of these facts the following references to the sanctuary are easily understood: Ps. 74:3, 7; 79:1; Isa. 63:18; 64:10, 11; Eze. 24:21; Jer. 51:51; Lam. 1:10; 2:7, 20; 4:1.

While Israel were thus dispersed among the nations, and their beautiful sanctuary at Jerusalem lay in ruins, God promised to be unto them *as* a little sanctuary, in the countries where they should come. Eze. 11:16. Toward the close of the seventy years' captivity, Daniel prayed thus to God, "Cause thy face to shine upon thy sanctuary that is desolate." Dan. 9:2, 17.

Chapter Fourteen.

THE SANCTUARY OFFERED BY EZEKIEL.

JERUSALEM, the temple, and the sanctuary, were destroyed in the eleventh year of the reign of Zedekiah, B. C. 588. Fourteen years after this, B. C. 574, Ezekiel, himself among the captives of Israel, was moved to describe a very remarkable sanctuary, into possession of which they were to come, if on their part they would comply with certain conditions. This is recorded in chapters 40 to 48, of his prophecy.

It is certain that this sanctuary has never been built. It becomes therefore a matter of interest to inquire why. Is it because the conditions were not complied with on the part of the people? or is it because, as some of late years have claimed, this prophecy pertains to the future, and the time has not yet come for its fulfillment?

Let us then see if we can ascertain from the specifications of the prophecy itself, in what dispensation it was to be fulfilled. The conclusion is very easily reached, that it was designed to be fulfilled, not in the future dispensation, which is the immortal state; not even in the present dispensation; but in the past. This will appear evident from a few of its statements.

1. It was to be fulfilled while circumcision was in force. Eze. 44 : 9. But circumcision was abolished at the first advent. Gal. 5 : 2; 6 : 12.

2. It was while divorce was allowed. Eze. 44 : 22. But this is now done away. Matt. 5 : 31, 32; 19 : 8, 9.

3. It was to be while the distinction between meats, clean and unclean, was recognized. Eze. 44 : 23, 31. But that does not now hold. Acts 10 : 11–16; Rom. 14.

4. Sacrifices, offerings, burnt-offerings, and sin-offerings, of bulls and goats, were then in force. Eze. 46. But they are not now acceptable to God. Heb. 10.

5. The feasts and the Jubilee were then in force. Eze. 45 : 21–25; 46 : 9, 11, 17. But they were nailed to the cross. Col. 2 : 14–17.

6. The Levitical priesthood was then in force. Eze. 40 : 46; 44 : 15. But the priesthood of Melchisedec, which passeth not to another, has taken its place. Heb. 5 : 6.

7. It was to be while "the middle wall of partition" existed, as all these ordinances prove, as

well as the acknowledged distinction between "the seed of the house of Israel" and the stranger. But this wall of partition is now broken down, and this distinction no longer exists. Eph. 2.

These facts point out with sufficient distinctness the time when this sanctuary was to be built, if it should be built at all. Why, then, was it not built? The answer is clear: The people did not comply with the conditions on which it was offered. It was to be established with them on the condition that they were ashamed of their iniquities, and put them away. Eze. 43:11. But Jeremiah, speaking prophetically of what would be, says, 6:15, that they were not ashamed when they had committed abomination. And this the event proved; for when the offer was made by Cyrus to all in the captivity to return to their own land, only a few availed themselves of the privilege to go back to Jerusalem. Thus they slighted the inestimable blessings offered them; and the sanctuary set before them in their captivity, which they might have had, was never erected.

What then shall we say of those who make this a prophecy to be fulfilled in the future age? A few considerations will show the folly of such an application.

1. In the future state, Christ is to be the Prince over Israel; and there is to be but one. Luke 1 : 32, 33. But the prince brought to view by Ezekiel is a poor, frail mortal, as is shown by the following representations made concerning him.

2. He is commanded to offer a bullock, as a sin-offering for himself. Eze. 45 : 22. But Christ, the Prince of the future state, is himself the great sin-offering for the world. 1 John 2 : 1, 2.

3. He was to offer all manner of offerings for himself. Eze. 46 : 1–8. But Christ caused all this to cease at his death. Dan. 9 : 27.

4. God says to the princes mentioned by Ezekiel, Take away your exactions from my people. Eze. 45 : 9. But when Christ reigns there will be nothing oppressive; for the officers will be peace, and the exactors, righteousness. Isa. 60 : 17–19.

5. Ezekiel's prince was to have sons and servants to whom he might, if he chose, give an inheritance; but it was to return to him in the year of Jubilee; and he was forbidden to oppress the people. Eze. 46 : 16–18. Surely it would be blasphemous to apply this to Christ, to whom it must apply if this prophecy has reference to the future state.

6. And finally, in the state of things Ezekiel brings to view, there are marriages, divorces, and *deaths.* Eze. 44 : 22, 24–27. But in the future state they neither marry nor are given in marriage, but are equal unto the angels, and can die no more. Luke 20 : 35, 36.

Thus it is demonstrated, first, That Ezekiel has no reference to the world or age to come; secondly, That he has no reference to the present dispensation; thirdly, That his prophecy refers wholly to the past or Mosaic dispensation; fourthly, That the prophecy was conditional, and the time having passed and the conditions never having been complied with, it never has been, and never is to be, fulfilled.

To the building offered by Ezekiel, the word sanctuary is eighteen times applied in the following instances: Eze. 41 : 21, 23; 42 : 20; 43 : 21; 44 : 1, 5 (verses 7, 8, refer to Solomon's temple), 9, 11, 15, 16, 27; 45 : 2, 3, 4, 18; 47 : 12; 48 : 8, 10, 21.

Chapter Fifteen.

THE SANCTUARY REBUILT.

WHEN the seventy years of Israel's captivity were expired, and the land of Judea had lain desolate and thus enjoyed her sabbaths, of which the wickedness of the people had deprived it, the Lord, in fulfillment of his word, stirred up the spirit of Cyrus, king of Persia, to make a proclamation throughout all the kingdom, that of all the people of the God of Heaven dwelling therein, whosoever would might return to Jerusalem. Two tribes only, as tribes, Judah and Benjamin, acknowledged the heavenly token, and availed themselves of the opportunity offered. The majority of the other tribes chose to remain in their iniquity, and to abide still in the land of the heathen. But some of all the tribes joined themselves to the returning company, so that all Israel was represented, and all the tribes were perpetuated in Judea after the captivity. Hence the idea sometimes advanced that there are ten lost tribes which are to be restored at some time in the future, is a figment of the imagination.

Forty-two thousand three hundred and sixty persons, enough to people quite a respectable city, returned, under the proclamation of Cyrus, to the site of Jerusalem, to rebuild the house of the Lord. And the sacred vessels which had been taken away were also restored. Fifty-two years after the complete destruction of the first temple, the foundation of the second was laid by Zerubbabel. The prophets, Haggai and Zechariah, encouraged the builders. Ez. 5:1; 6:14. Hindered fifteen years through the influence of the Samaritans and others, it was at length finished and dedicated in the sixth year of Darius Hystaspes, B. C. 515, twenty-one years after its commencement.

Though this temple was not, in some respects, equal to the first, yet the Lord promised that the glory should be greater, because to it, in the fullness of time, should come the Desire of all nations. Hag. 2.

What was wanting in the second temple? It was not with respect to size that the first house surpassed the latter; for this was of the same dimensions as the former, being built upon the same foundations. But those marks of the divine favor which were the main glory of the first temple, were wholly wanting in this. These the Jews reckon up in five particulars; namely, 1. The ark, and the mercy-seat which was upon it. 2. The shekinah, or divine presence. 3. The Urim and Thummim. 4. The holy fire upon the altar. 5. The spirit of prophecy.

What had become of the ark? Upon this question there has been expended much conjecture. That it was not carried to Babylon is generally admitted; as, if it had been, it would have been brought back with the other sacred treasures which had been carried thither. Ez. 1:8–11. It is supposed by some that it was hid away and preserved by Jeremiah. To sustain this view, reference is made to the book of Maccabees, which contains the following account of the matter:—

Jeremy the prophet, "being warned of God, commanded the tabernacle and the ark to go with him, as he went forth into the mountain where Moses climbed up, and saw the heritage of God. And when Jeremy came thither he found an hollow cave, wherein he laid the tabernacle and the ark, and the altar of incense, and so stopped the door. And some of those that followed him came to mark the way, but they could not find it. Which when Jeremy perceived, he blamed them, saying, As for this place it shall be unknown until the time that God gather his people again together, and receive them unto mercy." 2 Mac. 2:4–7. And from this latter expression some have inferred that it is to be discovered and brought forth again before the end.

"Most of the Jews will have it," says Prideaux, "that King Josiah, being foretold by Huldah the prophetess that the temple, speedily after his death, would be destroyed, caused the ark to be put in a vault underground, which Solomon, foreseeing this destruction, had caused of purpose to be built for the preserving of it." For proof, they produce 2 Chron. 35:3. But Prideaux argues that "these words import no more than that Manasseh or Ammon having removed the ark from where it ought to have stood, Josiah commanded it again to be restored to its proper place."

These are, perhaps, but little more than conjectures. And while there seems to be improbability that God would permit any work of his own hands, like the writing on the tables of the decalogue, to be destroyed by the hands of wicked men, there does not appear any positive proof that the ark and its contents were not destroyed with the temple, as were, probably, the show-bread table and the golden candlestick.

The want of the ark was, however, supplied as to the outward form; for an ark was made of the same shape and dimensions as the first, and placed in its appropriate position in the second temple ("Lightfoot on the Temple," c. 15, s. 4); but it contained no tables of the law, there was no appearance of the divine glory over it, and no oracular answers were given from it.

The Urim and Thummim. These were the third object specified as wanting in the second temple. What were they? Prideaux concludes that the words meant "only the divine virtue and power given to the breastplate in its consecration of obtaining an oracular answer from God, whenever counsel was asked of him by the high priest with it on, in such manner as his word did direct; and that the names Urim and Thummim were given hereto, only to denote the clearness and perfection which these oracular answers always carried with them; for these answers were not, like the heathen oracles, enigmatical and ambiguous, but always clear and manifest; not such as did ever fall short of perfection, either of fullness in the answer, or certainty in the truth of it. And hence it is that the Septuagint translate Urim and Thummim by the words *delosin kai aletheian, i. e.,* manifestation and truth, because all these oracular answers given by Urim and Thummim were always clear and manifest, and their truth ever certain and infallible. As to the use which was made of the Urim and Thummim, it was to ask counsel of God in difficult and momentous cases relating to the whole state of Israel."—*Connexion,* vol. i. p. 156.

Five hundred years elapse. The temple, as might well be supposed, became, during this time, in many respects sadly in need of repairs. Whereupon Herod the Great, to ingratiate himself with the Jews, conceived the idea of rebuilding it throughout. The old temple was pulled down to its foundation, and the building of the new one commenced B. C. 19. It was this temple to which the Jews referred when they said to the Saviour at his first passover, in the spring of A. D. 28, "Forty and six years was this temple in building." John 2:20. It had been completed the year before, A. D. 27, the very year in which Christ commenced his public ministry. To this temple, according to the prophecy of Haggai, the Desire of all nations had now come. Happy would it have been for the Jews, if, knowing the time of their visitation, they had received him as their Lord, and owned his mission.

Externally, this building was at once the admiration and envy of the world. "Its appearance," says Josephus, "had everything that could strike the mind and astonish the sight; for it was on every side covered with solid plates of gold, so that when the sun rose upon it, it reflected such a dazzling effulgence that the eye of the beholder was obliged to turn away from it; being no more able to sustain its radiance than the splendor of the sun." "It appeared at a distance like a huge mountain covered with snow; for where it was not decorated with plates of gold, it was extremely white and glistening."

Thus we are brought to the time of our Saviour. That covenant which had its ordinances of divine service in connection with "a worldly sanctuary," was drawing to a close. The great Sacrifice, to which the offerings of the sanctuary pointed, was about to be offered. The Lord was engaged in his solemn mission of love to man. Often would he have gathered them, to enlighten their blindness, heal their backslidings, and save from destruction. But they would not. Their incorrigible resistance at length wrung from him the mournful lamentation, "Behold, your house is left unto you desolate." Matt. 23:37, 38. Yes, their beautiful house, the

Spirit and presence of God driven therefrom, had become only a tomb of darkness and death. And as Christ departed with sad and lingering footsteps from the temple, the fearful doom which he saw awaiting that people obliged him to declare, not in anger, but in sorrow, that the temple should be thrown down, so that not one stone should be left upon another.

In the purpose of God, the services of this worldly sanctuary were now at an end. And when, amid the startling scenes, the darkness and the earthquake, that attended the crucifixion of the Son of God, unseen hands violently rent in twain the magnificent vail that hung before the holy of holies, its services came really to an end; for they were no longer of any virtue.

A few short years sufficed to bring the literal fulfillment of our Lord's prediction. The armies of Rome environed Jerusalem. The city fell. Titus desired to spare so gorgeous a trophy as the temple, but a Roman soldier, impelled by a blind spirit of infatuation, or perhaps by a divine impulse, climbing upon the shoulders of his comrade, thrust a blazing firebrand into the gilded lattice of the porch. The flames at once sprang up. No power could then save it. This scene has been so well described by Smith in his

"History of the World," vol. iii. p. 578, that we cannot forbear introducing a paragraph from his graphic picture:—

"The battering-rams began their work upon the defenses of the second court; but the massive stones withstood their shock; the scaling parties were dashed down upon the pavement, and their standards taken; and on the 8th of Ab (August), Titus gave orders to set fire to the great gates which he had attempted in vain to undermine. The flames spread to the cloisters, and blazed during all that day and night. On the second day the defenders burst out of the fiery circle and were hardly forced back by a cavalry charge led by Titus himself. The Roman now called a council of war to decide whether the temple should be saved. Though opinions were divided, he ordered the flames to be extinguished, and, having fixed the assault for the morrow, retired to rest. But another decree had long been registered by the Supreme Ruler; and the infuriated combatants were the instruments of his will. The indefatigable defenders, who had renewed their attacks on the soldiers engaged in putting out the fire, were driven back into the inner court, and pursued to the very gates of the temple. By one of those impulses which defy all discipline, a soldier, mounting on the shoulders of a comrade, threw a blazing torch into the gilded lattice of the porch. 'The flames sprang up at once. The Jews uttered one simultaneous shriek, and grasped their swords, with a furious determination of revenging and perishing in the ruins of the temple. Titus rushed down with the utmost speed; he shouted; he made signs to his soldiers to quench the fire: his voice was drowned, and his signs unnoticed in the blind confusion. The legionaries either could not or would not hear. They rushed on, trampling each other down in their furious haste, or, stumbling over the crumbling ruins, perished with the enemy. Each exhorted the other, and each hurled his blazing brand into the inner edifice, and then hurried to the work of carnage. The unarmed and defenseless people were slain in thousands; they lay heaped like sacrifices round the altar; the steps of the temple ran with streams of blood, which washed down the bodies which lay upon it.'

"The flames had not reached the sanctuary itself, when Titus entered the holy of holies. Admiration of its riches and splendor impelled him to a last effort for its preservation; but in his very presence, and in the midst of his earnest exhortations, a soldier thrust a lighted torch between the hinges of the door, and the building was presently in flames. This defiance of the sacred laws of Roman discipline is a most emphatic sign of the presence of a higher power than even the Cæsar. . . . Such was the resistance opposed by the immense and well-fitted stones to the work of destruction, that Titus is reported to have exclaimed, 'God has been my helper! God it was that pulled down the Jews from those formidable walls; for what could the hands of men or their engines have availed against them?'"

The date of this destruction, in A. D. 70, falls upon the same month, and the same day of the month, as the destruction of Solomon's temple by Nebuchadnezzar, six hundred and fifty-eight years before.

Standing here at the conclusion of its earthly history, it remains to inquire why this arrangement was ever instituted. What was the object of this earthly sanctuary and the services connected therewith?

Chapter Sixteen.

THE NEW-COVENANT SANCTUARY.

THE reader will now understand why we have dwelt so lengthily upon the history of the worldly sanctuary. It is because Paul, in plain and explicit language, declares that that building erected by Moses at the command of God, and which was perpetuated in the temples built by Solomon, Zerubbabel, and Herod, was the sanctuary of the first covenant; and it was important to see how prominent a place that held in the former dispensation. The word sanctuary occurs in the Old Testament one hundred and forty-two times, and in almost every instance refers to this building. It was no insignificant object, it was no trifle in the divine economy of that age. It is everywhere held before us as the sanctuary, the holy place, the sacred place, the dwelling-place of the Most High among the children of men. And Paul presents the complement to all these declarations when he declares so clearly that this was the sanctuary of the first covenant.

We desire the reader to appreciate the full

value which this statement possesses in this investigation. From this there is no appeal. Here all believers in the Bible must occupy common ground. Here, for the space of fifteen hundred years, we are all brought together on this subject. From Moses to Christ, this object, and no other, was the sanctuary of the Bible.

We have followed this to the close of its history. In A. D. 70 it disappeared forever from the face of the earth. Has there been no sanctuary since that time? Or has something else taken the place of that sanctuary? If this latter be the fact, we ask what that something else may be.

We have seen that only 490 years of the 2300 belonged to the Jews and Jerusalem. When that period ended, the services of the sanctuary of that people had come to an end. But yet 1810 years remained, bringing us down even to 1844. And it had been announced through the prophet that then the sanctuary should be cleansed. What sanctuary? and where? No sanctuary on the earth; for since A. D. 70 there has been none here. But a sanctuary cannot be cleansed that does not exist. There must therefore be a sanctuary somewhere, and that date must bring us to its cleansing, or the word of God prove incorrect.

Paul says that the sanctuary of Moses was the sanctuary of the first covenant. It was, as we have seen, one of the chief features of that covenant. But that covenant has given place to the new. Jer. 31:31; Heb. 8:10–12. Under this new covenant we are now living; for it was confirmed by the Messiah, the Prince, during the last week of the seventy, or the last seven years of the 490, by himself in person for the first half of the week, three years and a half to A. D. 31, and through his apostles during the remainder of that period, to A. D. 34. Heb. 2:3. The great features of that first covenant find their counterpart in the present. The sanctuary of that covenant must find its counterpart here. And the Bible nowhere recognizes anything as the sanctuary of God, except the sanctuary, or sanctuaries, connected with these two covenants. The new covenant therefore has a sanctuary, as well as the old.

This is proved directly by the words of Paul in the text in question, Heb. 9:1: "Then verily the first covenant had also ordinances of divine service, and a worldly sanctuary." Paul is showing the relation which the two covenants sustain to each other; and the word, *also*, shows that those things which he mentions pertained to both. One had ordinances of divine service; the other *also* has them. One had a sanctuary; the other *also* has a sanctuary.

The great question to which we have now come, and in which all the controversy is involved, is then simply this:—

What is the sanctuary of the new covenant?

The sanctuary of the old covenant must bear the same relation to the sanctuary of the new covenant, which the old covenant itself bears to the new. And on this point we suppose there is no controversy. All agree that they stand as type and antitype. The first was the type and shadow; this is the antitype and substance. The sanctuary of that dispensation was the type; the sanctuary of this is the antitype. But the sanctuary of that dispensation was the tabernacle of Moses. Of what, then, was the tabernacle of Moses a type, figure, or shadow?

The answer to this question is intimated in various scriptures to which we now call the attention of the reader. To Moses the Lord said: "Let them make me a sanctuary; that I may dwell among them. According to all that I show thee, after the *pattern* of the tabernacle, and the *pattern* of all the instruments thereof, even so shall ye make it." Ex. 25 : 8, 9. "And look that thou make them after their *pattern*, which was showed thee in the mount." Verse 40. "And thou shalt rear up the tabernacle according to the *fashion* thereof which was showed thee in the mount." Ex. 26 : 30. "As it was showed thee in the mount, so shall they make it." Ex. 27 : 8. "Our fathers had the tabernacle of witness in the wilderness, as He had appointed, speaking unto Moses, that he should make it according to the *fashion* that he had seen." Acts 7 : 44. "While as the first tabernacle was yet standing, which was a *figure* for the time then present, in which were offered both gifts and sacrifices." Heb. 9 : 8, 9. "For Christ is not entered into the holy places made with hands, which are the *figures* of the true." Verse 24.

These texts afford no material for an argument and conclusion. They make a plain, positive assertion, which, if we believe their testimony, we must admit. They declare that the tabernacle built by Moses, the sanctuary of the first covenant, was not an original structure; it was made after a pattern; it was simply a model or figure of something else, given for the time being to his people; and that from which it was modeled or fashioned, is declared to be the true sanctuary; and this true sanctuary must be the sanctuary of the new covenant; for God recognizes in connection with his work only these two: the true, and the figure or model which was made from it. The figure was the tabernacle of Moses. What is the true?

THE EARTH NOT THE SANCTUARY.—Having seen that the new covenant must have a sanctuary corresponding to that of the old, and that there must be something now recognized by the Bible as the sanctuary, the next step in the inquiry is to try to ascertain what this is. And here we are met by a variety of conflicting views which demand examination.

It is claimed by some that this earth is now the sanctuary.

By others, that it takes earth and Heaven together to constitute the sanctuary; the earth being the first apartment, and all Heaven the second.

By a third class it is claimed that the land of Canaan is now the sanctuary.

And a fourth class take the word in a more figurative sense, and apply it to the church.

Is the earth the sanctuary? We reply, No; and the reasons for this answer are at hand.

1. Definition of the word. According to Webster, Walker, Cruden, and the Bible, the

term sanctuary is defined to mean, "A holy place, a sacred place, a dwelling-place for the Most High." Is the earth such a place? or has it been such since sin entered therein to mar and defile it? We know it has not; and this fact alone is sufficient to strangle forever the idea that this earth is the sanctuary.

2. The antitypical nature of the new-covenant sanctuary. As we have seen, the sanctuary of the former dispensation was a type of the sanctuary of the present, whatever it may be. Is it now the earth? Then the former sanctuary prefigured it. But in what respect did it represent this earth? Can it for a moment be supposed that Moses when in the mount was shown this earth as a pattern from which he was to erect the sanctuary, and that the nearest resemblance he could make of it was an oblong building ten cubits in width, and three times that number in length? And we might extend the same inquiry to the furniture of the sanctuary. What is there on this earth that answers as the antitype of the ark, the altar of incense, the golden candlestick, and the table of show-bread? But this line of thought need not be pursued further to show the utter absurdity of such a view.

3. The use of the term. The word sanctuary occurs one hundred and forty-six times in the Bible, but is not in a single instance applied to the earth. The only texts which any one could imagine to have even a shadow of an application to this earth, are Isa. 60 : 13 ; Eze. 37 : 26–28 ; Rev. 21 : 1–3. But these refer, not to the present, but to the future, and show simply that this earth renewed is the place where the tabernacle of God will be located hereafter.

4. But finally, if the earth is the sanctuary now, it was just as much the sanctuary in the former dispensation. No change has taken place by which it has become the sanctuary now any more than it must have been then. But Paul says that the tabernacle built by Moses was the sanctuary then; hence the earth was not then the sanctuary, and therefore is not the sanctuary now.

This view being such apparent folly, what shall we say of that view which makes this earth only a part of the sanctuary, and looks to Heaven for the rest? It is strange that any person of common intelligence should conceive such an idea, or for a moment endeavor seriously to defend it. The only apology we can make for it is, that its advocates, misled by our common translation, suppose that the Bible calls Heaven the most holy place. But this is no apology; for no one has a right to set himself forth as a religious teacher, who on a point so plain is not acquainted with the correct reading.

THE LAND OF CANAAN NOT THE SANCTUARY.—The principles already presented on this subject go far toward proving the incorrectness of those views which apply the sanctuary to the land of Canaan or the church. See reasons 1, 2, 3, and 4 above stated. To prove the land of Canaan the sanctuary, appeal is made to Ex. 15: 17. But if this text proves that Canaan was ever the sanctuary, it was the sanctuary then, and of that covenant. But here come these good words of Paul again, which declare that the land of Canaan was not the sanctuary then, but that the tabernacle built by Moses was. This is sufficient to settle this point. But some will not be satisfied without a further notice of a few texts. Let Ex. 15:17, then, be explained by Ps. 78:53, 54, 69. David here speaks of the same events to which Moses referred. Moses gave them as matters of prediction; David, living after their accomplishment, spoke of them as matters of history. What Moses, in the poetical license of his fervent song of triumph, speaks of as the inheritance and sanctuary, David says in more explicit terms was the border of the sanctuary, and adds that the sanctuary was something which was built therein.

Good King Jehoshaphat makes the same distinction. 2 Chron. 20 : 7–9. He speaks of the *land* which had been given them, and the *sanctuary* which they had *built* therein, and then says that that sanctuary was the *house* (Solomon's temple) before which they stood. There is no mistaking such language, and any confusion in regard to the relation of the sanctuary to the land of Canaan is utterly inexcusable.

Isa. 63 : 18, refers to the overthrow and treading down of the house of God, the sanctuary of that time; stated in 2 Chron. 36 : 17–20; and Isa. 60 : 13, simply speaks of the new earth as the future glorious *place* of the sanctuary.

The land of Canaan was not, and is not, the sanctuary, but simply the place where the typical sanctuary was located.

THE CHURCH NOT THE SANCTUARY.—As regards the church, it is never once called the sanctuary. Ps. 114 : 2, speaks of Judah as God's sanctuary. But this at most would only prove that a portion of the church constitutes the sanctuary, not the whole, as Judah was only one of the twelve tribes. But again, when was Judah thus called the sanctuary? When Israel went out of Egypt. And what does Paul tell us was then the sanctuary? The tabernacle built by Moses. This settles the question again. Why, then, is Judah called the sanctuary? Simply because Mount Zion was located in Judah, and on Mount Zion the sanctuary was built.

But if Judah or the whole church was the sanctuary then, it would not be the sanctuary now; for the sanctuary of that dispensation has given place to the sanctuary of the new.

But if the church could be shown to be the sanctuary at any time, it could not even then be the sanctuary of Dan. 8:13, 14, the only one under discussion, for the church is expressly spoken of in connection with that as the host, or worshipers, related thereto. Here the church and the sanctuary are certainly separate and distinct objects.

Chapter Seventeen.

A SANCTUARY IN HEAVEN.

AS we have found that the earth is not the sanctuary, that the land of Canaan is not the sanctuary, and that the church is not the sanctuary, but little more remains upon this branch of the subject; for but one more object is left to be considered, and but one more class of texts to be examined.

This object is what is called the sanctuary, temple, or tabernacle in Heaven; and the texts that refer to it were spoken by David, Habakkuk, John, and Paul.

Paul uses language which cannot be misunderstood. Hear him: "Now of the things which we have spoken, this is the sum: We have such an high priest, who is set on the right hand of the throne of the Majesty in the Heavens; a minister of the sanctuary, and of the true tabernacle, which the Lord pitched, and not man." Heb. 8:1, 2.

In the seven preceding chapters of Hebrews, Paul has introduced the priesthood of Christ. He has compared it with that of Aaron in the light of prophecy. He shows the superiority of Christ's priesthood over that of Aaron. Christ is a priest forever, after the order of Melchisedec.

After plainly showing that a priest was to be provided like Melchisedec, he sums up his argument in the 8th chapter, already quoted. We have such an high priest. Who is he? Christ. Where is he? In Heaven. In what place does he minister? In the true sanctuary, not in the figure or model which existed here upon the earth. Who pitched this true tabernacle, or erected this sanctuary? Not man, as Moses erected the earthly sanctuary, but the Lord. Where is this true sanctuary? In Heaven, of course, where the High Priest is. Could not Christ be a priest upon earth? No; for provision was made in the Aaronic priesthood for all the work of that kind which was to be performed upon the earth; and they served, says Paul, "unto the example and shadow of heavenly things." Heb. 8:4, 5.

We invite the reader to dwell a moment upon this picture. The two dispensations are here set in juxtaposition before us; the relation they sustain to each other is clearly shown, together with the work that pertains to each, the place where it is carried forward, and the agents by whom it is performed. In the following epitome, let No. 1 represent the former dispensation, and No. 2, the present.

No. 1. Priesthood performed by Aaron and his sons.

No. 2. Priesthood performed by Christ, a priest forever, after the order of Melchisedec.

No. 1. Priesthood performed here upon the earth.

No. 2. Priesthood performed in Heaven.

No. 1. Performed in an earthly sanctuary, pitched by man.

No. 2. Performed in a heavenly sanctuary, which the Lord pitched, and not man.

No. 1. The type.

No. 2. The antitype.

Where is now our Priest? In Heaven. Where is now our sanctuary? In Heaven. Is the sanctuary in Heaven a literal sanctuary? Just as literal as the Priest, our Lord Jesus Christ, who ministers therein.

We have now found the great original from which Moses copied when he made the sanctuary for his dispensation. The sanctuary of Moses was simply copied from the sanctuary of this dispensation. The priesthood of that dispensation was copied from the priesthood of this dispensation. That owed its existence entirely to this. It was given in reference to this. It was designed simply to introduce this. This is the all-important object in the whole arrangement. That in due time came to an end; and this took its place. The work on earth ceased; and the work in Heaven commenced. We have now neither priest nor sanctuary on the earth; but we have both a Priest and a sanctuary in Heaven. Thank God that so momentous a truth, freighted with consequences of such infinite interest to us all, is so clearly revealed.

All these particulars are clearly and explicitly stated by Paul, and no believer in his inspiration can for a moment question his testimony. This should be an end of all controversy on this point.

This sanctuary in Heaven is called by David, Habakkuk, and John, "the temple of God in Heaven;" Ps. 11 : 4; Hab. 2 : 20; Rev. 11 : 19; 16 : 17; by Zechariah and Jeremiah, God's "holy habitation;" Zech. 2 : 13; Jer. 25 : 30; by Paul, a "greater and more perfect tabernacle, not made with hands," Heb. 9 : 11, "the true," verse 24, "things in the Heavens," verse 23, and the "holy places" (Greek), verses 8, 12, and chapter 10 : 19.

But some one may say, This sounds very well as an argument, yet there may possibly be some error in the premises or conclusions. But if any one had only been to Heaven and seen this sanctuary there, we could then believe. Will you take the testimony of such a one? You shall have it. John was taken to Heaven in vision, and shown things therein; and he has plainly told us of some of the things which he there saw. Rev. 4 : 5: "Seven lamps of fire burning before the throne," antitype of the golden candlestick of the earthly sanctuary with its seven branches. Rev. 8 : 3: Altar of incense, golden censer, and "much incense," all of which pertained exclusively to the sanctuary. Rev. 11 : 19: "And the temple of God was opened in Heaven, and there was seen in his temple the ark of his testament." What was the ark? An instrument of the sanctuary, and nothing else; to be seen in the most holy place, and nowhere else. Thus John beheld the sanctuary in Heaven, and has given us a description of its furniture. And what more need we? Moses says he made the sanctuary after a pattern which was shown to him; Paul says plainly that that pattern was the true sanctuary, and that it is now in Heaven; and John completes the evidence by saying that he saw it there. How could testimony be more comprehensive or complete? Reader, do you believe these things? If you believe God's word, you do!

But there is one consideration which in some minds weighs as an objection to the view here presented. It is said that if there is a sanctuary in Heaven, it cannot be the sanctuary of Dan. 8:14; for that is a sanctuary which is trodden under foot; but a sanctuary in Heaven cannot be trodden under foot.

This objection is surely uttered without thought. Where is Christ? In Heaven. Can he, while there, be trodden under foot? If so, the sanctuary where he ministers can also be trodden under foot. And Paul says emphatically that Christ is trodden under foot by a certain class of sinners, crucified afresh, and put to an open shame. Heb. 10:29: "Of how much sorer punishment, suppose ye, shall he be thought worthy, who hath *trodden under foot the Son of God?*" How do they do this? Simply by becoming apostate and counting his blood an unholy thing, and doing despite to the Spirit of grace. And how do they tread under foot the sanctuary? By erecting rival sanctuaries, and turning mankind away from the true. While the sanctuary was upon earth, this sometimes involved the literal destruction of the tabernacle; but this was only a subsidiary feature, not the main circumstance in this work.

The two powers which were to tread down the host and sanctuary were paganism and the papacy. How have they done it? In the days of the Judges and of Samuel, Satan's rival sanctuary was the temple of Dagon, where the Philistines worshiped. Judges 16 : 23, 24. After Solomon had erected a glorious sanctuary upon Mount Moriah, Jeroboam, who made Israel to sin, erected a rival sanctuary at Bethel, and thus drew away ten of the twelve tribes from the worship of the living God to that of the golden calves. 1 Kings 12 : 26-33; Amos 7 : 13, margin. In the days of Nebuchadnezzar, the rival of the sanctuary of God was the temple of old Belus in Babylon. At a later period, there was the Pantheon, or temple of "all the gods," at Rome, which, after the typical sanctuary had given place to the true, was baptized, and called Christian. Thenceforward Satan had at Rome a "temple of God," in which was a being "exalted above all that is called God, or that is worshiped," the man of sin, the son of perdition. And of this papal abomination it was expressly predicted that it should make war upon the saints, or tread under foot "the host," and make war upon the tabernacle of God in Heaven, or tread under foot the sanctuary above. Rev. 13: 6. And it has done this by turning away the worship of them that dwell on the earth from the temple of God in Heaven to its own sanctuary at Rome. It has trodden under foot the Son of God, the minister of the heavenly sanctuary, by making the pope the vicegerent of the Son of God, and the head of the church instead of Christ, and by leading men to worship this son of perdition as one not only able like God to forgive past sins, but to go beyond what God ever proposed, in forgiving them before their commission. Surely there is propriety in speaking of this work as treading under foot the host and the sanctuary, or "blaspheming God's tabernacle and them that dwell in Heaven." And thus the only seeming objection that can be urged to the position here taken is removed out of the way.

Chapter Eighteen.

MINISTRATION OF THE SANCTUARY.

SO far as the object itself is concerned, we have now before us the sanctuary of the Bible in its entirety. It consists, first, of the earthly sanctuary as embodied in the tabernacle of Moses, and the temples of Solomon, Zerubbabel, and Herod, and, secondly, of the more perfect tabernacle, temple, and sanctuary in Heaven, which the Lord pitched, and not man, and which took the place of the former when the typical dispensation gave place to the true. The Bible nowhere recognizes any other objects as the sanctuary of the Lord, and these cover both dispensations. Whatever, therefore, is said of the sanctuary which has its application in the former dispensation, refers to the sanctuary of that dispensation; and whatever has its application in this dispensation, refers to the sanctuary of the present dispensation, the sanctuary in Heaven. This is a self-evident conclusion from the premises already proved.

Another conclusion as speedily follows; namely, that the declaration of Dan. 8 : 14, " Unto two thousand and three hundred days, then shall the sanctuary be cleansed," has its application in this dispensation, and hence refers to the sanctuary in Heaven. For it has been before shown that only 490 years of the 2300 belonged to the Jews and the earthly sanctuary. There remain 1810 years, extending far down into this dispensation, even to 1844. There the 2300 days terminated, and there we come to the cleansing of the sanctuary, the sanctuary, of course, of this dispensation.

Gabriel himself showed this, before he completed his instructions to the prophet Daniel. He showed him, first, that the earthly sanctuary would be destroyed shortly after the rejection of the Messiah by his people, and that it would never be rebuilt, but be desolate until the consummation. Dan. 9 : 26, 27. Secondly, he brought to view the new covenant: "He [the Messiah] shall confirm the covenant [the new covenant] with many for one week." Verse 27. Thirdly, he brought to view the new-covenant church, or host, namely, the "many" with whom the covenant was to be confirmed. Fourthly, he brought to view the new-covenant sacrifice, namely, the cutting off of the Messiah, but not for himself. Fifthly, he brought to view the

Mediator of the new covenant, who should cause the sacrifices and services of the former to cease. Verse 27. See also Dan. 11 : 22; Heb. 12 : 24. And sixthly and lastly, he brought to view the new-covenant sanctuary when he said that seventy weeks were cut off . . . . "to anoint the most holy." Verse 24. This brings to view an act which was performed preparatory to the commencement of the ministration of the sanctuary, which was to anoint both the holy places and all the sacred vessels. Ex. 40 : 9–11. On this point the *Advent Shield*, No. 1, p. 75, contains the following :—

"And the last event of the seventy weeks, as enumerated in verse 24, was the anointing of the 'most holy,' or the 'holy of holies' or the 'sanctum sanctorum.' Not that which was on earth, made with hands, but the true tabernacle, into which Christ, our High Priest, is for us entered. Christ was to do in the true tabernacle in Heaven what Moses and Aaron did in its pattern. See Hebrews, chapters 6, 7, 8, and 9; Ex. 30 : 22–30; Lev. 8 : 10–15."

In this utterance, the *Shield* was not far from the kingdom of God; and it seems almost marvelous that any upon whose minds the truth had begun to dawn so clearly, should not have followed on to the full light on this glorious subject. No doubt, certainly, can remain concerning the object which the angel had in view when he said, "Unto two thousand and three hundred days, then shall the sanctuary be cleansed."

But it is at once objected that this application cannot be correct, and this cannot refer to any sanctuary in Heaven; for there is nothing there that needs cleansing; nothing there impure, to which such language can apply. And in some minds this mole-hill becomes magnified into a mountain, which they forever try in vain to surmount, and which eclipses from their minds all the strength of proof and array of evidence which may be brought upon this question from any other quarter.

It is not strange that upon the first introduction of this subject, this thought should arise as a seeming objection. But it can, upon a little thought, be fairly met and fully disposed of. It would be anticipating to enter at length upon the question here, inasmuch as it involves an examination of the ministration and cleansing of the heavenly sanctuary, where it will receive due consideration. Suffice it to say at this point that this cleansing is not a cleansing from any physical impurities. It is not accomplished with water, soap, sand, mops, and brushes. It is a cleansing accomplished with blood. But the use of blood is for the sake of remission or forgiveness of sin, nothing else; hence the cleansing is a cleansing from sin; and Paul testifies that such a cleansing does pertain to both the earthly and the heavenly building. He says, Heb. 9:23: "It was therefore necessary that the patterns of things in the Heavens should be purified with these; but the heavenly things themselves with better sacrifices than these." That is, to paraphrase and express more fully the meaning of this language, "It was therefore [because there is no remission or forgiveness of sin without the shedding of blood, verse 22] necessary that the patterns of things in the Heavens [that is, the earthly sanctuary] should be purified [or cleansed] with these [the sacrifices of calves and goats, verse 19, with which the earthly sanctuary each year was cleansed]; but [it was necessary for the same reason that] the heavenly things themselves [the true sanctuary in Heaven, should be cleansed] with better sacrifices than these [even with the precious blood of Christ]."

We confidently submit, to every one capable of understanding the meaning of language, that this is the exact idea which Paul here expresses; and this being so, Paul affirms in the clearest manner that the sanctuary in Heaven must be cleansed. Consistent or inconsistent, this is what Paul says. We leave the objector to settle the matter with the apostle.

We wish to know what this cleansing of the heavenly sanctuary is, which is predicted in Dan. 8:14; for this is the great event to which the prophecy points us. To learn this, we must acquire an understanding of the ministration of that heavenly sanctuary; but we can learn of this only from the ministration of the earthly sanctuary; for Paul says that the priests who here ministered, served "unto the example and shadow of heavenly things." Heb. 8:5. We therefore go backward in history thirty-three hundred years, to that law which was given to lead us to Christ, through which there was spread out here upon earth a shadow of heavenly things, and inquire into the services and ceremonies connected with its sanctuary, how they were performed, and what they signified.

The ministration of the earthly sanctuary was accomplished by the Levitical order of priesthood, and consisted of two great divisions: first, the daily ministration in the first apartment, or holy place, which went forward through the entire year, with the exception of, secondly, a special service in the second apartment, or most holy place, into which, says Paul, the high priest went once every year, not without blood, which he offered for himself and the errors of the people. This yearly day of service in the most holy place was called the day of atonement, and fell each year on the tenth day of the seventh month. Lev. 23 : 27.

The daily ministration embraced the regular morning and evening burnt-offering, Ex. 29 : 38–43, the burning of sweet incense on the golden altar of incense every morning when the high priest dressed the lamps, and every evening when he lighted them, Exodus, chapter 30, the additional work appointed for the Sabbaths of the Lord, and the annual sabbaths, new moons, and feasts, Numbers, chapters 28 and 29, besides the particular work to be accomplished for individuals as they should present their offerings throughout the year.

This latter was the larger and more important part of the service. It consisted of several impressive and solemn steps, chief among which were the following: When a person had sinned, he procured for himself such a victim as the law prescribed, which was to be put to death in his stead. This victim he brought to the priest, to the door of the tabernacle. He then laid his hand upon the head of the victim, and confessed over him his sin, through which act his sin was considered as transferred to the victim. With his own hands he then took the life of his offering, a most striking confession that through his sin he was worthy of death; and the priest took of the blood, and dipping his finger therein, sprinkled it seven times before the Lord, before the vail of the sanctuary, as near as he could approach to the ark till the great day of atonement. Thus was the sin transferred, first to the victim, and then through its blood to the sanctuary itself, and the transgressor went free.

In this manner went the typical service forward through the year. Day after day, week after week, month after month, we behold this round of service performed, the victims coming in solemn procession to the sanctuary, the work of confession going on, the crimson tide of expiation flowing, and the solemn-visaged priests in ceaseless service sprinkling this token of forfeited life before the broken law. There was thus a continual transfer of sins from the people to the sanctuary through the year. What became of these sins?

Chapter Nineteen.

CLEANSING OF THE EARTHLY SANCTUARY.

OUR last chapter closed with the query, What was further done with the sins which were borne into the sanctuary? The Bible fully informs us. Their transfer from the sinner to the sanctuary was not the final disposition of them. They were not borne into the sanctuary either to remain there forever or to be considered as blotted out and removed. But they were treated as still in existence, and as hateful and evil things, respecting which a further ministration must take place, in order that the camp of Israel might become forever free therefrom.

We have already noticed the service through which the sins of the people were borne into the sanctuary. We now come to notice that by which they were taken out. This work was performed only once a year, and was fixed invariably to the tenth day of the seventh month. The work itself was called the cleansing of the sanctuary, or the atonement; and the day upon which it was performed was called the day of atonement.

To accomplish this, an apartment of the sanctuary, into which no man through all the year had been permitted to enter on pain of death, was solemnly laid open, and the ministry of the high priest transferred thereto. So Paul says that into the second apartment of the sanctuary, or most holy place, "went the high priest alone, once every year, not without blood, which he offered for himself, and for the errors of the people." Heb. 9 : 7. When this was accomplished, a complete round of service in the sanctuary had been completed. Then the most holy place was closed again to mortal presence for another year, and the work in the first apartment, or holy place, went on as before till the next tenth day of the seventh month.

The description of this special or yearly ministration in the most holy place, which constituted the cleansing of the sanctuary, is found in Leviticus 16. Let us look briefly at some of the principal features of the scene. Through Moses the Lord gave the following instruction to Aaron the priest: "Speak unto Aaron thy brother, that he come not at all times into the holy place within the vail before the mercy-seat, which is upon the ark; that he die not; for I will appear in the cloud upon the mercy-seat." Lev. 16 : 2.

The Lord sometimes met with his people in other places; Ex. 29 : 42, 43, etc.; but in the earthly tabernacle, the place over the mercy-seat, between the cherubim, may be considered as the place where God generally manifested his presence, and from which he had ordained to commune with them. At all events, he promised to meet the priest there on the great day of atonement.

To come thus into the immediate presence of God was an act of fearful solemnity, and was not to be performed without suitable preparation, and certainly in no trivial or careless manner. Therefore the priest was to offer a young bullock for a sin-offering, and a ram for a burnt-offering, and make atonement for himself and his house. Lev. 16 : 6, 11–14. Having thus, so far as that service could go, become free from sin himself, he was prepared to act in the remaining solemn services of that day, as mediator between God and the people.

He was then to take of the congregation of the children of Israel two kids of the goats, and present them before the Lord at the door of the tabernacle of the congregation. Verse 5. One of these goats was to be slain, and his blood ministered in the most holy place; the other was to be the scape-goat. But which of these it should be was not left to Aaron to decide: the Lord determined that by the lot which Aaron was to cast for this purpose. Verse 8. This being decided, he was to slay the goat upon which the lot fell for the Lord, for a sin-offering for the people, and bear his blood within the vail, and sprinkle it with his finger upon the mercy-seat eastward, and before the mercy-seat seven times.

Two special purposes are stated for which this blood was offered: 1. To make an atonement for the transgression of the children of Israel in all their sins. 2. To cleanse, or make atonement for, the holy sanctuary. These vital facts are clearly stated in Lev. 16:15–22, a portion of which, for the benefit of the reader, we here transcribe:—

Verse 15. "Then shall he kill the goat of the sin-offering, that is for the people, and bring his blood within the vail, and do with that blood as he did with the blood of the bullock, and sprinkle it upon the mercy-seat, and before the mercy-seat. 16. And he shall make an atonement for the holy place, because of the uncleanness of the children of Israel, and because of their transgressions in all their sins; and so shall he do for the tabernacle of the congregation, that remaineth among them in the midst of their uncleanness. 17. And there shall be no man in the tabernacle of the congregation when he goeth in to make an atonement in the holy place, until he come out, and have made an atonement for himself, and for his household, and for all the congregation of Israel. . . . . 20. And when he hath made an end of reconciling the holy place, and the tabernacle of the congregation, and the altar, he shall bring the live goat; 21; and Aaron shall lay both his hands upon the head of the live goat, and confess over him all the iniquities of the children of Israel, and all their transgressions in all their sins, putting them upon the head of the goat, and shall send him away by the hand of a fit man into the wilderness; 22; and the goat shall bear upon him all their iniquities unto a land not inhabited; and he shall let go the goat in the wilderness."

The margin of this last verse reads, instead of a land not inhabited, a land of separation. This goat was separated from the people. He came no more into the camp. And with him, the sins he bore upon himself were considered as forever separated from the people, to appear no more against them. Tradition has it that this goat was hurled from a precipice, and so dashed in pieces. However this may be, beyond question he in some way miserably perished; and with him, also, perished the load of guilt he had borne away from Israel. The man who led away the scape-goat was obliged to wash both himself and his clothes with water before returning into the camp. The whole service was calculated to impress the Israelites with the holiness of God and his abhorrence of sin, and to show them that they could have no contact with it without becoming greatly defiled.

With the sending away of the goat, the people were free from the effect of those sins to which the atonement related. Till then, they were not. For every man was to afflict his soul while the work of atonement was going forward; and whoever refused to do this, was to be cut off from among the people. Lev. 23 : 29, 30.

The work of the priest in the cleansing of the sanctuary is again summed up in Lev. 16 : 29, 30, 33, 34: "And this shall be a statute forever unto you; that in the seventh month, on the tenth day of the month, ye shall afflict your souls, and do no work at all, whether it be one of your own country, or a stranger that sojourneth among you; for on that day shall the priest make an atonement for you, to cleanse you, that ye may be clean from all your sins before the Lord." "And he shall make an atonement for the holy sanctuary, and he shall make an atonement for the tabernacle of the congregation, and for the altar, and he shall make an atonement for the priests, and for all the people of the congregation. And this shall be an everlasting statute unto you, to make an atonement for the children of Israel for all their sins once a year. And he did as the Lord commanded Moses."

The view of the subject here presented suggests some pertinent thoughts relative to the forgiveness and remission of sin. The acceptance of a substitute for the sinner was not for the purpose of making in the body of that substitute an end of the punishment due to the transgressor's sin, but simply to remove the guilt from the sinner. The pouring out of the blood of that victim was not to cancel the sin, but to provide a means of its transfer to still some other object or party. Through the blood of the victim, the sin was transferred to the sanctuary. So far, the sinner's work was an acknowledgment to the law, through blood, of his guilt, and a desire for pardon through faith in a substitute. But he was as yet only relatively or conditionally free. The law still held him, and unless its claims should be more directly satisfied, the remission of his sins would not be secured.

On the day of atonement, the priest, taking an offering from the people, appeared with the blood of this general offering for the people, and sprinkled it upon the mercy-seat directly over the law, to make full satisfaction for its claims. Its demands being thus met, the law released its hold of all the sins in the sanctuary, and through them of the sinners from whom they had come. Then the high priest, if we may so express it, gathered the sins all upon himself and bore them from the sanctuary. Placing his hands upon the head of the scape-goat, he confessed over him all these sins, thus transferring them from himself to the goat. The goat then bore them away, and with him they perished.

Remission means a sending away. Remission of sins is that absolute disposal of them that removes them forever, so that they can no more appear against the sinner. Pardon of sin was secured through the sinner's offering; remission, only through the atonement. Pardon was conditional; remission, absolute.

We have now before us a general outline of the ministration and cleansing of the earthly sanctuary. This was performed, says Paul, unto the example and shadow of heavenly things. From this service, we are, therefore, to reason concerning the ministration and cleansing of the sanctuary in Heaven.

Chapter Twenty.

THE MINISTRATION OF THE HEAVENLY SANCTUARY.

IN entering upon this, the most important branch of the subject before us, we are not left to explore our way alone. Guides, appointed of Heaven to lead the inquiring mind into the right way, are present to direct us. Paul, in his divine commentary on the typical system, addressed to the Hebrews, draws out in plainest terms the parallel between the priestly work of that system and the ministry of our Lord, who is a priest after the order of Melchisedec. Arm in arm with the apostle we walk forward to the following conclusions:—

1. The earthly sanctuary meets its antitype in the true tabernacle, which the Lord pitched, and not man, of which, with its two holy places, it constituted a correct pattern or shadow. Heb. 8 : 2, 5; 9 : 8, 9, 12, 23, 24.

2. The typical offerings meet their antitype in the great offering on Calvary. Heb. 7 : 27; 9 : 11–14, 26; 10 : 10, 12, 14.

3. The typical priesthood meets its antitype

in the priesthood of our Lord. Heb. 4 : 14; 7 : 23, 24; 8 : 1, 2; 9 : 11, 24, 25.

4. As the priests on earth had offerings to make, it is necessary that Christ also have somewhat to offer. Heb. 8 : 3.

5. The work of the priest in the earthly tabernacle meets its antitype in the ministry of our Lord in the sanctuary above. Heb. 8 : 5, 6.

That Christ is our High Priest, and that he has ascended to Heaven, there to minister for us, will not be disputed by any of that class of people with whom we now argue.

When did he commence his ministry in the sanctuary on high? When he ascended up to appear in the presence of God for us. Heb. 9 : 8, 11, 12, 24; 10 : 12. On this there can be no diversity of opinion.

Where did he commence his ministry? Was it in a place corresponding to the first apartment or holy place of the earthly sanctuary, or in some place which corresponds to the most holy place? In other words, does Christ minister in two apartments in the sanctuary above, so that somewhere in his ministry he changes his work from one to the other? or, does he minister in only one apartment, and that the most holy place? While we answer unhesitatingly that Christ commenced his work in the first apartment of the heavenly sanctuary, others take issue, and claim that he ministers only in the most holy place. Their view in reality is, that there is in the antitype only a most holy place, and that is all Heaven; consequently, Christ has but one place in which to minister, and his work goes on without change of character or locality from beginning to end. Let us see what this view involves.

1. The ministration in the most holy place is the cleansing of the sanctuary, let it take place when it will, and continue as long as it may. So, according to this view, the cleansing of the sanctuary commenced when Christ ascended to Heaven, and he has been doing no other work for these 1800 years past, and it is not ended yet. Why, then, may it not just as appropriately continue 1800 years more, and indefinitely longer? This reduces the idea of the cleansing of the sanctuary to an absurdity.

2. The 2300 years reached to the cleansing of the sanctuary. They must, therefore, have ended at the ascension of Christ, if he then commenced the work in the most holy place, for that is the cleansing of the sanctuary. But such a claim is ridiculous, as the prophecy makes only

seventy weeks of the 2300 days reach to that event. The last of the seventy weeks, which were cut off from the 2300 days, brought us to the ascension of Christ, and the commencement of his ministry as priest at the right hand of God.

3. The earthly sanctuary was the shadow cast here by the heavenly; and the earthly had two apartments certainly; but if the heavenly has but one apartment, the most holy alone, how could it cast upon earth a shadow with two? When people will show us a monument with a single shaft casting in the light of the same sun a shadow with two shafts, then they may talk about a heavenly sanctuary with one apartment casting a shadow here upon the earth with two. Till then, if they have any regard for their reputation as men of common observation or philosophy, let them never hint such an idea. But if there are two apartments in the heavenly sanctuary, that settles the question of the ministration; for surely an apartment would not be provided in which no ministration was to be performed.

4. But the service of the priests was a shadow of heavenly things, just as much as the place in which they ministered. And by far the greater

portion of their ministry was performed in the first apartment, or holy place. Now, a ministry performed by the earthly priests in the holy place could not shadow forth a ministry performed by Christ in the most holy place. Therefore, on the view we are examining, all this service in the holy place for 364 days out of the year was performed unto the example and shadow—of nothing! Such a position stands related to both Scripture and common sense, negatively as 364 to 1. That is, it has only one claim out of 365 to either common sense or Scripture.

5. If Heaven is the most holy place simply, what is the vail dividing between it and the holy? Some quote Heb. 10:19, 20, and say that it is Christ's flesh. Then when Christ entered within the vail, as they say he did when he ascended, he entered within his flesh, which is absurd. These texts assert simply that his flesh is the new and living way consecrated for us, not that it is the vail. His flesh, or his sacrifice, is that with which we by faith enter into the true holy places, as these verses assert.

6. The text, "This man, after he had offered one sacrifice for sins forever, sat down on the right hand of God" (Heb. 10:12), has been urged as forbidding the idea of his ministering

in two holy places. We answer that, so far as the idea of sitting is concerned, it would be equally proper to represent him as standing on the Father's right hand. Acts 7 : 55, 56. And then we reply further, that even when he is seen coming in the clouds of heaven, he is said to be "sitting on the right hand of power." Matt. 26 : 64; Mark 14 : 62. Then he can certainly be at the Father's right hand in both the holy places. But Paul bears direct testimony on this point. He says that Christ is a minister of the sanctuary; and the word here rendered sanctuary (Heb. 8 : 2) is in the plural number, and signifies the holy places. This none can deny. It is by the Douay Bible rendered, "the holies;" and by Macknight, "holy places." We therefore justly conclude (1) that our Lord can be a minister of the two holy places, and yet be at the Father's right hand; and (2) that he must minister in both the holy places, or Paul's testimony that he is a minister of the holies (plural) is not true; for a priest that should minister simply in the holiest of all, would not be a minister of the holy places.

7. Again: Heb. 9 : 8, and also 10 : 19, are by some urged to prove that Christ ministers only in the most holy place. These texts both speak

of the holiest as though it were in the singular number; but we have already observed that the words thus rendered are not in the singular, but plural; not "hagia *hagion*," holy of holies, as in chapter 9 : 3, but simply "*hagion*," holies, plural, the same as is rendered sanctuary in chapter 8 : 2. Also the phrase in chapter 9 : 12, 25, rendered, "into the holy place," is the same as is in verse 24 literally rendered, "into the holy places" (plural). These texts, therefore, instead of sustaining what they are often quoted to prove, viz., that Christ has but one apartment in which to minister, furnish positive testimony to the reverse, by showing that there are holy places in the heavenly sanctuary, and that Jesus ministers in them both.

Chapter Twenty-One.

WITHIN THE VAIL.

WE have offered conclusive proof that Christ commenced his ministry in the first apartment of the heavenly sanctuary, and answered some objections which are offered against that view. A few more points remain to be noticed.

Paul's testimony in Heb. 6 : 19, 20, is quoted to prove that when Christ ascended he entered into the most holy place: "Which hope we have as an anchor of the soul, both sure and steadfast, and which entereth into that within the vail; whither the forerunner is for us entered, even Jesus, made an high priest forever after the order of Melchisedec."

The claim here instituted is that "the vail," within which Christ has entered, signifies the vail dividing between the holy and most holy places; and if Christ entered within that vail when he ascended, or if he was there when Paul wrote, he was in the most holy place.

If we grant this claim, some conclusions follow which demand consideration. If there is a vail dividing between the holy and most holy places, which the foregoing claim admits, then there is somewhere a holy place as well as a most holy. But if the most holy is all Heaven, where Christ has entered, then what and where is the holy place? It must be something outside of Heaven. Then what is it? Is it this earth, as some contend? If it is anything outside of Heaven, it must be; for this is the only place with which we have anything to do this side of Heaven. Then what is the vail dividing between earth and Heaven? Why are not our opponents thoughtful enough to give us some light on such points as these?

But, further, the holy place in the sanctuary was twice as large as the most holy; and if the earth is the holy place of the true sanctuary, and Heaven the most holy, it follows, the proportion being maintained, that this little diminutive earth, of which it would take two hundred and fifty-two thousand to equal the bulk of the sun, is twice as large as all Heaven!

And, still further, in fulfillment of the type, Christ must perform a portion of his ministry in the holy place. If this is the earth, he should have performed a portion of his ministry here. But Paul says explicitly that he could not be a priest upon earth; for there was another order of priests appointed to do all the work of this kind that was to be done on the earth. Heb. 8 : 4. And he says again that while the earthly tabernacle stood, while any service of that kind was performed here, the way into the holy places, both the holy and the most holy of the heavenly sanctuary, was not made manifest or laid open. Heb. 9 : 8.

We have already seen how this idea that Christ entered into the most holy place at his ascension, and commenced the work of cleansing the sanctuary, disarranges the period of 2300 days, that great central pillar of the prophecies. It throws the whole system of prophetic interpretation into inextricable confusion. It even destroys the Messiahship of Christ, by throwing the seventy weeks far back into the former dispensation. If these two pillars, the seventy weeks and the 2300 days, can be wrenched from their foundations in the temple of truth, as Samson lifted the pillars of the Philistine temple, the whole structure falls, and biblical interpreters of every school are involved in the ruin.

And what is the reason for all this? Why call the vail in Heb. 6 : 19 the second vail? Simply to avoid the conclusion that the Lord is doing any special work either in Heaven or on earth at the present time; for if the sanctuary is not now being cleansed, the position and work of our Lord differ in no respect from what they have been the past 1800 years; and the past Advent movement is all a failure. But if there is nothing to the past movement, there is certainly nothing to the present. Thus men labor hard to give the devil the whole field, and exhibit themselves as the victims of the thinnest of all delusions.

We inquire, then, Does the word vail in Heb. 6:19, mean the second vail? We answer, No; and this we will prove to the satisfaction of every candid mind. There are but two words rendered vail in the New Testament. These are *κάλυμμα* and *καταπέτασμα*. The first occurs four times only, in verses 13, 14, 15, and 16 of 2 Cor. 3, referring to the vail over Moses' face. The second is used six times, once each by Matthew, Mark, and Luke, all in reference to the vail of the temple which was rent in twain when Christ expired upon the cross, Matt. 27:51; Mark 15:38; Luke 23:45; and three times by Paul in the book of Hebrews: 6:19; 9:3; and 10:20. Is there anything peculiar in Paul's use of this word in Hebrews? Yes; when he means the second vail he specifies it. Heb. 9:3: "And after the *second* vail, the tabernacle which is called the holiest of all." Now if the term, "the vail," was used to signify invariably the second vail, why did Paul use the term second? Why did he not say, here, simply, "And after the vail"? Because a second must imply a first, and he well understood that there was at the entrance to the tabernacle a hanging, which was just as much a vail as that which divided between the holy and the most holy; and to carry out his purpose of instruction in reference to the sanctuary, which is one of Paul's great objects in the book of Hebrews, he accurately distinguishes between the two, and when he means the second, he says the second.

This word, vail, καταπέτασμα, is defined in Robinson's Gr. Lex. of New Testament as follows: "A covering, vail, which hangs down. In Sept. a vail, curtain, of the tabernacle and temple, of which there were two, viz., one at the entrance of the outer sanctuary, Heb., מָסָךְ, Sept., καταπέτασμα, Ex. 26:36; 40:5; Jos. B. J. 5. 5. 4; and the other before the holy of holies, separating it from the outer sanctuary."

Here is good testimony that the same word is used to designate both hangings, the one at the door, and the other in the interior, of the sanctuary. In the Hebrew, in Ex. 35 : 12; 39 : 34; 40 : 21; and Num. 4 : 5, both the terms that are used for hanging and vail are joined together to designate the inner vail before the most holy place, and it is called the vail of the covering. The Cyclopedia of Biblical Literature by M'Clintock and Strong, under the term "Hanging," says:—

"The hanging was a curtain or covering (as the word radically means, and as it is sometimes rendered) to close an entrance. It was made of variegated stuff wrought with needle-work (compare Esth. 1 : 6), and (in one instance at least) was hung on five pillars of acacia wood. The term is applied to a series of curtains suspended before the successive openings of entrance into the tabernacle and its parts. Of these, the first hung before the entrance to the court of the tabernacle (Ex. 27 : 15; 38 : 18; Num. 4 : 26) the second before the door of the tabernacle (Ex. 26 : 36, 37; 39 : 38); and the third before the entrance to the most holy place, called, more fully, vail of the covering. Ex. 35 : 12; 39 : 34; 40 : 21."

We have now before us sufficient evidence that the covering of the outer entrance to the tabernacle was a vail, as well as that which hung before the most holy place. The same Greek word, and the same Hebrew word, are applied to both.

The point now to be ascertained is, In what sense does Paul use the term, the vail? All hangs on the answer to this question, as he is the one who makes use of the language now under examination. As we have seen, with the single exception of the three references by the evangelists to the vail on the day of the crucifixion, Paul is the only New Testament writer who makes use of the term. And in accordance with the accuracy with which he is writing, he finds it necessary to discriminate between the two. And inasmuch as he once specifies the second vail when he refers to that, we must understand him as referring to the first vail when not thus specified. To understand otherwise, is to charge Paul with a degree of looseness in his writings altogether unpardonable in a man of his ability and education, and altogether unaccountable in one who wrote, moreover, by the inspiration of God.

We therefore assert that it matters not how other writers use the term. The evangelists by the vail may mean the second vail, as they doubtless do; and if other writers had used it in the same sense a thousand times, it would in nowise affect the case in hand; for Paul has shown us plainly how *he* uses the term, and that is all we have to know, to understand his writings in reference to it. And when he means the second, he says the second; and when he does not specify, he means the only remaining one, which is the first.

Now to show finally and conclusively that this is so, we quote Heb. 10:19, 20: "Having therefore, brethren, boldness to enter into the holiest [Greek, holies, plural,] by the blood of Jesus, by a new and living way, which he hath consecrated for us, through the vail, that is to say, his flesh." Paul here assures us that Christ by his flesh, his sacrifice, has consecrated a new and living way for us through the vail. And into what does that way through the vail lead? Into the holy places, plural, both of them, the holy as well as the most holy. Therefore to go into the holy place, or first apartment, is to go through or within the vail, as Paul uses the term. And this passage is exactly parallel with Heb. 6:19, 20. Christ, our forerunner, is entered within the vail, to make this living way for us into the holy places. But Christ does not minister, nor open the way for us, in both of the places at once. This would outrage all order, and do violence to the type. He ministers in the first apartment till the prophetic days expire, then goes within the second vail, to accomplish the last division of his solemn work, which is to cleanse the sanctuary, and make once for all a disposition of the sins of those who have sought pardon through his blood.

Here are harmony, reason, and Scripture, a divine triumvirate, to oppose which looks to us like willfully shutting our eyes to the light.

Chapter Twenty-Two.

BETWEEN THE CHERUBIM.

AND still another attempt is made to find an objection to the view we advocate, that Christ commenced his ministry as priest in the first apartment of the sanctuary in Heaven when he ascended up on high. It is framed on this wise: God is spoken of as dwelling between the cherubim. These cherubim were on the ends of the mercy-seat, which was the cover of the ark; and the ark was always in the most holy place, or second apartment of the sanctuary. This, therefore, being God's fixed location, when Christ ascended up to the right hand of the Father on high, he of necessity entered where God was, into the most holy place, and hence did not commence his ministry in the holy place.

The passages which contain the expression, "Between the cherubims," are the following: Ex. 25:22; Num. 7:89; 1 Sam. 4:4; 2 Sam. 6:2; 2 Kings 19:15; Ps. 80:1; 99:1; Isa. 37:16; Eze. 10:2, 6, 7. It will be noticed that all are from Old Testament writers. The first four refer directly to the ark of the tabernacle. Of the remaining passages, two refer to the one expression made by Hezekiah in his prayer, and two are used by David, the three being evidently borrowed from the sanctuary service. The passages from Ezekiel record what he saw when he had visions of God.

Before these passages can be made available for our opponents, it must be shown,

First, That God immovably fixed himself to that position between the cherubim on the ark, and did not meet nor commune with his people from any other place. But this is contrary to the record; for at times he met with both Moses and the children of Israel at the door of the tabernacle. Ex. 29 : 42, 43; 33 : 9, 10. And again, was God dwelling between the cherubim of the ark when the sons of Eli rashly took it out to battle, and it fell into the hands of the Philistines? It must be shown,

Secondly, That even though God did meet and commune with his servants from between the cherubim of the ark here below, so much so that it is spoken of as his dwelling-place, it must also be so in Heaven. But this would not inevitably follow; for in his intercourse with men this might be the best mode of procedure, but not necessarily so in Heaven. It must be shown,

Thirdly, That the cherubim between whom God dwells on high are the cherubim of the ark. But this cannot be shown; for it appears from Ezekiel's vision of God and his throne, in Ezekiel, chaps. 1 and 10, that the throne of God itself is a living throne, supported by the most exalted order of cherubim. And the most appropriate representation of this fact that could be given here on earth was to designate the locality between the cherubim over the ark, as his dwelling-place in his ordinary intercourse with the human race. It must be shown,

Fourthly, That God's throne in Heaven is immovably fixed to one place. But this cannot be shown; for in Ezekiel's vision above referred to it is represented as full of awful life and unapproachable majesty, and moving whithersoever the Spirit was to go. And as in the earthly tabernacle, so here, it sometimes stood at the door of the Lord's house. Eze. 10:18, 19. It must be shown,

Fifthly, That the declaration that Christ ascended to the right hand of the throne of the Majesty in the Heavens, signifies locality, rather than position in respect to exaltation and power. But this cannot be shown; for even when Christ appears coming in the clouds of heaven, he is said to be sitting on the right hand of power. Matt. 26 : 64.

Thus the argument of our opponents fails them at every step.

We have seen from Ezekiel's sublime description that God's throne is in itself a throne of life and motion. The Creator of the universe, the Upholder and Ruler of all this vast realm, is not immovably confined to any one locality. And yet he dwells between the cherubim, because his throne itself is upheld by those wonderful beings. We now have evidence to show that when Christ commenced his ministry above, on the throne of his Father, that throne was in the first apartment of the heavenly sanctuary.

1. John says, in the 4th chapter of the Revelation, "After this I looked, and, behold, a door was opened in Heaven." He thus introduces us, not merely into Heaven, but into some apartment in Heaven. Therein he saw the throne of God, in all its majesty and glory, and before the throne he beheld seven lamps of fire, which are, beyond question, the antitype of the candlestick with its seven lamps, which had its position in the holy place, or first apartment of the sanctuary. Christ is then introduced into the scene, described both as the lion of the tribe of Judah, and as a lamb as

it had been slain, signifying at once his sacrificial work as priest, and his position of exaltation and power with God; and he takes the book sealed with seven seals, and begins to break the seals and unroll the book for the benefit of his people. And the first seal opens with the first, or apostolic, church. Thus the scene opens with the commencement of Christ's ministry, and at that time the throne of God was in the first apartment of the sanctuary, where the antitype of the golden candlestick was seen.

2. This view of the matter is rendered sure by the testimony of Rev. 11 : 19, which declares that the temple of God where the ark is, the most holy place, was not opened till the sounding of the seventh trumpet, near the end of all earthly kingdoms. The scene of Rev. 4, where John first beheld the throne of God, was therefore certainly not in the most holy place.

3. The opening of the investigative Judgment is brought to view in Dan. 7 : 9, 10. And it is said that at that time "the Ancient of days did sit." The word here rendered "did sit," signifies both in Hebrew and in the Greek of the Septuagint, according to Gesenius and Liddell and Scott, "to sit enthroned," or "as judges to sit in court." Had not the Ancient of days been seated upon

his throne before this? Certainly; but the language clearly indicates that he here took a new position for a new purpose. Some move is therefore made on the part of the Father when the Judgment scene opens. He then occupies a position which he did not occupy before.

4. The relation of Christ to this move on the part of the Father, is indicated in verses 13, 14: "I saw in the night visions, and, behold, one like the Son of man came with the clouds of heaven, and came to the Ancient of days, and they brought him near before him. And there was given him dominion, and glory, and a kingdom," etc. This is not Christ's second coming to earth, for the Ancient of days is not here; but he came to the Ancient of days in Heaven, and came to receive dominion and a kingdom, which he will receive at the conclusion of his work as priest, but will not receive till then. This therefore brings to view a scene to transpire near, and at, the conclusion of Christ's work as priest. We have seen Christ on the throne with the Father in the holy place. But we have seen the Father changing his position and opening a new scene, a scene of judgment. To do this, he must first move to the place where this scene is to transpire. Then Christ, as the second essential actor

in the scene, is escorted by a multitude of heavenly beings, surrounding him like clouds of glory, into the presence of the Ancient of days in his new position, according to Dan. 7:13. On the supposition of a change of ministration from the holy to the most holy place of the heavenly sanctuary near the close of Christ's work therein, all these statements and movements have their appropriate place and explanation; but on no other ground can they be harmonized or explained.

Thus it becomes more and more apparent that the view that Christ entered the most holy place when he ascended, is at every step at war with both reason and Scripture; while every objection to the view that he commenced his ministry in the first apartment vanishes at the slightest touch; for God can dwell between the cherubim, and Christ be at his right hand, and both be, nevertheless, in the holy place.

Chapter Twenty-Three.

THE PRIESTHOOD OF CHRIST.

WE rest with all confidence upon the great fact now fully proved in the course of this investigation, that there is in Heaven a real, literal sanctuary, the antitype of the earthly building, called the temple, the temple of God, and the temple of Heaven; and that Christ, when he ascended up on high, opened his grand work of priestly ministry in the first apartment of that heavenly tabernacle, in accordance with the work of the earthly priests, who, ministering unto the example and shadow of heavenly things, began their round of service in the first apartment of the earthly building.

And this fact established, is a nail in a sure place. Other conclusions, of overwhelming importance to the church and the world, follow inevitably and in quick succession, as we shall presently see.

We pause a moment, before passing, to notice one more query, the only remaining one now coming to mind as pertaining to this subject previous to the opening of Christ's ministry in Heaven.

The work in the typical sanctuary virtually came to an end when the real sacrifice was offered upon the cross, and the vail of the temple was rent in twain from top to bottom. It was of no account for the sinner to present, any longer, his victims there. But Christ did not ascend for forty-three days after this, and of course could not commence his ministry before his ascension. And the question is asked, What was the condition of the world during that time? With no service of any virtue here upon the earth, and the work in the heavenly sanctuary not yet commenced, is there not a perplexing break of at least forty-three days and probably of three years and a half to the end of the seventy weeks, during which the sinner was left without a mediator?

In answering this, we might go back to the time before the earthly tabernacle was erected, and before a regular order of priesthood was instituted, even to those offerings in reference to which Adam and Eve were instructed, when sin had forced them to turn their backs on holy Eden in the world's earliest infancy. No priests were then ordained; the sinner presented his offering in his own behalf. There were no holy places laid open, and no priestly work was established in Heaven. Yet the offerings there made, if offered in a proper manner, were as efficacious as any offered at any time previous to Christ. The great offering was not made, but these all looked forward in faith to it; and faith in the Redeemer to come gave them all their virtue.

It may be said that during these antecedent ages, though there was no ministry in Heaven, men had effectual sacrifices which they could offer, which they could not do after the vail of the temple was rent and its services ceased. Very true; but that very moment they had a sacrifice provided for them, the merits of which they could present to God in their behalf. There was really no break in the work. The two systems, typical and antitypical, touched each other upon the cross. There the shadow, all the way from Eden down, met the substance, and there was no blank between the two. As men by their sacrifices could manifest their faith in a Redeemer to come, though there was no ministration going on in Heaven, and as those offerings were efficacious up to the cross, so from that very moment men could manifest their faith in a sacrifice which had been offered, though the actual commencement of Christ's work as priest might still for some years be delayed.

The way thus being all cleared up to this important division of the subject, let us consider a moment the nature of that priesthood upon which Christ now entered. The work in the earthly tabernacle was performed by mortal men, subject to disease and death, and was hence cumbered with such imperfections as were inseparable from the defective instruments by which it was performed. The priesthood of Christ is a superior priesthood, in which the imperfections of the earthly system find no analogy. This may be stated in a few particulars:—

1. Christ is a priest after the order of Melchisedec, and not after the order of Aaron. Heb. 5 : 6.

2. Perfection was not of the Levitical priesthood; for if it had been, says Paul, what further need was there that another priest should arise after the order of Melchisedec, and not after the order of Aaron? Heb. 7 : 11.

3. Those priests were many, because they were not suffered to continue by reason of death; but this man continueth ever, and hath an unchangeable priesthood. Verses 23, 24.

4. It was necessary for the priests of the house of Levi to offer up sacrifices daily, embracing all the various offerings that were made by those who had transgressed. But all this

Christ did by one act when he offered up himself. Heb. 9 : 25, 26, 28; 10 : 10, 12, 14.

5. The round of service in the earthly tabernacle was many times repeated; but the ministry of Christ is accomplished once for all. Heb. 9 : 11, 12, 24, 25; chapter 10.

6. All the blood which was offered in the former dispensation, was offered for past transgressions only, and made no provision for the future; while the merits of that blood which was shed on Calvary applied not to the past alone, but to the future also. Heb. 9 : 14, 15.

7. As the blood of Christ is the only blood ministered in connection with the heavenly sanctuary (whether by actual presentation or by virtue of its merits is immaterial), the same blood must be ministered in both apartments.

8. As long as Christ fills the office of priest, so long he is mediator between God and man.

The chief difference, then, between the priestly work of Christ and that of the Levitical order, results from these facts: that Christ has but one offering to make for his entire ministry that he ever lives, and hence need not repeat his work, but perform it once for all; that his offering pertains to the future as well as to the past; and that it does make perfect, or really and absolutely take away the sins of, those who avail themselves of its merits. There is nothing in the fact that Christ is a priest after the order of Melchisedec and not after the order of Aaron, to show that he does not perform a work exactly like that performed by Aaron, as near as the perfect things of Heaven may resemble the imperfect things of earth. And Paul assures us that he does perform just such a work; for he says that the Aaronic priesthood in their work were simply acting out the shadow of the work performed by Christ in Heaven.

The conclusion becomes evident, therefore, that as the sins of the people were borne into the earthly sanctuary in type through the blood of beasts, they are now borne into the heavenly sanctuary in reality through the blood of Christ. A comparison of Leviticus and Hebrews will make this plain.

The blood of all the offerings, it appears, was not borne into the sanctuary by the priest, and sprinkled before the vail. It was the blood of some of the offerings called sin-offerings which was thus treated. Of these offerings, Wm. Smith, in his Dictionary of the Bible, says:—

"The sin-offering represented that covenant as broken by man, and as knit together again by God's appointment, through the 'shedding of blood.' Its characteristic ceremony was the sprinkling of the blood before the vail of the sanctuary, the putting of some of it on the horns of the altar of incense, and the pouring out of all the rest at the foot of the altar of burnt-offering. The flesh was in no case touched by the offerer; either it was consumed by fire without the camp, or it was eaten by the priest alone in the holy place, and everything that touched it was holy. This latter point marked the distinction from the peace-offering, and showed that the sacrificer had been rendered unworthy of communion with God. The shedding of the blood, the symbol of life, signified that the death of the offender was deserved for sin, but the death of the victim was accepted for his death by the ordinance of God's mercy. . . . Accordingly we find (see quotation from the Mishna in Outr. *De Sacr.* i. c. xv., § 10) that, in all cases, it was the custom for the offerer to lay his hand on the head of the sin-offering, to confess generally or specially his sins, and to say, 'Let *this* be my expiation.' Beyond all doubt, the sin-offering distinctly witnessed that sin existed in man, that 'the wages of that sin was death,' and that God had provided an atonement by the vicarious suffering of an appointed victim."

Provision was made for all to present this kind of offering, the blood of which was borne into the sanctuary, and sprinkled before the vail. First, for the priest. Lev. 4 : 3–12. Secondly, for the whole congregation, collectively. Verses 13–21. Thirdly, for the ruler. Verses 22–26. And, fourthly, for any one of the common people. Verses 27–35.

In Lev. 6 : 30, we read: "And no sin-offering, whereof any of the blood is brought into the tabernacle of the congregation to reconcile withal in the holy place, shall be eaten. It shall be burnt in the fire." Now, it appears from Paul's testimony to the Hebrews, that of all the offerings, those sin-offerings, the blood of which was carried into the sanctuary, and their bodies burned without the camp, especially prefigured the offering of our Lord. He says, Heb. 13 : 11, 12: "For the bodies of those beasts, whose blood is brought into the sanctuary by the high priest for sin, are burned without the camp. *Wherefore* Jesus *also,* that he might sanctify the people with his own blood, suffered without the gate." Of these offerings Christ was especially the antitype. And as by these the sins of the people were anciently transferred to the sanctuary (for Paul says their blood was borne in there *for sin*), so through the blood of Christ, which is ministered wholly in the sanctuary above, our sins are transferred to that heavenly temple.

Chapter Twenty-Four.

CLEANSING OF THE HEAVENLY SANCTUARY.

A PORTION of the evidence was presented in the preceding chapter to show that our sins are transferred to the heavenly sanctuary through the blood of Christ. This is still further confirmed by 1 Pet. 2 : 24 : "Who [Christ] his own self bare our sins in his own body on the tree." On the cross, Christ bore our sins as a sacrifice. In this sense he bears them at no other time or place. Here he was set forth as "the Lamb of God that taketh [margin, beareth] away the sin of the world." John 1 : 29. Here he was offered as the "propitiation for the sins of the whole world." But how much is implied in these expressions, that he bare our sins on the tree, and that he is the Lamb that taketh away the sin of the world? Simply that here a sacrifice was provided, the merit of which was sufficient to avail with God to cancel the guilt of the entire world; that here an offering was given, upon which all who would, might lay their sins. But if none had come or should come to Christ, his offering would have been in vain. Whether or not his sacrifice shall be of benefit in any individual case, depends on the action of that individual.

Having provided the sacrifice, Christ commences his work as priest in the sanctuary above, and the invitation is sent out to all the world, Come unto me for pardon and everlasting life. The way of our coming is described in Acts 20 : 21 : "Repentance toward God, and faith toward our Lord Jesus Christ." We confess our sins to God through Christ as our sacrifice. As the penitent in the former dispensation laid his sins upon his victim, by confessing over him his transgressions, so we lay our sins upon Christ by confessing them to God through him. Thus the confession and offering of the sinner of old finds its antitype in our confession of sin to God through Christ. By the Mosaic offering, the sin was borne into the earthly sanctuary; by faith in Christ as our offering, and by our confessions through him, we transfer our sins to the sanctuary in Heaven, where he ministers for us. Thus the Lord carries forward the great work which he commenced when he bore the sins of the world at his death, by pleading the cause of penitent sinners through his blood shed in their behalf. And thus there is in this dispensation, as in the former, a transfer of sins; there in figure, here in fact. There is nothing strange or fanciful in this. Every one can easily understand it. Such was the service of the type, which was a shadow of the heavenly things; and such, therefore, is the heavenly ministration itself.

As, in the case of sins transferred to the earthly tabernacle, the question arose, What became of those sins? we have here the same question to answer respecting the sins transferred through Christ to the heavenly sanctuary: What is to become of these sins? Do they remain there forever? No; they will be removed, just as they were in the type; for the heavenly sanctuary is to be cleansed even as was the earthly.

That sins are transferred to the sanctuary, is evident from the fact that there exists a necessity for its cleansing; and there can be nothing there but the presence of sin to render such a work necessary. We look to the type. A work of cleansing was performed every year in the most solemn manner by divine appointment. Why was this? What was there to render the cleansing of that sanctuary necessary? Into the most holy no man entered but the high priest, and he but *once a year*. In a place so sacredly guarded, could there have been anything physically impure? By no means. And yet that sanctuary, the most holy as well as the holy, had to be cleansed. Again we ask the reader, and especially the objector, to ponder well the question, Why? But one answer can be returned. The sins of the people were represented there; and from their presence it must be freed. And this work of cleansing, as we have seen, was not a purification from material uncleanness, but simply a ceremony by which imputed sins were removed and borne away forever.

So in the antitype. There is nothing literally impure or unclean in the heavenly sanctuary. But the sins of all those who have sought pardon through the merits of Jesus have been transferred there; and these must be removed. This is its cleansing. No other is brought to view. In reference to no other act or ceremony is the expression, "cleansing of the sanctuary," ever used. No mind can fail to understand this, and none need to revolt at the idea.

We have already referred to Paul's testimony in Heb. 9:22–24, which forever settles this point. We scarcely need repeat that the burden of Paul's argument is remission, which is the removal of sin. He shows in these verses that the earthly sanctuary had to be cleansed because sin was to be remitted, and that it must therefore be accomplished with blood. He then explicitly states that it was necessary for the same reason that the heavenly sanctuary should undergo a cleansing of the same nature, and by the same means, only that now the sacrifice was infinitely better, being the blood of Christ, instead of the blood of beasts. On this point we need not longer dwell. No statement is needed to add to such a plain declaration by the apostle, no additional light is called for to help the rays of the noon-day sun.

It would seem that no one can now fail to understand the nature of the cleansing of the sanctuary: It is accomplished by blood, not by fire. It is a part of Christ's work as priest, not as king. It is the ministration performed in the most holy place to complete the round of service, and end the work.

This, then, is what was to take place at the end of the 2300 days, when the sanctuary was to be cleansed. But some still cling to the idea that the sanctuary of which this is said, the sanctuary of Dan. 8 : 14, must be the very sanctuary that Daniel had in view, in the land of Palestine, not a sanctuary in Heaven. In reply we point the objector to the fact that there is no sanctuary now in Palestine. There was none there when the 2300 days ended, in 1844. And how can a sanctuary be cleansed that does not exist? They must first show a sanctuary there, before they can talk of its cleansing.

Still they ask, If a man should promise to cleanse a meeting-house in Battle Creek which had become defiled, and then should go and cleanse one in Detroit, would that be fulfilling the promise? Such a question betrays at once their utter misapprehension of the question. In the first place, the cleansing of the sanctuary is not made necessary by its being trodden under foot. It has reference to another feature of the question entirely. In the answer to the question, enough was given for us to know; namely, the time when the closing scene in its work should commence, which after a brief but indefinite space of time would bring us to the end. Secondly, the sanctuary in Palestine, and the sanctuary in Heaven, are not like two meeting-houses, one in Battle Creek and the other in Detroit, having no connection with each other. These are counterparts of each other. They stand as type and antitype. When one had fulfilled its design, it gave place to the other, which thenceforward became the sanctuary. The first was given to lead us to the second, and instruct us in reference thereto. Therefore whatever is said in reference to the sanctuary which applies to the former dispensation, has reference to the sanctuary of that dispensation; and whatever applies to this dispensation, has reference to that which is the sanctuary of this dispensation, namely, the sanctuary in Heaven. But as we have shown, the 2300 days reach far down into this dispensation; and consequently the sanctuary to be cleansed at the end of those days is the sanctuary of this dispensation, the tabernacle on high.

This is illustrated by what is said of the host. The host was to be trodden under foot the whole length of time covered by the vision. Who were the host, the people of God, when Daniel wrote? The Jews. But the vision reaches over into this dispensation, and who are the host, the people of God, now? The Jews? No; but Christians who are called in by the gospel. When the dispensation changed, the Jews were no longer recognized as the host, but Christians are now such, and to them Dan. 8:13 now applies. So, likewise, when the new covenant was introduced, the sanctuary of the vanished dispensation was no longer recognized as the sanctuary of the Bible, but the true sanctuary in Heaven, which then took its place. And to this, Dan. 8 : 14 now applies.

To return to the illustration of our opponents: If it was arranged that a meeting-house in Battle Creek should be *the* meeting-house of a certain society for ten years, and then it should be destroyed, and give place to a meeting-house in Detroit which should thenceforward for ten years be *the* meeting-house of that society, and at the end of twenty years the meeting-house of that society should be cleansed, to which would it apply? To the meeting-house in Battle Creek, which had been destroyed? or to the meeting-house in Detroit, which was the meeting-house of the society at that time? To the one in Detroit, of course. This would be an illustration adapted to the subject of the sanctuary; for this is just what the Bible asserts in relation to it. It said that while the former dispensation lasted, the earthly sanctuary should be the sanctuary connected with God's worship; that then that sanctuary should be destroyed and give place to the true tabernacle and sanctuary in Heaven, which the Lord pitched, and not man, which should thenceforward be *the* sanctuary of God's worship and of this dispensation; and finally, that at the end of 2300 days, 1813 years and six months down in this dispensation, the sanctuary should be cleansed. What sanctuary? The earthly one, which had served its purpose, been destroyed, vanished away with the system to which it belonged, and had given place to the new? No; but the sanctuary of this dispensation, of course. It is only when thus stated that this is a fair illustration of the subject. But thus stated it is taken out of the hands of the objector; for it sets forth just the points which we maintain. The sanctuary in Heaven is therefore the one to be cleansed at the end of the 2300 days.

Striking about for some other pretext to object to our conclusion, our opponents next assert that the language, "then shall the sanctuary be cleansed," means that the cleansing should be finished at the end of the 2300 days, whereas we assert that then it just begins. The answer to this is not long nor difficult. The cleansing of the sanctuary, as we have seen, occupies a space of time; and in speaking of such events, the Bible brings us to the beginning of the work, not to its close. It does not say, Then shall the sanctuary have been cleansed, but, Then shall it be cleansed. When the Scriptures speak of accomplished events, they so express it; as of the two witnesses, Rev. 11:7: "When they shall have finished their testimony," or of Christ, 1 Cor. 15:24: "When he shall have delivered up the kingdom." But when they say, "Then shall be great tribulation," Matt. 24:21, it means that it shall then begin, and continue; and when they say, "Then shall that Wicked be revealed," 2 Thess. 2:8, it means then shall begin the period during which he will stand revealed before the world. So, "then shall the sanctuary be cleansed," simply refers to the time when the work shall commence.

Therefore are we held inevitably to the conclusion that at the end of the 2300 days, in the autumn of 1844, the ministration of the sanctuary above was changed from the holy to the most holy place. Then the temple of God was opened in Heaven, and there was seen in his temple the ark of his testament. Rev. 11:19. There the Ancient of days then placed his throne, and "did sit," as the prophet Daniel saw. Dan. 7:9. Then, escorted by the retinue of holy angels, Christ, our priest and mediator, moved into the inner temple to receive from his Father the result of his long work of mediation for man. Dan. 7 : 13, 14. Then opened the solemn Judgment scene of verses 9 and 10 of Dan. 7. Then the seventh angel sounded, and the work of finishing the mystery of God began. Rev. 10 : 7. These are the sublime events involved in the cleansing of the sanctuary which then commenced. In the scene now presented before us, we behold the climax of the grandeur, glory, and solemnity that center in this great subject.

Chapter Twenty-Five.

A WORK OF JUDGMENT.

AN examination of the work called the cleansing of the sanctuary leads us into a series of subjects of the most important and timely character, subjects which explain some statements of the Scriptures which are otherwise obscure, harmonize lines of prophecy otherwise disconnected, and answer some otherwise unanswerable queries which arise concerning events connected with that crowning of all events, the second coming of our Lord Jesus Christ.

For instance, when Christ comes, a change passes instantaneously upon the people of God, and all others are passed by. The righteous who are in their graves are raised in power, glory, and immortality, and the rest of the dead are left in their graves for a thousand years, and the righteous who are living are changed from mortality to immortality, while the rest of the living are given over to perish under the judgments of the Almighty. And this change for God's people is wrought instantaneously at the last trump. But before this change can be wrought, it must be decided who are the people of God, and who are the incorrigibly wicked. This matter must be determined before the Lord comes; for there is no time then for investigation and decision of character. But this work of decision is a work of judgment; and such a work of judgment must transpire before the Lord comes.

We know of no system of belief which has a place for this preliminary work of judgment, except that held by S. D. Adventists. It has been a source of perplexity to many, and to meet it, they have been obliged to resort to such unscriptural conclusions as these: 1. That all the race, good and bad, are raised indiscriminately together; whereas the Bible plainly declares that there are a thousand years between the resurrection of the righteous and that of the wicked. Rev. 20 : 5. 2. That when the righteous are raised, they are raised mortal, judged, and then changed; whereas the Bible assigns no place for any such work of investigative judgment after Christ appears, and, moreover, explicitly declares that the righteous are raised in power, in glory, with spiritual bodies, and in incorruption. 1 Cor. 15 : 42–44. Thus every attempt made by any other system to explain how it is that immortality can be conferred upon the righteous when Christ comes, without this preliminary work of judgment, for which we find an appropriate place in the work of the sanctuary, runs directly against the Scriptures at every step. And no system which contradicts such plain statements of the Bible can be worthy of the least credit.

The subject of the sanctuary, correctly understood, removes all these difficulties. The cleansing of the sanctuary provides the very place for this preliminary work of judgment, and brings to view a work of just exactly this nature.

The cleansing of the sanctuary is a work of judgment. A few considerations will make this proposition plain. The priesthood of Christ continues up to the time when he takes his own throne as king. He passes directly from the first position to the second; and when he takes his position as king, his work as priest is done. Now, his work as priest being for the purpose of gathering out from the human family a people for his name and kingdom, his priestly office cannot close till this result is declared. When his work is finished, it will have been decided who have availed themselves of his mediation, and have thus become his people. It is the putting away of sin that determines this; but this is the very work that Christ performs in the most holy in the conclusion of his ministry. He here puts away the sins of his people; and this is the cleansing of the sanctuary.

This involves an examination of the books; for the rule that God has laid down in this matter is that all judgment shall be rendered according to each man's works as they stand upon the record. "And the dead," says John, "were judged out of those things which were written in the books, according to their works." Rev. 20:12. From the reference in this and numerous other passages, to the books, the book of life, the names or the things written therein, and the blotting out to take place, but one conclusion can be drawn; and that is that a faithful record is kept of each one's actions, the thoughts, words, and deeds that make up the texture of his character, and the course of his life. If the person repents, all these recorded sins are to be blotted out of this book. So Peter declared, "Repent ye, therefore, and be converted, that your sins may be blotted out, when the times of refreshing shall come from the presence of the Lord." Acts 3:19. Of the same class Christ speaks in Rev. 3:5: "He that overcometh, the same shall be clothed in white raiment; and I will not blot

U of M

out his name out of the book of life, but I will confess his name before my Father, and before his angels." Again he says, "Whosoever, therefore, shall confess me before men, him will I confess also before my Father which is in Heaven. But whosoever shall deny me before men, him will I also deny before my Father which is in Heaven." Matt. 10 : 32, 33 ; Luke 12 : 8, 9. And this is when Christ is about to be sent the second time to earth, Acts 3 : 20, and when he is prepared to come as a thief on all them that do not watch. Rev. 3 : 3.

The two divisions of this great proposition are thus established: If we secure the pardon of our sins, the time comes, just before the end, when these sins are blotted out of the books, and our names are retained in the Lamb's book of life, and the Saviour confesses our names to the Father as those who have accepted of salvation through him. Our cases are then decided, and we are sealed for everlasting life. If, on the other hand, we do not repent, our sins are not blotted out of the record where they stand, but our names are blotted out of the book of life, and Christ denies our names before his Father, as those who have slighted his mercy, and are not entitled to everlasting life through him.

Thus the cleansing of the sanctuary involves

the examination of the records of all the deeds of our lives. It is an investigative Judgment. Every individual of every generation from the beginning of the world thus passes in review before the great tribunal above. So Daniel, describing the opening of this scene, calls it a work of judgment, and expressly notices the fact that the books were opened. Dan. 7 : 9, 10.

This work has been going forward in the sanctuary above, since the end of the prophetic period in 1844. Beginning, according to the natural order, with the earliest generation, the work of examination passes on down through all the records of time, and closes with the living. Then the sealing message, Rev. 7, will have performed its work, and all antecedent questions being determined, all cases decided, everything will be ready for the coming of the Lord.

For nearly thirty-three years already this solemn work has been in progress. How much longer can it continue? Nearly thirty-three years of this decisive work of investigative Judgment already past, and yet how few of all the masses of the earth dream of their position! O church of Christ, lift up the voice like a trumpet, sound an alarm which shall cause all the inhabitants of the land to hear and tremble; for the great day of the Lord is near, and hasteth greatly.

Chapter Twenty-Six.

THE OPENING OF THE TEMPLE.

"AND the temple of God was opened in Heaven, and there was seen in his temple the ark of his testament." Rev. 11 : 19.

We have seen that the temple in Heaven is the sanctuary, the true tabernacle, which the Lord pitched, and not man. The opening of this temple, brought to view in this passage, is that which reveals the ark of God. The ark had its position invariably in the second apartment of the sanctuary. This, then, is the opening of the most holy place of the heavenly sanctuary. And when does this take place? At the sounding of the seventh trumpet. Rev. 11 : 15. The events mentioned to take place under this trumpet are, 1. The anger of the nations, verse 18, commencing especially when so many European thrones toppled to the dust in 1848, and continuing to the present time. 2. "And thy wrath is come," referring to the seven last plagues in the near future. 3. The kingdoms of this world become the kingdom of our Lord and of his Christ. Verse 15. This will be fulfilled when Christ takes the throne of his kingdom. 4. "And the time of the dead, that they should be judged, and that thou shouldest give reward unto thy servants the prophets, and to the saints, and them that fear thy name, small and great; and shouldest destroy them which destroy the earth." Verse 18. This must reach over to the final destruction of the wicked at the end of the one thousand years. 5. "And the temple of God was opened in Heaven." We know, from the argument on the sanctuary and the 2300 days, that this took place in 1844. And, conversely, as it does not take place till the sounding of the seventh trumpet, the last of that series, we know it must take place somewhere near the end, and could not have taken place at the opening of this dispensation, as some vainly imagine. This is the earliest event mentioned that takes place under the sounding of the seventh trumpet, and hence the inference is necessary that the seventh trumpet commenced to sound at that point. The 2300 days ended, the seventh trumpet began to sound, the temple of God was opened in Heaven, and the work of the cleansing of the sanctuary was entered upon.

And what results from the opening of this

temple? "There was seen," says John, "in his temple the ark of his testament." He does not say simply, I saw it, but it "was seen." John, standing here as the representative of the church, clearly teaches that the church would then by faith behold the ark in the tabernacle above. The sight of the ark suggests one thing, and one only, and that is the law of God contained in the ark. The ark was called the ark of the testament because it contained the tables of the testimony which God gave to Moses, the ten commandments. It owed its name to the fact that the tables of the law were therein. Had it not contained the tables it never would have been called the ark of the testament; and whenever and wherever it is called the ark of the testament it is proof that the law of God is there.

With these remarks, we ask the reader to mark well the fact that the ark as seen in Heaven by John, down under the sounding of the seventh trumpet, is still called "the ark of his testament." What does this prove? It proves that that ark in Heaven contains the law. What law? The same law that gave it that name in the days of Moses; namely, the tables of the testimony, the ten commandments.

And how may we suppose that those commandments read in the ark in Heaven? Just the same, of course, as they read in the ark on earth. Of this there can be no question. This forever precludes the idea of any change in the law. Talk about changing or abolishing the law? Not until we can change or abolish those tables in Heaven. Oh! what a vain and futile work are they engaged in, who are laboring to show that the law of God as a whole, or even the fourth commandment alone, has been in the least respect altered, much less done away.

The conclusion is therefore not only plain and scriptural, but beautiful as well, that as the ark in Heaven is the great original, after which the ark on earth was formed, so the law in the ark above is the great original, of which the law given on earth was but a transcript or copy. This great truth has been well embalmed by the poet, in the following language:—

> "For God well knew perdition's son
> Would ne'er his precepts love;
> He gave a duplicate alone,
> He kept his own above."

Having now found a sanctuary, an ark, and a law in Heaven, where Christ is ministering, another thought is at once suggested, in relation to the object to which the earthly and heavenly ministrations have reference. We have seen the relation which these two ministrations sustain to each other, namely, that of type and antitype. The first was a figure, the second the reality; the first a shadow, the second the substance. But everything pertaining to that dispensation was not a figure and a shadow. There was something there real; and that was sin. Men were actual transgressors. But sin, or transgression, is a violation of law. Hence there was a real law there which they were guilty of breaking; and that was the law contained in the ark, the ten commandments. All that was typical was the ministration connected with that law. There was real law, and actual sin; and the ministration, the service of the priesthood, was for the purpose of taking away that sin. But this could be done only in figure; for the blood of beasts, the only blood they had to offer, Paul says, could not in reality take away sin. But this typical ministration looked forward to one to come, to be performed by our Lord, which should in reality take away sin.

The offerings of that time were types of the offering of our Lord. Those offerings had reference to the law contained in the ark. The offering of our Lord must, therefore, have reference to the law contained in the ark; for what they were in figure, this must be in fact. The idea could not for a moment be conceived that those offerings should have reference to one law, and yet be types of an offering which would have reference to *another* or a *different* law. This could not be possible. In this case the one would not and could not be a type of the other. The established relation of type and antitype existing between these offerings shows that they must have reference to identically one and the same law. Therefore, the law in the ark in Heaven, before which Christ ministers, must be, word for word, letter for letter, jot for jot, tittle for tittle, the same as the law that was deposited in the typical ark here upon the earth.

Such is the bearing which the subject of the sanctuary has upon the law of ten commandments. It is an absolute demonstration of their perpetuity and entire immutability. And this is perhaps the reason why those who have set their hearts against the law shut their eyes to the plain light on the subject of the sanctuary. They cannot receive the one without adopting the other.

The temple has been opened in Heaven, and

John says there was seen there the ark of the testament, seen of course, through faith, by the church on earth. What further evidence can we show that this has been fulfilled? We answer, The great movement in behalf of the law now going forward in the land through the efforts of the S. D. Adventists. They have received the light on the subject of the sanctuary. They see the temple opened in Heaven. They behold there the ark, and our Lord making his last offering on the mercy-seat, the cover of the ark, in the most holy of the sanctuary on high. They see that the requirements of the law in that ark are neither relaxed nor altered. And they are going forth to vindicate its claims, and lead men to the reform necessary in its observance. This movement has come up in the right time and manner to fulfill the prophecy and confirm the application we make of this important subject.

The temple is opened, and no man can shut it. The ark is seen, and no man can obscure it. The corresponding movement on the earth is in progress, and no man can stop it. Reader, fall into line, and go with us to the kingdom.

Chapter Twenty-Seven.

FINISHING OF THE MYSTERY OF GOD.

IT was shown in the preceding chapter that at the time when the 2300 days ended, and the cleansing of the sanctuary commenced, then the temple of God, that apartment where the ark is, was opened; and that that took place under, and marked the commencement of, the sounding of the seventh trumpet. When the seventh trumpet, the last of the series of trumpets which covers the gospel dispensation, sounds, the temple of God is opened in Heaven, and the cleansing of the sanctuary commences.

There is another remarkable prediction concerning what takes place at the sounding of the seventh trumpet, which now invites our attention. It was said to John, Rev. 10 : 7: "But in the days of the voice of the seventh angel, when he shall begin to sound, the mystery of God should be finished, as he hath declared to his servants the prophets." What is meant by the mystery of God, and its finishing? In a number of passages Paul speaks very definitely concerning the mystery of God. In Eph. 3 : 3–6, he says:

"How that by revelation he made known unto me the mystery (as I wrote afore in few words, whereby, when ye read, ye may understand my knowledge in the mystery of Christ), which in other ages was not made known unto the sons of men, as it is now revealed unto his holy apostles and prophets by the Spirit; that the Gentiles should be fellow-heirs, and of the same body, and partakers of his promise in Christ by the gospel."

Here Paul states explicitly that the mystery was made known to him by revelation. In his epistle to the Galatians he tells us what was made known to him by revelation. Gal. 1:11, 12: "But I certify you, brethren, that the gospel which was preached of me is not after man; for I neither received it of man, neither was I taught it, but by the revelation of Jesus Christ." This is what he had written "afore," or a little before, "in few words." The epistle to the Galatians was written six years before the letter to the Ephesians. And what in Ephesians he calls the mystery made known to him by revelation, in Galatians he calls plainly the gospel as preached to the Gentiles.

Again he says, Eph. 1:9, 10: "Having made known unto us the mystery of his will, according to his good pleasure which he hath purposed in himself; that in the dispensation of the fullness of times he might gather together in one all things in Christ, both which are in Heaven, and which are on earth, even in him." Again, in Col. 1 : 25–27, we have this declaration: "Whereof I am made a minister, according to the dispensation of God which is given to me for you, to fulfill the word of God; even the mystery which hath been hid from ages and from generations, but now is made manifest to his saints; to whom God would make known what is the riches of the glory of this mystery among the Gentiles; which is Christ in you, the hope of glory." Eph. 3 : 9: "And to make all men see what is the fellowship of the mystery which from the beginning of the world hath been hid in God, who created all things by Jesus Christ." Rom. 16 : 25, 26: "Now to him that is of power to stablish you according to my gospel, and the preaching of Jesus Christ, according to the revelation of the mystery which was kept secret since the world began, but now is made manifest, and by the scriptures of the prophets, according to the commandment of the everlasting God, made known to all nations for the obedience of faith."

All these texts speak to the same point, and testify unmistakably to the fact that the mystery of God, the mystery of Christ, etc., is no more nor less than the gospel of Jesus Christ, through which the Gentiles are brought in to be members of the commonwealth of Israel and partakers with the household of faith. This being the mystery, its finishing would be the close of the proclamation of the gospel, the completion of the work which it was designed to accomplish. This of necessity closes the period of man's probation, and finishes the plan of salvation.

But this, as we have seen, is the very result involved in the cleansing of the sanctuary. That concludes Christ's work as priest, finishes his mediation, decides the cases of all mankind, and concludes the work of the gospel.

The reader will now perceive another beautiful link in the faultless chain of harmony which the Bible presents to us on this subject. When the seventh angel sounds, then commences the work called the finishing of the mystery of God. But it will occupy some years; for it is "in the days," years, "of the seventh angel when he shall begin to sound" that this mystery is to be finished. This work will occupy the first years of the sounding of this trumpet. But this trumpet commenced to sound at the end of the 2300 days, in 1844, when the temple of God was opened in Heaven. We are now, therefore, in the period of the finishing of the mystery of God; and this finishing work we find to be the same as the cleansing of the sanctuary there introduced, and the ministration in that apartment of the heavenly temple then opened. Could facts more completely harmonize than these?

"The mystery of God shall be finished," proclaimed the angel, "as he hath declared to his servants the prophets." Where had he declared this? This is but a part of the declaration of the angel, which includes the preceding verses; and in these we find him uttering a solemn oath that "time shall be no longer." Rev. 10:6. This cannot mean literal time; for the angel immediately speaks of the days of the seventh angel to succeed. It cannot mean probationary time; for John, as a representative of the church, is commissioned to proclaim another message to the people after that. But one other kind of time remains, and that is prophetic time; and to this, therefore, the passage must refer. But the period of 2300 days is the longest prophetic period given in the Bible, and reaches down to the latest point. Therefore this oath of the angel has its application at the point where the 2300 days terminate; and the expression is equivalent to a declaration that then prophetic time should end, or the 2300 days would terminate. Then the angel states what shall immediately follow; namely, the mystery of God should be finished, as he had declared to his servants the prophets. What had God declared to the prophets should take place at the end of the 2300 days? Why, it had been shown to Daniel that then the sanctuary should be cleansed. Here, then, is where he had declared to his servants the prophets that the mystery of God should be finished; which is the same thing. Such is the unquestionable parallel between these prophecies.

Chapter Twenty-Eight.

THE ATONEMENT.

IN the long retinue of subjects with which the question of the sanctuary stands so intimately connected, and in the understanding of which it exerts so controlling an influence, the doctrine of the atonement occupies a prominent place.

We have already seen that the cleansing of the sanctuary, the investigative Judgment of the saints, the blotting out, or remission, of sin, and the finishing of the mystery of God, are all one and the same thing. We now make the additional statement that this is also the atonement.

The frequency with which the expression is made that Christ atoned for our sins upon the cross, shows how widely the idea is entertained that the shedding of his blood and the atonement are the same thing. But this leads to two ultra and fundamental errors. Men have been driven by this idea to the extremes of error in opposite directions, and have spent their time in an unnecessary and fruitless warfare.

The Scriptures plainly declare that Christ died for all. Now, with the view that the death of

Christ is the atonement, the conclusion is easily reached that the sins of all have been atoned for, and hence that no condemnation can ultimately remain to any. This branch of the argument blossoms at once into Universalism.

But the Scriptures just as plainly assure us that all will not be saved; that some do now, and will in the end, rest under condemnation. For these, of course, no atonement is made; and if the atonement and the death of Christ are the same thing, it follows that his death reaches no farther than the atonement, and hence that he did not die for all, but only for a chosen few. On this branch of the argument we find the bitter fruit of ultra Calvinism.

The subject of the sanctuary relieves us from the false claims of both these errors. The trouble in either case lies in the premise common to both, which is defective; and with a false premise, however sound the reasoning based upon it, it is impossible to reach a correct conclusion. The death of Christ and the atonement are not the same thing. And this relieves the matter of all difficulty. Christ did not make the atonement when he shed his blood upon the cross. Let this fact be fixed forever in the mind.

But does it not say that he bore our sins in his

own body on the tree? And as he died for all, did he not thus bear the sins of all? He did, indeed; but in what sense? What office was he fulfilling in the shedding of his blood? For light on this, we turn again to the types. The idea and doctrine of the atonement are drawn from the typical system.

To reach the atonement, several steps were necessary: 1. The confession of sin upon the head of the victim. 2. The sacrifice of the offering. 3. The work of the priest. And this work was performed three hundred and sixty-four days in the year before the day of atonement came. The work of atonement was the last ceremony of the year, and completed the round of sanctuary service. The offering and the service of the priest preceded the atonement. The offering was not the atonement, nor was the service of the priest, until the day of atonement arrived, and the work was commenced in the most holy place of the sanctuary.

The parallel between the earthly and the heavenly sanctuary has been sufficiently drawn to make at once the application. The antitypical atonement, which is the real removal of sin, was not made when the offering for this dispensation was provided, nor by the service of the priest in the first apartment of the sanctuary, but is accomplished only by the service of the priest in the most holy place, which is the closing work of our Lord's ministration, the cleansing of the sanctuary, and did not commence, as we have seen, till 1844.

In this case, as in the type, the offering and the usual priestly work precede the atonement. But when Christ suffered for us, in what capacity was he acting? Not as our priest, but only as the offering; for he was put to death by wicked hands, even as the victims of old were slain by the sinner. It was as the sacrifice and offering that he bore our sins in his body on the tree. Here the blood was provided with which he was to minister. This was an act preparatory to the priestly work he was to perform; the atonement is the last. Those who make the offering to be the same as the atonement, confound together events that are more than 1800 years apart. The offering was general. Christ died for all the world. The sacrifice was offered to all who would accept of it. But the atonement at the close is specific; it is made only for those who seek the benefits of his redeeming work.

It is not the place here to introduce a dissertation on the subject of the atonement. It is mentioned in this connection simply to show that the great sanctuary question locates the atonement, and guards us against the error of confounding the offering with the atonement, and placing it at the commencement of Christ's ministry, instead of at its close. And thus we are provided with a safeguard against the errors of Universalism and Calvinism above noticed.

But does not Peter say, Repent and be baptized for the remission of sins? Acts 2:38; and if sins are remitted in the act of baptism, how can we look forward to a future time for the atonement and remission? So some minds may query. But the text does not say that sins are remitted in baptism. It is only for, or "in order to" remission that this rite is performed. It looks forward to a future time, when all the requirements of God having been complied with in faith, sins will be blotted out, and the times of refreshing come from the presence of the Lord.

It may be asked again if Rom. 5:11, does not say that we have already received the atonement. The word *katallage,* there rendered atonement, should be rendered reconciliation, as in the margin. Reconciliation is effected between ourselves and God, but the atonement, or the removing of sins so that they can be remembered no more against us, is the last act of priestly service performed by the Lord for us.

But are not our sins forgiven now? and, if forgiven, are they not put away? We answer, Forgiving sin and blotting out sin are not the same. Forgiveness is conditional, the condition being that we comply with certain requirements upon which it is suspended, till the end of our probation. If we fail, we stand at last unforgiven, and no atonement can be made for us. The doctrine on this point is stated by Ezekiel, and an illustration is given by the Saviour himself.

The doctrine. Eze. 18:26: "When a righteous man turneth away from his righteousness and committeth iniquity, and dieth in them; for his iniquity that he hath done, shall he die." In chapter 33:13, it is added, "All his righteousnesses shall not be remembered." That is, he shall be treated as though he had never been righteous. But the righteousness of the righteous is by faith; therefore, if he turn, and commit iniquity, he shall be treated as if he never had faith; the forgiveness, conditionally extended, is withdrawn.

The illustration. Matt. 18:21–35. We will not take space to quote it, but simply epitomize the facts: A king had a servant who owed him an enormous sum of money; but, having nothing wherewith to pay, his lord forgave him the debt; but this same servant had a fellow-servant who owed him a small sum, and, having nothing with which to pay, asked to be forgiven the debt. But his fellow-servant would not, but cast him into prison till he should pay all. His lord, hearing of it, immediately withdrew his own offer, and delivered the unmerciful debtor over to the officers till he should pay all that was due. Christ puts the fearful point to this illustration by adding, "So likewise shall my Heavenly Father do also unto you, if ye from your hearts forgive not every one his brother their trespasses." This plainly illustrates the conditional nature of forgiveness, and shows how past forgiveness may be nullified by present or future sin.

How, then, if the atonement is yet future, do we receive of its benefits? How are we justified? In reply, we would ask the questioner, How, if the atonement was made on the cross, did those who lived before that time secure its benefits? And just as the people of God who lived and died before Christ could receive the benefits of the atonement if it was made on the cross, just so both they and we can receive its benefits, if it is deferred to be the closing work of this dispensation. It is by faith. The patriarchs were justified by faith, and so died. So with the righteous ever since that day. All their life-work, their acts of faith, stand faithfully written out in the heavenly books of record. The time comes for the investigative Judgment, for the last division of Christ's work as priest, for the sanctuary to be cleansed, for sins to be blotted out, for the atonement to be made. The books are opened. Every case is examined. Then the sins of those whose record shows their last acts to have been acts of repentance, faith, and obedience, are atoned for, or blotted out.

Chapter Twenty-Nine.

THE TENTH DAY OF THE SEVENTH MONTH.

WE have seen that the closing work in the sanctuary is the work of atonement. In the type, one day out of the year, called the day of atonement, was allotted to this work. This was the tenth day of the seventh month. Lev. 16 : 29, 30.

It will be noticed that in the fulfillment of the types, scrupulous exactness is observed in reference to the time; that is, the fulfillment occurs in the same month of the year, and on the same day of the month, as that on which the type was set forth. The fulfillment of the types of the spring is recorded in the New Testament, so that we have a divine exposition of this part of the typical system.

Thus, the passover was killed on the fourteenth day of the first month. Ex. 12 : 6 ; Lev. 23 : 5. Christ is our passover ; and he was sacrificed for us in the same month and on the same day, the fourteenth day of the first month. 1 Cor. 5 : 7 ; Mark 14 : 12 ; John 18 : 39, 40 ; 19. The sheaf of first-fruits was waved on the sixteenth day of the first month. This met its antitype in the resurrection of our Lord, the first-fruits of them that slept, the sixteenth of the first month. 1 Cor. 15 : 20; Luke 24 : 21. The feast of weeks, or Pentecost, occurred on the fiftieth day from the offering of the first-fruits. The antitype of this feast, the Pentecost of Acts 2, was fulfilled on that very day, fifty days from the resurrection of Christ, in the outpouring of the Holy Spirit upon the disciples.

The fulfillment of these types shows us these facts: That the great events for which the passover, the day of first-fruits, and the Pentecost were respectively noted, met their antitype on the very days of the types. Applying the same principle to the work on the tenth day of the seventh month, we are led to expect the antitype of the great work which characterized that day of atonement, namely, the cleansing of the sanctuary, on the tenth day of the seventh month of that year in which the 2300 days ended, as it was at that point that the sanctuary was to be cleansed.

As those days ended in 1844, an effort was made to find the tenth day of the seventh month, Jewish time, of that year; and it was found to fall on the 22nd of October. The historical and numerical arguments on the 2300 days have shown that those days terminated in the autumn of that year; and the argument from the types would confine us to that month and that day. This is why that day was set for the coming of Christ. While it is marvelous that so critical an examination of the types should not have revealed to the Adventists of that time the fact that the cleansing of the sanctuary was not the coming of Christ, nevertheless, their eyes being so holden that they did not perceive this point, and supposing that the cleansing of the sanctuary was inseparably connected with the coming of Christ, they were left no alternative but to fix that day for his appearing.

In the light of the preceding argument, it is unnecessary to add that all any one had a warrant to conclude was that on that day the great work in the second apartment of the heavenly sanctuary would commence.

Another point should be borne in mind relative to typical fulfillment; namely, that the antitype commences upon the day of the type, but may extend forward a great distance. We are still partaking of Christ our passover, as the church has been for the past eighteen centuries.

We are still keeping the feast of unleavened bread. And the Holy Spirit which came down on the day of Pentecost, as the antitype of the feast on that day, still abides with the church of Christ. Read carefully 1 Cor. 5 : 7, 8; John 14 : 16. So with the work in the holiest on the day of atonement, the tenth day of the seventh month. Its antitype must commence at that time, and, of course, must occupy a space of time corresponding to its magnitude and importance.

But right here some set up the claim that the 2300 days do not extend to the cleansing of the sanctuary, but only to the antitypical day of atonement; and that as there were preliminary offerings to be made on that day, before the real work of cleansing the sanctuary, so now, although the 2300 days have ended, we are yet only in that preliminary work, and the cleansing of the sanctuary has not yet commenced.

But few words are needed in reply to this proposition. We do not read anywhere in the Bible of such a period as the antitypical day of atonement. It may be proper enough to apply this expression to the time actually covered by the work of the antitypical cleansing of the sanctuary. We may speak of this as the antitypical day of atonement, confining it to the time while the sanctuary is being cleansed; but as the Bible nowhere uses the expression, so it nowhere countenances the idea of any antitypical day of atonement, extending outside of that work.

To say that the 2300 days do not extend to the cleansing of the sanctuary, is squarely to contradict Dan. 8:13, 14, which says that at that time the sanctuary shall be cleansed. It is only by corrupting the words of the text and making it read, Then shall the antitypical day of atonement commence, instead of, "Then shall the sanctuary be cleansed," that any one is able to insert any time between the ending of the days and the commencement of the work of the cleansing of the sanctuary. But who knows that the extra offerings of the day of atonement, as mentioned in Num. 29, were to transpire before the high priest entered the most holy place? Who knows but they were made after the high priest came out of the holiest, at the time mentioned in Lev. 16:23, 24? All this has to be assumed; because the Bible is silent upon it.

But if it could be proved that these offerings were made prior to the work in the most holy place, no such conclusion as is set forth could then be drawn from it; for in some of the types of the spring, to which reference has already been made, as, for instance, the day of first-fruits and the feast of weeks, or the Pentecost, there was the same work of burnt-offerings, etc., as on the day of atonement. Lev. 23:10–21; Num. 28:16–31. Yet, in the fulfillment, no allowance of time was made for these; but the antitype commenced on the very day of the type.

From these considerations, it follows that if we are to have a long preliminary work preceding the cleansing of the sanctuary, that work must transpire before the 2300 days end. If these days ended in 1844, then this supposed preliminary work had transpired prior to that time. But if the preliminary work is now going on, the 2300 days have not yet ended. But the evidence that the 2300 days have ended is unanswerable. Therefore, the cleansing of the sanctuary must now be transpiring.

Chapter Thirty.

THE CLOSE OF PROBATION.

THE idea seems to have taken strong hold of some minds, that when the work of atonement commences in the most holy place of the sanctuary above, mercy can no longer be offered to sinners, but probation must close. And this is offered as an objection to our view that the cleansing of the sanctuary commenced in 1844; for, say they, had that been the case, there could have been no conversions since that time; but as sinners have been converted since that point, they conclude that the cleansing of the sanctuary did not then commence.

But who has said that probation must close when our Lord commences to minister in the most holy place? No inspired writer has said such a thing, and it is not in the type. It is answered that all offerings for sin were to be presented at the door of the tabernacle; this is true; but an assumption must be superadded to that fact to make it available as an objection; and that assumption is this: that our prayers, supplications, and confessions of sin, are our offerings; that consequently we can present them nowhere else than at the door of the tabernacle, and can present them there only while the High Priest ministers in the first apartment; for after he has changed his position to the second apartment, no such offerings can longer be accepted, no more mercy be offered, nor probation continued.

Such betray an utter misapprehension of the whole question; for they make our prayers and confessions the antitype of those ancient offerings. What! can any one for a moment suppose that when a person offered up his victim at the earthly tabernacle, it signified that people under the gospel dispensation would pray, and confess their sins! This we are indeed to do; but the ancient offerings had no connection with this; for they all pointed forward to Christ; and when our friends will take the right antitype, they may lay as much stress as they please upon the locality where it is to be offered; for Christ also "suffered without the gate." Heb. 13:12.

But if Lev. 17, which is supposed to prove that forgiveness of sin can be found only in the first apartment, be examined as far as verse 7, it will be seen that the great object of the special charge to bring their offerings to the door of the tabernacle, was to prevent the people from sacrificing in the fields to devils. This therefore in no way contradicts the testimony of Lev. 16, that the high priest with the blood of sin-offering did make atonement in the holiest because of the transgression of the people in all their sins.

Reference was made in the preceding chapter to those offerings which are supposed to be preliminary to the work of atonement or the cleansing of the sanctuary. As already stated, the position is taken by some that we are now in this preliminary work, and the matter of continued probation is got along with on the supposition that these preliminary offerings might have reference to individual cases, and have reference to particular sins.

We inquire for the foundation upon which this supposition rests. It is said that the work in the holiest was not the offering of blood for particular individuals, but for all the people. Then we answer that these preliminary offerings, to which reference has already been made, were of precisely the same nature. They were not offered by individuals, but, like the daily morning and evening sacrifices, were offered in behalf of the whole people. So there is just as much mercy implied in the sin-offering in the holiest, as in the other offerings presented on that day. We do not deny, but on the other hand fully maintain, that these offerings did imply mercy and the forgiveness of sin for the people. But if so, there was forgiveness of sin to be found while the high priest was presenting his offering in the most holy place.

If it be said that the work in the holiest was to cleanse the sanctuary, we reply that it cannot be said that it was *only* to cleanse the sanctuary, which would make quite a different statement of it. It is true it was to cleanse the sanctuary, but this is not the whole truth on this point. It was also for the people, availing for sins committed up to the moment of its offering. The high priest made atonement for the sins of the people on that day just as much as he did for his own sins. Read carefully Lev. 16 and Heb. 9:7.

Now, we affirm that what was done in the type for the people as a body, is done in the antitype for the people as individuals; and the blood of sin-offering ministered in the most holy place, avails for their sins, even as it did in the outer apartment, till it comes to an application in their individual cases. The twofold work of the high priest in the earthly sanctuary seems fitly to typify this twofold work of our High Priest above. For the sins of the whole church for six thousand years may be disposed of as individual cases, and all the while that this great work is being accomplished, the blood of Jesus may avail for us in the presence of God.

There seems, therefore, to be no difficulty involved in the idea that the offering of the High Priest in the holiest, can avail for sins committed while he is there before God. Some additional considerations go to sustain this idea. In the type, so far as we know, during the whole work of the year, the transgression preceded the offering. The sin was committed before the victim was brought. And no offering was brought to the priest for sins that would be committed in the future. This was at least as much so in the holy place as in the most holy.

But how was it with our Lord? He shed his blood before entering the tabernacle in Heaven at all. And that blood, once shed, avails for sins committed after his death just as effectually as for those which, as in the type, were committed before his offering was made. And, as we have seen, this blood is ministered by our Lord in both apartments of the heavenly sanctuary. Now, if its offering in the most holy place cannot avail for any sins only those committed before it began to be offered there, by parity of reasoning it would follow that it could not avail in the holy place, or first apartment, for any sins only those which had been committed before it began to be offered there. And then we should have no forgiveness anywhere in all this spiritual, life-giving dispensation. But this would be proving too much; and any position which involves such an issue, or any line of argument which leads to such a result, must be abandoned.

And finally, the testimony of the New Testament is conclusive on the point that the blood of Jesus avails for us in both the holy places of the heavenly tabernacle: Heb. 10:19: "Having therefore, brethren, boldness to enter into the holiest by the blood of Jesus." The word here rendered holiest is plural in the original, signifying holy places; and so Macknight renders it: "Well, then, brethren, having boldness in the entrance of the holy places by the blood of Jesus."

These words are a complete refutation of the doctrine that probation closes with our Lord's entrance within the second vail. We enter into the most holy as well as into the holy by his blood; and we do it with boldness, because of the promise of the forgiveness of our sins. Thank God that we can still thus enter by the blood of Jesus.

We therefore conclude that probation does not end when the work in the most holy place commences, but that it ends with each individual, as the work shall reach his or her individual case. The natural order would seem to be that this work, which we have shown to be the investigative Judgment, would begin with the earliest generations of men, that is, with those who are now in their graves (but their record lives on high), and so come down through all successive generations till it reaches the living, the decision of whose cases would be the very closing act of this last work. And we may perhaps consider our experience since the cleansing of the sanctuary commenced, a demonstration of this point.

But at length the cases of all the generations of the dead will have been examined, and it will come to the living; and then, as each individual case is taken up and passed upon, his probation will end and his destiny be fixed. This is the scene our Lord brings to view when just before his coming he says that this fearful fiat shall go forth: "He that is unjust, let him be unjust still; and he which is filthy, let him be filthy still; and he that is righteous, let him be righteous still; and he that is holy, let him be holy still."

And how near are we to this solemn moment? We know not. For thirty-three years already has this closing sanctuary work been in progress. It cannot much longer continue. Its whole duration is to be spanned by one generation. This much we know, as taught by the type, that if we would have Christ's blood avail for us to atone for our sins when our cases shall come up in that grand review, the record must show that we have sincerely repented of all our sins, and sought pardon for them through our Advocate on high. In the type the people were required on the day of atonement to afflict their souls. Are we thus faithfully crucifying ourselves to this world, that we may live in the world to come? How solemn is this time! Let us endeavor to feel the force of the following impressive lines of the poet, and give them in our memory the place they so well deserve:—

"There is a time, we know not when,
A point, we know not where,
That marks the destiny of men,
To glory or despair.

"There is a line, by us unseen,
That crosses every path,
The hidden boundary between
God's patience and his wrath.

"To pass that limit is to die,
To die as if by stealth;
It does not quench the beaming eye,
Or fade the glow of health.

"The conscience may be still at ease,
The spirit light and gay;
That which is pleasing, still may please,
And care be thrust away.

"But on that forehead God has set
Indelibly a mark
Unseen by man; for man, as yet,
Is blind, and in the dark.

"And yet the doomed man's path below
Like Eden may have bloomed;
He did not, does not, will not, know
Or feel that he is doomed.

"Oh! where is this mysterious bourn
By which each path is crossed,
Beyond which God himself hath sworn
That he who goes—is lost?

"How far may we go on in sin?
How long will God forbear?
Where does hope end—and where begin
The confines of despair?

"An answer from the skies is sent:
Ye that from God depart,
While it is called to-day, repent,
And harden not your heart."

Chapter Thirty-One.

THE SEVEN LAST PLAGUES.

WE have now brought our investigation of this subject down to the time when all cases have been examined and decided. The investigative Judgment in the most holy place has then transpired. The mystery of God is finished. Christ is no longer an intercessor. Probation has closed. We have endeavored to anticipate and answer all queries that properly arise in reference to this subject thus far; and we now turn our attention to what follows the work of this awful moment, upon the decisions of which hangs the gain or loss of an eternity of bliss.

When Christ ceases to plead, and steps out from between God and rebellious and incorrigible man (for such are all those who at this time stand unreconciled to God), there is nothing to longer stay the vials of long-merited judgments from the shelterless heads of the wicked. Then can be fulfilled the punishment threatened by the third angel's message against the worshipers of the beast, which is the visitation of God's wrath with no mixture of mercy; Rev. 14:10; and then we can have, as described in chapter 15:1, the pouring out of those vials in which is filled up his indignation. Neither of these could be fulfilled while a divine mediator stood between God and men. For so long as God regards the pleading of his Son, which he will do so long as he pleads at all, he could not visit upon men judgment in which no mercy was mingled, nor pour out any vials filled up with wrath alone. This is proof that the third angel's message is addressed to the last generation of men; for on no others can the punishment threatened be visited.

We now propose to show that these judgments are the seven last plagues, and that they immediately follow the close of our Lord's work in the sanctuary above.

In the 15th of Revelation, verse 5, John speaks of the opening of the tabernacle of the testimony in Heaven. This is the opening of the most holy place of the sanctuary, as elsewhere explained. After this, seven angels come out of the temple having the seven plagues, represented as seven golden vials full of the wrath of God. They go forth to pour these out upon men, and the temple or sanctuary is filled with smoke, so that no man, or no being, as it might be translated, is able to enter therein, or carry forward a work of ministration there, till the seven plagues of the seven angels are fulfilled.

In verse 1 of this chapter it is said that in these plagues is filled up the wrath of God, which shows that they are poured out after probation is ended, and the sun of mercy has withdrawn its last warming ray from this apostate earth.

The statement of verse 8, that no one was able to enter into the temple till the seven plagues were fulfilled, is another proof of the same point, and if possible still more positive. For, ever since Christ commenced his work in Heaven, there has been some one in the sanctuary. So this scene has not transpired in the past, and it is certain that the seven last plagues have not yet commenced to be poured out. And until Christ closes forever his service as priest, there will be some being in the sanctuary; for there is no break in this work from beginning to end. The scene of verse 8 cannot, therefore, transpire till the sanctuary work is done.

The prototype of this scene is found in Ex. 40 : 34, 35 : "Then a cloud covered the tent of the congregation, and the glory of the Lord filled the tabernacle. And Moses was not able to enter into the tent of the congregation, because the cloud abode thereon, and the glory of the Lord filled the tabernacle." This was at the commencement of the typical work here on earth, as the scene described in Rev. 15 is at the close of the real work in Heaven. Thus this work, so far as it relates to man, is bounded at its beginning and close with an overpowering manifestation of the glory of God. The great God takes sole possession of his own dwelling-place, and thus sets his seal to the work which has been accomplished therein.

Passing out from the sanctuary, we are now called upon to look at the effects of the close of this work in scenes to transpire here among men. A dissertation upon the subject of the plagues is not called for in this place. See the subject discussed more at length in "Thoughts on the Revelation," chapter 16. We only glance here at simply the most prominent features.

As we have shown that these plagues are future, and are visited upon men at the close of probation, so there is just as clear evidence that they will be literal. The first falls upon the men who are guilty of that sin against which the third message is warning the world to-day.

A sore, noisome and grievous, more corroding than the leprosy, more stinging than blains, more painful than boils, breaks forth upon those who, contrary to light and warning, have received the mark of the beast, and worship his image.

The second vial throws the sea into the most infectious and deadly condition that can be conceived of: it becomes like the blood of a dead man. If this applies to the oceans of our globe, as we see not why it may not, we leave each one's imagination to grapple with the problem, what the condition of the earth would be with three-quarters of it enveloped in this deadly substance.

The third plague strikes at a still more vulnerable spot, and the rivers and fountains become blood; as if the earth in her last agony was pouring forth blood from every aperture, even as it oozed from the Saviour's pores, as he wrestled with the world's sin and darkness in lonely Gethsemane. This plague, as perhaps the preceding, will probably be of short duration, as it would seem that none could long survive should this cup of blood be pressed continually to their lips.

The fourth plague lights up the sun with an

unwonted flame. Vegetation withers beneath its scorching rays; the streams evaporate; the heat burns to the very bones of men; and an air of desolation spreads over the face of nature. Thus under these plagues the woes of men increase in a regular ratio: first, sores; then, as a consequence, fever and thirst; then blood to quench that thirst; and finally, blazing, glaring, intolerable heat from a sun on fire.

The fifth angel pours the contents of his vial upon the seat of the beast, old Rome, gray and crumbling from its long years of sin. And the kingdom of the beast, the whole Catholic world, is full of darkness. The similar plague on Egypt, produced darkness so gross that it could be recognized by the sense of touch; and in the dark night following the dark day of May 19, 1780, even dumb animals were filled with such terror that horses could not be forced from their stables. So here the darkness summons around the followers of the papal apostasy its legions of undefinable terrors till they dare not stir, but gnaw their tongues for their pains and their sores.

The sixth angel stations himself over the symbolic Euphrates, and pours his vial upon the Turkish empire; and its waters (people), which have for many years already been growing weaker, or drying up, will then be clean dried up, and the way of the kings of the East will be laid open, that they may come up to the battle of the great day of the Lord. Then the spirits of devils from the three great systems of false or apostate religion, the dragon, beast, and false prophet, paganism, popery, and a dead and back-slidden Protestantism, go forth to gather the nations to the last strife. And they march up, goaded by their own sufferings and torments, the results of the previous plagues, and impelled by devils, to the valley of slaughter, the great antitypical Megiddo.

The seventh angel hurls the contents of his vial around the globe. The air is tainted, and every breathing thing inhales the deadly miasma. Then the voice of God, which has once shaken the earth, is heard again, and shakes both earth and heaven. That voice proclaims the controversy ended. It is done. And the majestic utterance rends the earth with the mightiest convulsion it has ever felt. The cities fall; great Babylon is forced to taste the fierceness of God's wrath; every island flees away, the mountains disappear, and when thus every hiding-place and refuge is taken away, the mighty treasures of hail which God has reserved against the time of trouble, against the day of battle and war, Job 38 : 22, 23, are dashed upon them out of heaven. The last prayer of the wicked is for rocks and mountains to hide them from the presence of the Lamb; but so completely are they transformed by sin that their last ejaculation is one of blasphemy against God; for the plague of the hail is exceeding great. Thus amid the convulsions of the last day, this poor earth, which has long groaned under the weight of the curse and been torn by the wild disorders of sin, is laid in its coffin for a thousand years.

We ask the sinner to study well this picture, and haste, while a few precious hours of probation linger, to seek a shelter beneath that wing which shall safely cover the righteous during the time of trouble, and bring them everlasting deliverance at its close.

Chapter Thirty-Two.

THE SCAPE-GOAT.

AFTER the ministry in the most holy place was accomplished, one thing more remained for the priest to do, before the work was entirely finished. Having, by presenting before the law in the ark the blood of the appropriate offering, released from the sanctuary the sins for which that blood made atonement, those sins were canceled as related to the forgiven sinner, but were not by this act destroyed. The high priest having performed the ministry which took them from the sanctuary, they were left for him to dispose of in a manner plainly pointed out. He came out of the sanctuary, and laying both his hands on the head of the scape-goat, held in waiting at the door, confessed over him "all the iniquities of the children of Israel, and all their transgressions in all their sins, putting them upon the head of the goat." Lev. 16:21. This is a plain statement that the sins taken from the sanctuary were transferred to the goat. The goat, with these sins upon him, was then by the hand of a suitable person sent away into the wilderness, into a land of forgetfulness, implying, probably, the destruction of the goat, in the death of which the sins of the people which he bore also perished.

The ceremony of thus sending away the sins of the people in the type, Lev. 16 : 20–22, has already been noticed. The question now arises, What service in the real ministry of Christ, in the more perfect tabernacle above, answers to this, and how is it to be performed?

The principal question here to be decided is, What being shall we regard as the antitypical scape-goat? When the typical goat, anciently, loaded with the sins of the people, went forth from the camp of Israel, to be heard of no more forever, what did it foreshadow to be fulfilled in this dispensation? Here again we are led to differ very materially from the views which have obtained on this subject.

The idea very generally held is that the scape-goat typified Christ. Because John the Baptist said, John 1 : 29, "Behold the Lamb of God which taketh [margin, beareth] away the sin of the world," and because it is said of the scape-goat that he "shall bear upon him all their iniquities into a land not inhabited," it is, without further thought, concluded by some that the latter was a type of the former.

From such a view we dissent, for the following reasons:—

1. If Christ, in bearing the sin of the world, fulfilled the antitype of the scape-goat, he must have filled this office at the time of the crucifixion; for Peter says of him, "Who his own self bare our sins in his own body on the tree;" 1 Pet. 2:24; and this is the only time when, and the only sense in which, he is said to have borne our sins. But in the type, the scape-goat did not bear away the sins of the people till after the cleansing of the sanctuary; hence the antitype of this work cannot take place till after the cleansing of the antitypical sanctuary, which work, as has been proved, did not commence till the termination of the 2300 days in 1844. Dan. 8:14; Heb. 9:23. It is therefore impossible to carry this work back to the crucifixion of Christ, which was even before he commenced his ministry in the heavenly sanctuary at all. Christ cannot therefore be the antitype of the scape-goat.

2. The scape-goat, after being loaded with sin, was sent away by the priest. He could not therefore be the priest himself. But in this dispensation Christ is priest; he cannot therefore be the antitypical scape-goat to be sent away by

the priest. Christ cannot send away himself. The conclusion is hence inevitable that the scape-goat must be some being whom Christ, after placing upon him the sins borne from the sanctuary, shall send away into a land not inhabited.

3. The scape-goat was sent away from Israel, into the uninhabited wilderness. If our Saviour is its antitype, he also must be sent away, not his body alone, as some suppose who refer it to his death, but in his entire being (for the goat was sent away alive) from, not to, nor into, his people; neither into Heaven; for that is not a wilderness, or land not inhabited. But instead of thus being sent away, Christ is to dwell in the midst of his people, the true Israel of faith, for evermore.

4. The scape-goat received and retained all the iniquities of the children of Israel; but when Christ appears the second time, he will be "without sin."

5. It is impossible that two goats, one of which was chosen by the Lord, and is called the Lord's, while the other is not so called, but was left to perform an entirely different office,—it is impossible that these both should typify the same person. But the goat on which the Lord's lot fell,

the blood of which was ministered in the sanctuary, did certainly typify Christ. Just as surely the scape-goat did not typify him.

Having thus proved by evidence which must be conclusive to every candid mind, that Christ cannot be the antitype of the Levitical scape-goat, the direct question, Who is the antitype of that goat? now presents itself for solution.

1. The definition of the word is sufficient to suggest an application. In the common acceptation of the word, the term scape-goat is applied to any miserable vagabond who has become obnoxious to the claims of justice; and while it is revolting to all our conceptions of the character and glory of Christ, to apply this term to him, it must strike every one as a very appropriate designation for a certain character whom the Scriptures style, the accuser, adversary, angel of the bottomless pit, Beelzebub, Belial, dragon, enemy, evil spirit, father of lies, murderer, prince of devils, serpent, tempter, seducer, etc.

2. We are not without direct evidence to the same purpose. The Hebrew word for scape-goat, as given in the margin of Lev. 16:8, is *Azazel.* On this verse, Jenks, in his Comprehensive Commentary, remarks: "Scape-goat. See different opinions in Bochart. Spencer, after the oldest

opinion of the Hebrews and Christians, thinks *Azazel* is the *name of the devil;* and so Rosenmüller, whom see. The Syriac has, *Azzail,* the 'angel (strong one) who revolted.'" These authorities unmistakably point out Satan. Thus we have the definition of the Scripture term for scape-goat, in two ancient languages, with the oldest opinion of both Hebrews and Christians, in favor of the view that the scape-goat is a type of Satan.

3. Charles Beecher, in "Redeemer and Redeemed," pp. 67, 68, says:—

"What goes to confirm this is, that the most ancient paraphrases and translations treat Azazel as a proper name. The Chaldee paraphrase, and the targums of Onkelos and Jonathan, would certainly have translated it if it was not a proper name, but they do not. The Septuagint, or oldest Greek version, renders it by ἀποπομπαῖος *(apopompaios)*, a word applied by the Greeks to a malign deity sometimes appeased by sacrifices. Another confirmation is found in the book of Enoch, where the name Azalzel, evidently a corruption of Azazel, is given to one of the fallen angels, thus plainly showing what was the prevalent understanding of the Jews at that day.

"Still another evidence is found in the Arabic, where Azazel is employed as the name of the Evil Spirit. In addition to these we have the evidence of the Jewish work Zohar, and of the Cabalistic and Rabbinical writers. They tell us that the following proverb was current among the Jews: 'On the day of atonement, a gift to Sammael.' Hence Moses Gerundinensis feels called to say that it is not a sacrifice, but only done because commanded by God.

"Another step in the evidence is, when we find this same opinion passing from the Jewish to the early Christian church. Origen was the most learned of the Fathers, and on such a point as this, the meaning of a Hebrew word, his testimony is reliable. Says Origen: 'He who is called in the Septuagint ἀποπομπαῖος, and in the Hebrew Azazel, is no other than the devil.'

"In view then of the difficulties attending any other meaning, and the accumulated evidence in favor of this, Hengstenberg affirms with great confidence that Azazel cannot be anything else but another name for Satan."

On page 70, Mr. Beecher further says: "The meaning of the term [scape-goat] viewed as a proper name, was stated, in 1677, by Spencer, Dean of Ely, to be powerful Apostate, or mighty Receder." Prof. Bush is also quoted on page 72, as regarding Azazel as a proper name of Satan.

It is but just to Mr. B. to remark that while he thinks that Azazel is the name for Satan, he does not regard the goat as representing Satan, but looks upon the ceremony as performed in some sense in reference to Satan. This he thinks implied in the words engraved on the lots which the high priest drew for the goats on the day of atonement; one, La-Yehovah, for Jehovah, the other, La-Azazel, for Azazel, for the devil; and he takes the transaction to signify that subjection of Christ to Satan which is implied in the sentence that the serpent should bruise the heel of the seed of the woman. But as this was done at the crucifixion, it can have no reference to the ceremony of the scape-goat, a ceremony not performed till the work in the sanctuary is finished. And inasmuch as the goat upon which the lot fell for the Lord typified Christ himself, so the goat upon which the lot fell for Azazel would typify Azazel, or Satan himself.

Another reason for considering the scape-goat a type of Satan is the very striking manner in which the ceremony of sending away the goat into the wilderness harmonizes with the events to transpire in connection with the cleansing of the heavenly sanctuary, so far as revealed to us in the Scriptures of truth.

Thus in the type we see the following acts performed: 1. The sin of the transgressor is imparted to the victim. 2. That sin is borne by the priest in the blood of the offering into the sanctuary. 3. On the day of atonement, the priest, with the blood of the sin-offering for the people, removes all these sins from the sanctuary, and lays them upon the head of the scape-goat. 4. The goat is then sent away into a land not inhabited.

Answering to these several events in the type, we have in the antitype the following: 1. The great offering for the world was made on Calvary. 2. The sins of all those who avail themselves of the offer of Christ's blood by faith in him, are represented in that blood, with which he entered into the sanctuary on high, Heb. 9 : 12, and are through that transferred to that sanctuary. 3. After Christ, the minister of the true tabernacle, Heb. 8 : 2, has finished his ministration, and by the atonement has released the sins of his people from the sanctuary, he will lay them upon the head of their author, the antitypical scape-goat, the devil. 4. The devil will then be sent away, loaded with these sins, into a land not inhabited.

And we apprehend that we find a description of this latter event in plain terms in Rev. 20: 1–3: "And I saw an angel come down from Heaven, having the key of the bottomless pit, and a great chain in his hand. And he laid hold on the dragon, that old serpent, which is the devil and Satan, and bound him a thousand years, and cast him into the bottomless pit, and shut him up, and set a seal upon him, that he should deceive the nations no more till the thousand years should be fulfilled."

This is just such a movement in reference to Satan as we might expect to occur on the supposition that he is the antitype of the ancient scape-goat. Looking upon him as such antitype, we watch for some transaction which will correspond to the sending away of the goat anciently, loaded with sins, into the waste wilderness.

And as we reach a point just subsequent to the cleansing of the heavenly sanctuary, when, in the order of the sanctuary work, the scape-goat should be sent away in antitype, lo, an angel comes down from Heaven, lays hold upon Satan, binds him, and casts him into the bottomless pit for a thousand years. And as we look upon this scene, we can but involuntarily exclaim,

Here is the sending away of the antitypical scape-goat.

With this view we can show the relation of the scene described in Rev. 20 : 1–3, to other events, and give a reason why it occurs. Without this, it comes in abruptly; and who can tell why just this disposition, instead of some other, is at this time made of the devil?

This scene occurs at just the right time to fulfill the antitype; for it is immediately after Christ has finished his work as priest. Secondly, the right agent is employed. The goat anciently was not led away by the high priest, but by the hand of another person. So here it is not Christ, our great High Priest, who casts Satan into the bottomless pit, but an angel; which admirably answers to the type. Thirdly, he is cast into the right place. Anciently, the goat was sent away into a waste wilderness, a land not inhabited. The devil is cast into the bottomless pit, corresponding most fittingly to the former, as we shall see.

This word, bottomless pit, in the original signifies an abyss, bottomless, deep, profound. Its use seems to be to denote any place of darkness, desolation, and death. Thus in Rev. 9 : 1, 2, it is applied to the barren wastes of the Arabian desert, and in Rom. 10:7, to the grave. In Gen. 1:2, the same word is rendered "deep" in the declaration that "darkness was upon the face of the deep;" and here it must apply to the whole earth in its state of primeval chaos. And we have reason to believe that it means precisely this in Rev. 20:3, when it is made the dreary prison-house of Satan. At this time, let it be borne in mind, the earth is a vast charnel-house of desolation and death. The voice of God has shaken it to its foundations, the islands and mountains have been moved out of their places, the great earthquake has leveled to the earth the mightiest works of man, the seven last plagues have left their withering and blasting foot-prints over all the fair face of nature, the burning glory attending the coming of the Son of man has borne its part in accomplishing the general desolation, the wicked have been given to the slaughter, and their putrefying flesh and bleaching bones lie unburied and unlamented from one end of the earth to the other. Thus is the earth made empty and waste, and turned upside down. Isa. 24:1. Thus is it brought back again to its original state of chaos; for Jeremiah, describing the scenes of the last days, says, "I beheld the earth, and, lo, it was without form, and void; and the heavens, and they had no light." Jer. 4:19–26. And what better term could be used to describe it rolling on in its disorganized condition of darkness and desolation for a thousand years, than the term abyss or bottomless pit, which was used to describe it in the beginning?

Here is a desolate wilderness, or "land not inhabited," well befitting the great antitypical scape-goat. And what more fitting retribution could at this point overtake the author of all our woe, than that he should, through all these slow-circling thousand years, be confined amid the ruin which his own hands have indirectly wrought, unable to flee from his habitation of woe, or to repair in the least degree its hideous wretchedness.

But it may be asked if Paul does not show by the expression that Christ "appeared to put away sin by the sacrifice of himself," that he did put it away upon the cross. The answer is that that must be understood only as making provision for the putting away of sin; for sins cannot be put away in advance, and millions of those who will be saved, were yet unborn when Christ suffered.

But a still stronger objection to the view here

advocated, that Satan is the antitype of the scape-goat, is urged from the expression used in reference to that goat in Lev. 16:10: "But the goat on which the lot fell to be the scape-goat, shall be presented alive before the Lord, to make an atonement with him, and to let him go for a scape-goat into the wilderness." How, it is asked, can the scape-goat be a type of Satan when an atonement was made with him? does Satan have anything to do in making the atonement? Assuredly not; and we do not think such an idea is presented in the text. It does not read that the goat should be presented alive before the Lord that he might make an atonement for the sins of the people, or to assist in making the atonement. But the goat shall be "presented alive before the Lord," by whom? By the priest. "To make an atonement with him." Who to make an atonement? The priest. Then the atonement is all made by the priest. No one shares with him in this work. But in making the atonement, or in carrying out, or completing, the work of the atonement, the high priest has something to do with the scape-goat, and that is to heap upon him the foul load of the sins of the people and send him away to the waste wilderness.

So, as the antitype, Satan has nothing to do of himself in making the atonement. He has no share in the work; but our High Priest has something to do with him in carrying out the result of his work, by making him bear away the sins which have been taken from the sanctuary, that he may perish with them, and thus a final disposition be made of both them and him. So far, therefore, as concerns the relation which Satan bears to the atonement, no objection exists to the view here advocated.

While Satan is passing his thousand years upon this desolate earth, bound, that is, restrained by the very circumstances of his position from carrying forward his nefarious work, the righteous being in Heaven, and the wicked in their graves, and so all being beyond his power, the saints are accomplishing that work of judgment which they perform in connection with Christ in Heaven, 1 Cor. 6 : 2; Rev. 20 : 4, that is, apportioning to the wicked the punishment due to each one, to be inflicted upon them at the end of the thousand years.

This work being accomplished, the thousand years expire, the wicked dead are raised, Satan is loosed, for he now has something to do, and he goes out to deceive those wicked multitudes that are brought out of their graves. Having gathered them around the holy city, which has then come down out of Heaven, fire descends from God and devours them all, root and branch, Satan and all his followers. Here the wicked receive in their own persons the punishment due to their sins, while Satan suffers under the accumulated load of the sins of all the righteous, which, at the beginning of the thousand years, were laid upon him as the antitypical scape-goat.

Chapter Thirty-Three.

THE END OF SIN.

THE division of the subject now under consideration, is one of exceeding interest. The great burden of the penitent, reaching out for a Saviour, is, "Who shall deliver me from the body of this death?" And the great joy of the new convert is, "There is now no condemnation to them who are in Christ Jesus." The question of becoming free from sin, and the process by which this is accomplished, has power to affect the heart of the awakened sinner, as no other question can.

With scarcely less interest we go forward to the final disposition of sin, when it shall be forever put away. We have now traced it, in the work of salvation, from the sinner to the sacrificial victim, from the victim to the sanctuary, from the sanctuary to the scape-goat, which in the antitype is Satan, and are led to the conclusion that sin, of which he is himself the author, comes to its end in his destruction.

A query may here arise relative to the punishment of sin in the person of Satan. If Satan is punished for the sins of the righteous, are not those sins punished twice, once in the person of Christ, who suffered for our sins, and again in the person of Satan, upon whom they are finally laid? We answer that the sins of the righteous are no more punished twice than the sins of the wicked. Christ suffered for all alike, just as much for those who will be finally lost, as for those who will be saved. But the lost will all be punished at last for their own sins.

The trouble arises from a misapprehension of the position of Christ as our substitute. The idea seems to be generally entertained that Christ in his own person suffered all the punishment due to the sins of all the saved, which they would themselves have endured had they been lost. This leaves those who believe in eternal misery to grapple with an insurmountable problem; and it leads to the most ultra Calvinism. The truth seems rather to be that Christ appeared before the law as an innocent victim to meet in behalf of others the sentence, "The soul that sinneth, it shall die." The offering was voluntary, and therefore involved no injustice; it was from one of so exalted a position that God could accept it; and it was of such infinite value that the law could honorably relax its claims from all those who would accept of it, even if all the world should do so. But we have seen from the type that the removal of sin from the penitent did not cancel the sin itself, but only transferred it to some other object. The forgiveness was relative, not absolute; that is, as related to the sinner it was forgiven, but the sin itself was considered still in existence, to be disposed of in some other way. Christ has done for us in fact what the ancient offering did for the sinner in figure; that is, he has provided a medium through which sin with its guilt may be removed from us and transferred to some other party. Thus we can be saved, but the sin must meet its just desert in some other quarter.

Let us now consider where this, in the case of the sinner, would naturally fall. Sin did not have its origin with mankind. They were not the original agents of this evil, but were seduced and led away under the power of temptation by another. And this we apprehend to be the difference between the condition of men and that of Satan and his angels. With the one, sin had its origin; and an outbreak so unprovoked and causeless could have no forgiveness. It would not be safe to re-instate to favor those with whom such a course could originate. But with the other, with men, sin was an evil into which they were led by another party; hence their case could be commiserated, and provision be made for their restoration.

Sin may therefore be represented as a partnership business. Satan is the senior party, the sinner the junior. The latter, having been seduced into that position, is allowed, under certain conditions, to leave the company and step out from under the obligations of the business. Upon whom then will they fall? Upon the only remaining member of the firm, the instigator of the whole business, the senior partner, Satan. If the sinner chooses to maintain the partnership in that illegitimate business, he can do so, and receive in his own person at last the punishment of his deeds. But it is in his power, if he so desires, to leave his present relation, unite himself to Christ; and leave his former business with him who is primarily responsible for it.

And this is what we are taught by the doctrine of the scape-goat. The sinner goes free, and Satan receives the sins he has incited the sinner to commit back upon his own head, to answer therefor in the settlement which he at last must meet.

Viewing in this light the work of Satan among mankind, it is evident that the matter has been so overruled that he has been playing a losing game, in seducing men to sin. It would have been far better for him if he had done nothing of the kind. But having entered upon this work, we see that he has a personal interest of the most powerful kind to induce him to hold persons in sin to the last; for then they receive the punishment for their own sins which he otherwise must suffer. And every one who escapes from his power and secures salvation through Christ, adds an additional weight to his accumulating load of woe.

And it must strike every one as right and consistent that this should be so. The sinner has been seduced into sin, but he repents. Yet standing back of the scene, there is one who is the primary author and instigator of all, the inciting agent in every sinner's deeds; and when the transgressor awakes to the true nature of his course, and sees the enormity of his crimes, and seeks to put away his sins, what could be more fitting than that they should fall back upon the head of him who first gave birth to sin, and who has fostered the growth of every branch from that baleful root. In this, the decision of every right-minded intelligence must be, that God is just, and Satan receives no more than his due deserts.

Satan, having thus received the load of sins from which the righteous have become free, and being confined to this desolate earth, is reserved to the day of perdition. The thousand years at length expire, the lake of fire prepared for the devil and his angels, appears. They are cast therein, and all the wicked in league with them share the same fate. Then every sin ever committed is punished, and in the persons of the wicked, evil angels, and Satan, it perishes forever.

And here is reached that point of transcendent interest when one of the most cheering prophecies in all the Bible can be fulfilled. For at this point, but not before, can that universal song of jubilee be raised to God, which the seer of Patmos foretold in these inspiring words: "And every creature which is in Heaven, and on the earth, and under the earth, and such as are in the sea, and all that are in them, heard I saying, Blessing, and honor, and glory, and power, be unto Him that sitteth upon the throne, and unto the Lamb for ever and ever." The quenchless flames of the fiery lake have spent their force in consuming the rebel hosts. The earth is purified by the fervent heat. No sinner and no taint of sin is left. The new earth appears, the abiding habitation of the just.

No room for Universalism here; for the wicked have all been destroyed. No place for an endless burning hell; for all who are found worthy at last to live, are in harmony with God's will, and filled with sympathetic joy and praise.

Chapter Thirty-Four.

THE SUBJECT CONCLUDED.

THE reader will now understand why we consider it difficult, as stated on page 11, to come to wrong conclusions in reference to important prophecies connected with this question, when this subject is correctly understood, and almost impossible to reach correct ones, if such understanding does not exist.

To illustrate: In the light of the sanctuary, we at once perceive that no prophetic period reaches to the coming of Christ; and this fact determines the whole aspect of the Advent movement; for without this view, we must extend the longest period to that event, and hence go forth with an admission fatal to all our claims as interpreters of the prophecies, that the prophecies cannot be understood; or, secondly, we must fix upon some point of time for the Lord to come. And of this latter work we have seen enough in some branches of the Adventist body to irredeemably disgrace their cause, and disgust all sensible people. From all this we are saved by an understanding of the sanctuary work; for the cleansing of the sanctuary, at the beginning of which the longest and latest prophetic period terminates, is a work the duration of which cannot be measured by any data given in the Bible. Hence we can set no time for the conclusion of this service, and the second coming of Christ.

At the same time we are immovably established on the great doctrine that the second advent of our Lord is right at hand. For we behold, in this view of the sanctuary, the whole work of this dispensation spread out in one view before us; and we see that that work is almost finished. All the service in the holy place, or first apartment, is already accomplished. That in the second apartment we know is very brief, and that it has been now almost thirty-three years in progress. When that is finished, Christ's work as priest is done; and his second coming in his new office of King of kings, immediately follows. What, then, must be our view of the second coming of Christ? We must regard it as at the door. To do otherwise would be to willfully ignore all the mighty array of evidence by which the sanctuary subject is sustained. Had we no other evidence, had no signs been foretold, nor any other lines of prophecy been given, we have enough in this to show us, beyond the possibility of question, that this dispensation is almost finished, and that the second coming of Christ in such overpowering glory that no sinner can behold it and live, is at the very door.

We are, furthermore, saved from the fearful step of denying the existence of the law of God. In the sanctuary we behold that law, reposing beneath the eye of Jehovah, and guarded by the highest and brightest seraphs that surround his throne. We behold it there just as it read upon the tables, God-written, which were deposited in the sanctuary here below, and just as it was heard, when, uttered by the Creator's lips from the summit of Sinai thirty-three hundred years ago, it reverberated around the earth, in echoes that shook the world. It still exists; it is unchanged; the seventh day is still the Sabbath. A sight of the sanctuary as it now exists, is an end of all controversy on these vexed questions. He who receives what we here set forth as the truth on this subject will inevitably keep the seventh day as the Sabbath. There is no avoiding it. And he will believe in the soon-coming of Christ. In other words, he will be a SEVENTH-DAY ADVENTIST.

Again, we are guarded by this subject against the error of supposing that the dead are conscious, and the soul immortal; for it is at once seen that the atonement, which is the canceling, in behalf of the penitent sinner, of the debt incurred by sin, is not applied to a single soul (save only by anticipation in a few exceptional cases) till this closing division of our Lord's ministry. The righteous dead are not therefore with Christ, nor are they receiving their reward; for their sins must be atoned for, or be blotted out, before they can receive these blessings. They are therefore sleeping in their graves.

We are also held to our view that the seven last plagues are future; for they cannot fall till Christ's mediation ceases; and this determines the chronology of the third angel's message, and the work of the two-horned beast to the present time, while the work in the sanctuary is closing.

We are now prepared to take a retrospective view of this important subject. The questions proposed in the beginning of this work, are now answered.

To the question, "The Sanctuary—what is it?" the answer has been plainly found. It is not the earth, not the land of Palestine, not the church; but, as revealed to us in the Scriptures, it is, first, the dwelling which the Lord provided for himself here among men, in the tabernacle of Moses, and afterward in the temple of Jerusalem; and, secondly, we behold it as the temple of God in Heaven, his dwelling-place on high.

To the question, "When is it?" the answer has come. In all its most important aspects, it is now. Beginning with Moses, fifteen hundred years before Christ, it becomes an object of ever-increasing interest, till, as we reach our own generation, and the work connected with it is about to close, the issues there to be decided make it an all-important center of consideration and study.

To the question, "Where is it?" the answer is equally plain. During the typical dispensation, it was here upon earth; in the present antitypical dispensation, it is in Heaven.

"What are its uses?" It is the center around which all the worship of God revolves, and to which every act of devotion points. "And why?" Because it is the habitation of God, and there in the most holy, he placed the transcript of his will, the ten commandments; and there on the mercy-seat, the cover of the ark, is the focal point in the work of redemption, where "mercy and truth meet together, and righteousness and peace kiss each other." There reposes the law which shows transgression; and there is presented the blood which satisfies the law, and, so far as the sinner's record is concerned, blots out the sin.

"What are its relations, and how extensive?" The previous chapters of this work have partially and imperfectly answered this question. It relates to everything in the plan of salvation, and has to do with every individual who comes within the range of Christ's redeeming work.

"What prominence is given to it on the inspired pages of the book of God's revelation to men?" Great prominence. The word occurs one hundred and forty-four times, not merely as casual mentions, but often as the theme of the discourse itself.

"What bearing has it upon the interpretation of the prophecies?" A bearing the most intimate. It shows that no prophetic period reaches to the coming of the Lord, but only to the short but indefinite work called the cleansing of the sanctuary which just precedes that coming. It thus saves us from the folly of time-setting. It clears up and explains the mystery of the disappointment in the past Advent movement. Mistaking the sanctuary to mean the earth, it was supposed that the cleansing of the sanctuary meant the purifying of the earth by fire; and as the Lord is to be revealed in flaming fire, it was argued that the Lord must then come. Hence the coming of the Lord was looked for at the end of the 2300 days in 1844. But the prophecy only says, "Then shall the sanctuary be cleansed," which we now see to be the closing work of our High Priest in the temple above. It explains the parable of the wedding garment, Matt. 22: 11–13, shows where that preliminary work of Judgment comes in, which must precede the coming of Christ, and shows how and when that sentence which eternally fixes every man's condition, whether he be filthy or righteous, unjust or holy, can go forth before the Lord appears. Rev. 22:11.

"How is its past history calculated to interest, or its present work concern, us?" Its past history interests us because it is the text-book from which we learn the nature of the work of our great High Priest above, and the manner of his ministration; and its present work concerns us, because in connection with the declaration of the prophecies concerning it, we learn more definitely than from any other source, our proximity to the end.

"In what way are our dearest interests connected with it?" Our dearest interests are there because there is our only hope of life and salvation. There is to be found the only means that can cleanse our souls from guilt, and there the only Advocate who can plead our cause. If we accept his mediation on the free terms offered, our case will go well; if we reject it, all is lost. The court is now sitting; its session soon will close, and its eternal decisions be rendered.

These are the claims it now has upon our attention, the strongest and most urgent that can ever be brought to bear upon men.

All through its history are epochs of interest. It was a point of great interest when the tabernacle was first erected in this world of ours, and an outward symbol of the work of salvation was given to men.

It was a point of interest when the tabernacle gave place to the larger and more glorious structure of the temple, and when in the dedication of that temple the most imposing religious ceremony was performed which the world has ever witnessed.

It was a point of still greater interest when the typical dispensation closed, and a transfer was made from the sanctuary below to the sanctuary on high. Henceforward we come directly to Jesus, the mediator of the new covenant, and turn our attention to Jerusalem above.

A point of still deeper interest to us was reached when at the end of the 2300 days in 1844 the time came for the cleansing of the sanctuary, and the ministration was moved from the holy into the most holy place. Then the temple of God was opened in Heaven. Then was discerned, by faith, the ark of God's testament there. Then the position of the moral law was seen, enthroned in the very presence of Jehovah, immutable, eternal. Then was discovered the connection between this subject and the seal of the living God, the sealing work, the last message of mercy, and the closing up of the great Advent movement of the present generation. Then the foretold Judgment hour began, and the church entered upon the great Sabbath reform. With this subject all portions of the message are connected; this is the grand center and citadel of the present truth.

Then it was seen that the time of probation could last but a little longer; for the final work in the sanctuary must be brief. Should it be otherwise it would destroy the type, and show in the plan and work of God a want of consistency and harmony, which we know does not exist. And already for nearly thirty-three years this work has been going forward. We understand that, beginning with the human race at the opening of the world's history, the examination passes down through successive generations, in consecutive order, till at length the cases of the last generation, the living, are reached, who come latest into this investigative Judgment, and the work closes. And what generation has the work now reached? Has it come down to the age of Noah? of Abraham? of Job? of Moses? of Daniel? Has it reached the age of the apostles and the early Christians? Are their cases now in review before the great tribunal above? Has it come down to the setting up of the papacy, to the Dark Ages, when the Waldenses and other few faithful witnesses in obscurity and concealment kept the light of God's truth alive in the world? Has it come down to the great Reformation, to the times of Luther? of the Wesleys? We know not. We know only that it is passing down somewhere through these generations, and rapidly approaching the living, when our cases will come up for decision, and our destiny be decided forever. And here we now stand waiting; may we not also say, preparing?

But with considerations of such thrilling interest even as these, our view of this subject does not end. We go forward a little in the future, and behold thé sins of all the righteous loaded upon the head of the antitypical scape-goat, to be put away forever. We see Satan bound, and the saints forever free from his power. This is a point of transcendent interest to all the righteous. Then we take our first draughts from the cup of immortality. Our sins are borne away. They come up to trouble us no more. We cannot recall them; and even God says that he will forget them. He who instigated them will then have received them back again. Here the serpent's head is effectually bruised by the seed of the woman. Here the strong man armed (Satan), who has been shutting up even the followers of Christ in his prison house, the grave, for six thousand years, will be bound by a stronger than he (Christ), and his house be spoiled of its precious treasures. Then will the tares have been bound in bundles for the burning, and the wheat have been gathered into the heavenly garner. Then our High Priest will have come forth from the sanctuary to pronounce the everlasting blessing upon his waiting people. Then we shall have come, not by faith merely, but in deed and in truth, unto Mount Zion, and the city of the living

God, the heavenly Jerusalem, and to an innumerable company of angels. Then will the redeemed, placing the foot of triumph upon the world, the flesh, and the devil, raise their glad voices in the song of Moses and the Lamb. Glorious and longed-for day! The Lord hasten it in his time.

One more scene remains: the kindling of those final fires prepared for the devil and his angels, at the end of the thousand years. Here is also the perdition of ungodly men. And here all the agents of evil, root and branch, Satan and all his followers, be they angels or men, are destroyed from the universe of God. The deepest taint of the curse is burned out of the earth; the last vestige of disgrace is removed; and from the ashes of the old system, by a new act of God's creative energy, who says, "Behold, I make all things new," there spring forth a new heavens and new earth, fitting abode of the redeemed forever. And of Satan's original rebellion, then nothing remains but the great and solemn lesson of sin and its fearful results, which will ever tend to confirm in uprightness and holiness all other intelligences in all the universe.

Thus triumphantly for God's name and glory does his controversy with sin and sinners end.

Here are finished the results of all Christ's work as connected with the sanctuary. Redemption is successfully completed. The original purpose in regard to this world, that it should be the beauteous abode of holy beings, is carried out. The requisite number to people it is secured, and the earth is renewed to be their eternal abode. Here the righteous are called to inherit the kingdom prepared for them from the foundation of the world.

And from this height of ineffable bliss, away through the ever-revolving cycles of eternity, there open before us boundless vistas of

EVERLASTING LIFE AND ETERNAL GLORY.

COMPLETE LIST

OF

TEXTS CONTAINING THE WORD SANCTUARY.

There are two Hebrew words rendered sanctuary. The first of these is *mikdash*, מִקְדָּשׁ, which is translated sanctuary sixty-nine times, as follows :—

Ex.	15 : 17.	(in) *the sanctuary*, O Lord, which thy
	25 : 8.	let them make me *a sanctuary ;*
Lev.	12 : 4.	nor come into *the sanctuary*,
	16 : 33.	make an atonement for *the* holy *sanctuary*,
	19 : 30.	*and* reverence *my sanctuary :*
	20 : 3.	to defile *my sanctuary*,
	21 : 12.	Neither shall he go out of *the sanctuary*,
		nor profane *the sanctuary of* his God ;
	23.	profane not *my sanctuaries :*
	26 : 2.	*and* reverence *my sanctuary :*
	31.	*your sanctuaries* unto desolation,
Num.	3 : 38.	keeping the charge of *the sanctuary*
	10 : 21.	bearing *the sanctuary :*
	18 : 1.	shall bear the iniquity of *the sanctuary :*
	19 : 20.	he hath defiled *the sanctuary of* the Lord :
Josh.	24 : 26.	that (was) *by the sanctuary of* the Lord.
1 Chron.	22 : 19.	build ye *the sanctuary of* the Lord God,
	28 : 10.	to build an house *for the sanctuary :*
2 Chron.	20 : 8.	have built thee *a sanctuary*
	26 : 18.	go out of *the sanctuary ;*
	29 : 21.	for *the sanctuary*, and for Judah.
	30 : 8.	enter *into his sanctuary*,
	36 : 17.	the house of *their sanctuary*,
Neh.	10 : 39 (40).	(are) the vessels of *the sanctuary*,

Ps. 73 : 17. Until I went into *the sanctuary of* God ;
74 : 7. They have cast fire into *thy sanctuary*,
78 : 69. he built *his sanctuary* like high (palaces),
96 : 6. strength and beauty (are) *in his sanctuary*.
Isa. 8 : 14. he shall be *for a sanctuary ;*
16 : 12. he shall come to *his sanctuary* to pray ;
60 : 13. to beautify the place of *my sanctuary ;*
63 : 18. our adversaries have trodden down *thy sanctuary*.
Jer. 17 : 12. the place of *our sanctuary*.
51 : 51. strangers are come into *the sanctuaries of*
Lam 1 : 10. the heathen entered into *her sanctuary*,
2 : 7. he hath abhorred *his sanctuary*,
20. the prophet be slain *in the sanctuary of*
Eze. 5 : 11. because thou hast defiled *my sanctuary*
8 : 6. I should go far off from *my sanctuary ?*
9 : 6. *and* begin *at my sanctuary*.
11 : 16. yet will I be to them *as a* little *sanctuary*
23 : 38. they have defiled *my sanctuary*
39 they came the same day into *my sanctuary*
24 : 21. I will profane *my sanctuary*,
25 : 3. Because thou saidst, Aha, against *my sanctuary*,
28 : 18. Thou hast defiled *thy sanctuaries*
37 : 26. will set *my sanctuary* in the midst of them
28. *my sanctuary* shall be in the midst of them
43 : 21. without *the sanctuary*.
44 : 1 the gate of *the* outward *sanctuary*
5. with every going forth of *the sanctuary*.
7. to be *in my sanctuary*,
8. keepers of my charge *in my sanctuary*
9. shall enter into *my sanctuary*,
11. they shall be ministers *in my sanctuary*,
15. kept the charge of *my sanctuary*
16. They shall enter into *my sanctuary*,
45 : 3. in it shall be *the sanctuary*
4. the ministers of *the sanctuary*,

Eze. 45 : 4. *and an holy place for the sanctuary.*
18. cleanse *the sanctuary:*
47 : 12. they issued out of *the sanctuary:*
48 : 8. *the sanctuary* shall be in the midst
10. *the sanctuary of* the Lord shall be in the
21. *and the sanctuary of* the house
Dan. 8 : 11. the place of *his sanctuary* was cast down.
9 : 17. cause thy face to shine upon *thy sanctuary*
11 : 31. they shall pollute *the sanctuary*
Amos 7 : 9. *and the sanctuaries of* Israel

This word occurs in only four other instances, and is translated once "hallowed part," twice "holy places," and once "chapel."

The other word is *kodesh*, קֹדֶשׁ, which is translated sanctuary seventy one times in the following instances:—

Ex. 30 : 13, 24. After the shekel of *the sanctuary.*
36 : 1. for the service of *the sanctuary*
3. of the service of *the sanctuary*
4. the work of *the sanctuary*
6. the offering of *the sanctuary*
38 : 24, 25, 26. after the shekel of *the sanctuary.*
27. the sockets of *the sanctuary.*
Lev. 4 : 6. before the vail of *the sanctuary*
5 : 15. after the shekel of *the sanctuary*
10 : 4 your brethren from before *the sanctuary*
27 : 3. after the shekel of *the sanctuary.*
25. according to the shekel of *the sanctuary*
Num. 3 : 28. keeping the charge of *the sanctuary*
31. the vessels of *the sanctuary*
32. that keep the charge of *the sanctuary*
47, 50. after the shekel of *the sanctuary*
4 : 12. wherewith they minister *in the sanctuary.*
15. made an end of covering *the sanctuary.*
— and all the vessels of *the sanctuary.*
16. *in the sanctuary*, and in the vessels
7 : 9. the service of *the sanctuary*

Num. 7 : 13, 19, 25, 31, 37, 43, 49, 55, 61, 67, 73, 79, 85, 86, after the shekel of *the sanctuary.*
8 : 19. come nigh unto *the sanctuary*
18 : 3. they shall not come nigh the vessels of *the sanctuary*
5. ye shall keep the charge of *the sanctuary.*
16. after the shekel of *the sanctuary*
1 Chron. 9 : 29. all the instruments of *the sanctuary*
24 : 5. the governors of *the sanctuary*
2 Chron. 30 : 19. the purification of *the sanctuary.*
Ps. 20 : 2. send thee help from *the sanctuary*
28 : 2. (margin) the oracle of *thy sanctuary*
29 : 2. (margin) in his glorious *sanctuary*
63 : 2. as I have seen thee in *the sanctuary*
68 : 24. my King, in *the sanctuary*
74 : 3. the enemy hath done wickedly in *the sanctuary*
77 : 13. Thy way, O God, (is) in *the sanctuary*
78 : 54. to the border of *his sanctuary*
96 : 9. (margin) in the glorious *sanctuary*
102 : 19. he hath looked down from the height of *his sanctuary.*
114 : 2. Judah was his *sanctuary.*
134 : 2. Lift up your hands (in) *the sanctuary*
150 : 1. Praise God in *his sanctuary*
Isa. 43 : 28. profaned the princes of *the sanctuary*
Lam. 4 : 1. the stones of *the sanctuary* are poured out.
Eze. 41 : 21. the face of *the sanctuary*
23. the temple and *the sanctuary* had two
42 : 20. make a separation between *the sanctuary*
44 : 27. the day that he goeth into *the sanctuary,* to minister in *the sanctuary*
45 : 2. Of this there shall be for *the sanctuary*
Dan. 8 : 13. to give *both the sanctuary* and the host
14. then shall *the sanctuary* be cleansed.
9 : 26. destroy the city *and the sanctuary*
Zeph. 3 : 4. her priests have polluted *the sanctuary*

This word is also translated fifty-two times *holy* or *most holy* place, referring to these apartments of the sanctuary.

In the New Testament the word *hagion*, ἅγιον, is rendered sanctuary in the following four instances:—

Heb. 8 : 2. a minister of the *sanctuary* and
9 : 1. divine service and a worldly *sanctuary*
9 : 2. which is called the *sanctuary*
13 : 11. brought into the *sanctuary* by the

This word occurs in only six other instances, in which it is rendered holy place, holiest, and holiest of all, all referring to the sanctuary.

It will thus be seen that the original terms in Hebrew and Greek which are employed to describe the sanctuary, or some part of it, are used 202 times with direct reference to that object, and are 144 times translated sanctuary in our English version.

NOTE. The statement is once or twice made in this work that the word sanctuary occurs in the Bible 146 times. The foregoing list from the Englishman's Hebrew, and Greek, Concordances, will be a sufficient correction.

AUTHORS QUOTED.

INDEX.

Catalogue of Publications

For sale at the Office of the Review and Herald, Battle Creek, Mich., and at the Pacific Press, Oakland, Cal.

BOUND BOOKS.

Pages. Price.

History of the Sabbath and of the First Day of the Week, by ELDER J. N. ANDREWS. This work contains an outline of the history of the Sabbath for the period of Six Thousand years. Part First is the Biblical history of the Sabbath and of the first day of the week. Part Second is the secular history of these two days since the time of the apostles. The several steps by which Sunday observance was introduced are carefully traced, and the acts by which the observance of the Sabbath of the Lord was abandoned are distinctly stated. The true reasons why the Sabbath is of priceless value are given, and the ultimate triumph of this divine institution is shown in prophecy, when all flesh shall keep it with one heart.

This volume has been prepared with most careful and patient study. In all cases of quotations from secular history, book, chapter, and page

	Pages.	Price.
are given. And book, chapter, and verse are given of all quotations from the word of God..................	528	1 00
The Sanctuary and the 2300 Days of Dan. 8 : 14, by ELDER U. SMITH. This question has developed the people known as Seventh-day Adventists, and is the pivotal doctrine upon which their applications of prophecy largely depend. It explains the past Advent movement, shows why those who looked for the Lord in 1844 were disappointed, reveals the fact so essential to be understood, that no prophetic period reaches to the second coming of Christ, and shows where we are, and what we are to expect in the future. But the greatest beauty of the subject is seen in the light it throws upon the progressive steps of the remedial system, the types and shadows of the former dispensation, and the position and work of our Lord in the present. It determines absolutely the question of the nearness of the second coming of Christ, the perpetuity of the law of God, the nature and time of the atonement, and the work of Judgment that precedes Christ's coming. A knowledge of this subject is indispensable to a correct application of the more important prophecies pertaining to the present time.................	352	1 00
Condensed edition, paper, ...	224	30

	Pages.	Price.
Thoughts on Daniel, Critical and Practical, by ELDER U. SMITH. An exposition of the book of Daniel, verse by verse. We are now living in times plainly pointed out in this prophecy, and it is important to understand it; for Daniel himself says that in the time of the end the wise shall understand; while, if we fail, we are equally guilty with the Jews, who knew not the time of their visitation, Luke 19 : 42–44, and shall meet a similar fate............	384	1 00
Condensed edition, paper, ...	256	35
Thoughts on Revelation, Critical and Practical, by ELDER U. SMITH. This work presents every verse in the book of Revelation with such remarks as serve to illustrate or explain the meaning of the text. It is a new and harmonious exposition of that important book, and is designed to create an interest in its study............................	352	1 00
The Nature and Destiny of Man, by ELDER U. SMITH. This work, as its title implies, treats upon the constitution of man, his consequent condition in death, and destiny beyond the resurrection. All the passages in the Bible which have a bearing upon these questions are taken up and explained in full, thus giving the most comprehensive view of this whole question that has yet been presented. The object has been to find a definite and satisfactory answer to the ques-		

Pages. Price.

tion, "What saith the Scriptures?" as they are the only source of authority upon this subject. The result is a harmonious and consistent presentation of their testimony. Of the importance of being well informed upon this question it is not necessary to speak while spiritualism is making such havoc in the land. This is the only safeguard against that great delusion; but it is an effectual one; for before the true light on the intermediate state, spiritualism with its foul brood flees away, and purgatory, saint worship, universalism, and a host of other errors, all go down. There is a daily-increasing agitation on this question, and it is a hopeful sign that this doctrine is making rapid progress among people of the best minds and hearts. 3. 1 00

Life of William Miller, with portrait. This work comprises sketches of the Christian Experience and Public Labors of this remarkable man, gathered from his Memoir by the late Sylvester Bliss, many years editor of the *Advent Herald*, published at Boston, Mass., with Introduction and Notes by ELDER JAMES WHITE. This book sets forth the true principles and real character of the man who was the leading spirit in the great American Second-Advent Movement of 1840–1844. It maintains that Mr. Miller was correct on the nature and object of the Second

	Pages.	Price.
Advent, in his application of the prophetic symbols of Daniel and John, and in his calculations of the prophetic periods; and that he was mistaken only in the event to occur at the close of the great period of 2300 prophetic days. For a full explanation of the nature of the disappointment in 1844, see the works entitled, The Sanctuary and 2300 Days, and The Three Messages of Rev. 14.	408	1 00
Life of Elder Joseph Bates, with portrait. This is a reprint of his Autobiography, with introduction, and closing chapters relative to his public ministry, and last sickness, by ELDER JAMES WHITE. The closing chapters relate to his labors in the ministry, and in moral reforms, and the triumphant close of his long and useful life. This book should be in every family library. Fine tinted paper,	352	1 00
Plain white paper,	"	85

The Spirit of Prophecy; or, the Great Controversy between Christ and his Angels, and Satan and his Angels, in four volumes, by MRS. ELLEN G. WHITE. These volumes cover the time from the fall of Satan to the destruction of sin at the close of the one thousand years of Rev. 20:—

Vol. I. The first of these volumes contains, first, a Biblical argument in defense of the doctrine that Spiritual Gifts

Pages. Price.

are to be perpetuated in the Christian church till the end of probation. The work proper commences with the fall of Satan, upon which it sheds great light; next it treats upon the creation of the earth; the temptation and fall of our first parents; and then opens the plan of salvation in a most instructive and deeply-interesting manner. Thence it traces the history of redemption as illustrated by the lives of good and evil men down to the time of the flood, which event it narrates in a most interesting and instructive chapter. Thence it pursues the history of redemption till the wanderings in the wilderness, which it dwells upon very fully, and then continues this record till the time of Solomon. 416 1 00

Vol. II. In her second volume, Mrs. White with increasing interest treats upon the Life, Ministry, Miracles, and Teachings of Christ. The reader will find that this volume furnishes invaluable aid in studying the lessons of Christ as set forth in the Gospels. 400 1 00

Vol. III. The teachings of Christ are continued in the third volume. Mrs. White dwells very fully upon the sufferings and death of Christ, his resurrection and his ascension to Heaven, and closes with the lives, teachings, and persecutions of the Apostles. Being aided in the study of the Scriptures, and in her work as a re-

	Pages.	Price.
ligious teacher, by the special enlightenment of the Spirit of God, she is peculiarly qualified to present the great facts of the New Testament connected with the divine plan of human redemption................	400	1 00
The Biblical Institute. This is the title of a work containing a synopsis of the lectures given at the Institute held in Oakland, Cal., April 1–17, 1877. These cover all the main points of our faith, giving facts and dates, and the heads of the arguments. Review questions are appended to each lesson, adapting it to the use of Sabbath-schools and Bible Classes. It is nicely bound in muslin, and makes an elegant volume................	352	1 00
Hymn Book. "Hymns and Tunes for those who keep the Commandments of God and the Faith of Jesus," is the title of our new book. It has 537 hymns and 147 tunes.	416	1 00
Constitutional Amendment; or, the Sunday, the Sabbath, the Change, and the Restitution. A discussion between W. H. Littlejohn and the editor of the *Christian Statesman*. This work discusses the proposed religious amendment to the Constitution, especially in its bearing upon the subject of the Sabbath and first day of the week. This involves an examination of the alleged change of the Sabbath........................	384	1 00
In paper covers,................	336	40

	Pages.	Price.
Sabbath Readings for the Home Circle. In two volumes, containing moral and religious reading carefully compiled for the use of Sabbath-schools and family libraries. Extra binding. Each volume, ...	400	75
The United States in the Light of Prophecy; or, an Exposition of Rev. 13 : 11–17, by ELDER U. SMITH. Dealing with our own land and applying to our time, this is a portion of prophecy which should possess surpassing interest for every American reader. This work shows by conclusive arguments the position which the United States government holds in prophecy, and the important part it is to act in the closing scenes of time. Issues are even now arising which it is of the greatest importance that all be prepared to meet.	160	40
In paper covers, ...		20
The Bible from Heaven, by ELDER D. M. CANRIGHT. This work is what its name implies, an argument to show that the Bible is not the work of men, but is in deed and in truth the word of God. It is a candid, forcible, conclusive argument, sustained by a large array of facts and such deductions of science as rest upon any tolerable certainty. Just the work to put into the hands of honest skeptics, and those who are exposed to infidel influences. Adapted to the use of any and all persons who believe in the Bible......................	300	80

	Pages.	Price.
A Word for the Sabbath; or, False Theories Exposed. A Poem, by ELDER U. SMITH. The principal points of the Sabbath argument are set forth in this work in verse, in order to secure the attention of some, who perhaps would not at first peruse a prose work upon this subject. No strength of argument is sacrificed to the style, and whoever will peruse it will get a general idea of the weakness and absurdities of the Sunday argument. Handsomely bound in colored muslin, stamped in black, with gilt title, ...	60	30
In glazed paper covers, ...		15
Bible Lessons for Little Ones. This is a Sabbath-school book designed for the use of beginners, and prepared with special regard for the wants of very young children. The language is simple and direct, and such as children can most easily understand. It contains directions to the teacher, and questions to help in bringing out and impressing upon the mind the main points in the lesson. Without the questions the lessons form a continuous story, commencing at creation and extending to the time of Moses. Bound in flexible cloth, ...	84	15
In paper covers, ...	"	10
Gems of Song. This is the title of a vest-pocket song book containing hymns only. A choice collection. 96 pp. 119 hymns. Bound in flexible cloth,		15
In paper covers, ...		10

PAMPHLETS.

	Pages.	Price.
Facts for the Times: a Collection of Valuable Extracts from Eminent Authors..	224	25
Eleven Sermons on the Sabbath and Law, by ELDER J. N. ANDREWS..........	226	25
History of the Immortality of the Soul, by ELDER D. M. CANRIGHT..........	200	25
Modern Spiritualism. Nature and Tendency of Modern Spiritualism, by ELDER J. H. WAGGONER. This is a thorough exposure of the system of spiritualism. The author has carefully studied the subject, and has given such copious extracts from a large library of spiritualist publications as to fully condemn them in their teachings and their practices by their own testimony. It is also shown from the prophetic scriptures that spiritualism is one of the most impressive signs of the times.	184	20
Refutation of the Age to Come, by ELDER J. H. WAGGONER. This is a most decisive refutation of the view that men may find forgiveness of sins after the Saviour has closed his work in the Sanctuary above. No age-to-come writer has ever attempted a reply to it.	168	20
The Atonement, by ELDER J. H. WAGGONER. An examination of a remedial system in the light of Nature and		

Pages. Price.

Revelation. It fully refutes the idea so extensively held, that an atonement is inconsistent with reason; it shows the principles involved in the subject of the atonement, the nature of the work and the manner of its accomplishment, and the harmony of the Law and the Gospel; and sheds great light upon the work of Christ as our High Priest......... 168 20

The Ministration of Angels, and the Origin, History, and Destiny of Satan. By ELDER D. M. CANRIGHT..........144 20

Our Faith and Hope. Sermons on the Coming and Kingdom of Christ. By ELDER JAMES WHITE..............182 20

Miraculous Powers. The Scripture Testimony on the Perpetuity of Spiritual Gifts, with Narratives of Incidents and Sentiments carefully compiled from the Eminently Pious and Learned of various denominations...128 15

Resurrection of the Unjust. A vindication of the doctrine, by ELDER J. H. WAGGONER...... ....100 15

The Spirit of God, its Gifts and Manifestations to the end of the Christian Age, by ELDER J. H. WAGGONER. This is a brief but comprehensive argument on the solemn and important subject of the Spirit of God, and its gifts and manifestations.....144 15

The Three Messages of Revelation 14:6–12, particularly the Third Angel's Message and the Two-Horned Beast, by

	Pages.	Price.
ELDER J. N. ANDREWS. This work is designed to show that these proclamations are a prophetic representation of the great Advent movement.	144	15
The Two Laws, as set forth in the Scriptures of the Old and New Testaments, by ELDER D. M. CANRIGHT..	104	15
The Morality of the Sabbath, by ELDER D. M. CANRIGHT....................	96	15
The Complete Testimony of the Fathers of the First Three Centuries Concerning the Sabbath and First Day of the week, by ELDER J. N. ANDREWS.	112	15
Life of Christ, in six Pamphlets. By MRS. ELLEN G. WHITE:—		
No. 1. His First Advent and Ministry....	104	10
No. 2. His Temptation in the Wilderness.	96	10
No. 3. His Teachings and Parables......	126	15
No. 4. His Mighty Miracles............	128	15
No. 5. His Sufferings and Crucifixion....	96	10
No. 6. His Resurrection and Ascension..	80	10
Life of the Apostles, in two Pamphlets:—		
No. 1. The Ministry of Peter..........	80	10
No. 2. The Teachings of Paul...........	80	10
Christ and the Sabbath; or, Christ in the Old Testament and the Sabbath in the New, by ELDER JAMES WHITE. This is a new and carefully-written work, very important to those who hold that the Sabbath belongs exclusively to the Old Testament, and Christ to the New Testament......	56	10
Redeemer and Redeemed, by ELDER JAMES WHITE. This is a new work; in		

	Pages.	Price.
which the plan of human redemption in its three stages is set forth.	48	10
Matthew Twenty-Four. A clear, concise, and forcible exposition of our Lord's discourse upon the Mount of Olives, by ELDER JAMES WHITE.	64	10
Appeal to the Baptists for the Restoration of the Bible Sabbath. An Address to the Baptists from the Seventh-day Baptist General Conference.	46	10
The Sunday-Seventh Day Examined. A Refutation of the Teachings of Mede, Jennings, Akers, and Fuller, by ELDER J. N. ANDREWS. It most effectually demolishes the theory that Sunday is the original seventh day, and shows what absurdities and contradictions men involve themselves in, in laboring to prove that Sunday is the true Sabbath.	88	10
Review of Gilfillan; or, Thoughts Suggested by the Perusal of Gilfillan and other authors on the Sabbath, by THOMAS B. BROWN, Pastor of the Seventh-day Baptist church at Little Genesee, N. Y.	64	10
The Seven Trumpets. An Exposition of the subject, as set forth in the eighth and ninth chapters of the Revelation.	96	10
The Date of the Seventy Weeks of Dan. 9 Established; or, A Treatise on the Commandment to Restore and Build Jerusalem, by ELDER J. N. ANDREWS. This work gives the date from which the 70 weeks and		

	Pages.	Price.
2300 days are to be reckoned, and shows what constitutes the commandment of the prophecy..............	56	10
Review of Baird. A Review of Two Sermons against the Sabbath, and Seventh-day Adventists, by ELDER J. H. WAGGONER..................	64	10
The Truth Found. The Nature and Obligation of the Sabbath of the Fourth Commandment. By ELDER J. H. WAGGONER.....................	64	10
Vindication of the True Sabbath, in two parts, by ELDER J. W. MORTON, formerly missionary of the Reformed Presbyterian Church, to Hayti.....	68	10
The Ancient Sabbath. Forty-four Objections Considered..................	88	10
Sermon on the Two Covenants, by ELDER J. N. ANDREWS..................	48	10
Hope of the Gospel, by ELDER J. N. LOUGHBOROUGH.......................	80	10
Saints' Inheritance; or, The Earth Made New, by ELDER J. N. LOUGHBORO',	80	10
The State of the Dead. By JOHN MILTON, author of "Paradise Lost." This work shows that Milton was a decided believer in, and an able defender of, the doctrine that in death man is unconscious......................	32	5

TRACTS.

	Pages.	Price.
Redemption	32	4
The Second Advent	32	4
The Sufferings of Christ	32	4
The Present Truth	32	4
Origin and Progress of S. D. Adventists	32	4
The Two Thrones	32	4
The Rejected Ordinance	32	4
The Seventh Part of Time	32	4
The Ten Commandments not Abolished	32	4
The Two Covenants	32	4
Address to the Baptists	32	4
Systematic Benevolence	32	4
Spiritualism a Satanic Delusion	32	4
Samuel and the Witch of Endor	32	4
The First Message of Rev. 14	16	2
The Second Message of Rev. 14	20	3
The Third Message of Rev. 14	36	4
Who Changed the Sabbath?	24	3
The Lost-Time Question	24	3
Scripture References	24	3
The End of the Wicked	24	3
Infidel Cavils Considered	24	3
Sabbaton: An Exposition of Matt. 28: 1	24	3
Christ in the Old Testament	16	2
The Sabbath in the New Testament	16	2
The Spirit of Prophecy	16	2
The Old Moral Code Not Revised	16	2
The Sanctuary of the Bible	16	2

	Pages.	Price.
The Judgment	16	2
Much in Little	16	2
The Millennium	16	2
The Two Laws	16	2
Seven Reasons for Sunday-Keeping Examined	16	2
The Definite Seventh Day	16	2
Departing and Being with Christ	16	2
The Rich Man and Lazarus	16	2
Elihu on the Sabbath	16	2
The Coming of the Lord	8	1
Perfection of the Ten Commandments	8	1
Without Excuse	8	1
Thoughts for the Candid	8	1
Appeal on Immortality	8	1
Which Day Do You Keep? and Why?	8	1
Is the End Near?	8	1
Can We Know?	8	1
The Sleep of the Dead	8	1
The Sinner's Fate	8	1
Is Man Immortal?	8	1
One Hundred Bible Facts upon the Sabbath	8	1
What the Gospel Abrogated	8	1
Sunday not the Sabbath	8	1
The Christian Sabbath	8	1
Why not Found out Before	8	1

Health Publications

For sale at the Office of the Review and Herald, Battle Creek, Mich., and at the Pacific Press, Oakland, Cal.

	Pages.	Price.
The Uses of Water in Health and Disease. A carefully-written treatise, the objects of which are, 1. To present a careful and candid account of the nature of water and the physiological effects of its use; 2. To explain the effects of water as a remedial agent, and to demonstrate its value as a remedy for disease; 3. To show that the use of water as a therapeutic agent has been practiced by the most eminent physicians of all ages. 4. To expose those absurd and erroneous practices which have brought the use of water as a remedy into disrepute. 5. To provide a convenient manual for the various methods of applying water. Neatly bound in cloth,	160	60
In paper covers,	136	25
The Household Manual. This work contains instruction relating to domestic hygiene, foods and drinks, the treatment of common diseases, accidents and emergencies, and useful hints and recipes, together with treatises upon various other important topics. Bound in cloth,	176	75

	Pages.	Price.
Plain Facts about Sexual Life. A book for the times, treating upon all subjects pertaining to the anatomy and physiology of reproduction. It should be read by everybody. Hundreds who have read the book pronounce it invaluable. Many physicians and clergymen have given it most unqualified commendation. The *Boston Journal* says of the work: "A great deal of crime and wretchedness would be spared if the principles laid down in this volume were even approximated in the life of the people. A book so intelligently written as this, therefore, should not lack for readers." Tinted paper, handsomely bound, ...	360	1 50
In flexible covers, ...	260	75
The Physical, Moral, and Social Effects of Alcoholic Poison as a Beverage and as a Medicine. This work defines true temperance, explains the nature of alcohol and the manner of its production, describes its physical effects upon the human body, exhibits by statistics its moral and social effects, points out the causes and the proper cure of intemperance, answers the drunkard's arguments in favor of drinking, exposes the fallacy of alcoholic medication as commonly practiced, and defends the Bible against the imputation that it advocates or favors the use of alcoholic drinks. Paper covers, ...	128	25

	Pages.	Price
Healthful Cookery. A Hand-Book of Food and Diet; or, What to Eat, When to Eat, and How to Eat. It contains a large number of recipes for the preparation of wholesome and palatable food without condiments. Enamel paper covers, ...	128	25
Proper Diet for Man. The object of this work is to present a concise summary of the principal evidences which can be drawn from anatomy, physiology, and experience, in support of a vegetarian diet. Paper covers, ..	48	15
The Evils of Fashionable Dress, and How to Dress Healthfully. As stated in the preface to this work, its main objects are, 1. To call attention to the numerous physical evils growing out of the present fashionable modes of dress; 2. To point out the simple remedy for these evils by describing a mode of dress which is wholly free from injurious qualities; 3. To convince those who have recognized the necessity for a reform in dress, but have been deterred from any attempt at reform by an unwillingness to expose themselves to ridicule by adopting a peculiar style, that all the most essential features of a healthful dress may be adopted without subjecting the wearer to embarrassment on account of peculiarity of appearance. Paper covers, ...	40	10

Health and Temperance Tracts.

	Pages.	Price.
Dyspepsia. An account of its causes, how to prevent it, and how to cure it.	32	4
Healthful Clothing. A description of the evils of fashionable dress. The subject is treated candidly, and the writer admits the possibility of making a commendable reform in dress without exposing the wearer to ridicule on account of external peculiarities.	32	4
Startling Facts about Tobacco. A vivid portrayal of the evil effects arising from the pernicious habit of tobacco-using. Scores have been reformed by perusing it....................	32	4
Tea and Coffee. In this tract are given the principal objections to the use of these popular beverages. Many persons have been convinced of their injurious qualities by its perusal......	32	4
Wine and the Bible. A candid consideration of the Bible view of the wine question, in which it is shown conclusively that the Bible affords no support to the use of intoxicating drinks as a beverage under any circumstances.	24	3
Principles of Health Reform. A brief *résumé* of the principles which underlie the teaching of health reform, which forms an appropriate introduction to the subject for one who wishes to investigate it...........	16	2

	Pages.	Price.
Twenty-five Arguments for Tobacco-Using Briefly Answered. This tract sweeps away every shadow of a pretense which the tobacco slave can devise in favor of the continuance of the habit........................	24	3
Pork. In this tract many startling facts with which the public are generally unacquainted are brought out in a comprehensible manner. No lover of swine's flesh can read it without losing his relish for that kind of food. The tract contains an engraving of the terrible trichina worm, together with a full description of the parasite.	16	2
The Drunkard's Arguments Answered. A complete refutation of the arguments commonly urged by the drunkard and the moderate drinker in favor of alcoholic drinks.................	16	2
Alcoholic Medication. An exposure of the numerous evils arising from the popular use of alcohol as a remedy for disease........................	16	2
Moral and Social Effects of Alcohol. This tract is a collection of facts and statistics which are sufficient to astonish those who have not considered this phase of the subject............	8	1
Causes and Cure of Intemperance. The real causes of drunkenness are pointed out where they are least likely to be suspected. The evil is traced to its true source, and the only remedy pointed out......................	8	1

	Pages.	Price.
Alcohol: What is it? The question is answered by a description of the chemical and physical properties of alcohol, and the mode of its production.	4	½
Alcoholic Poison. A personal appeal to young men just entering upon a career of drunkenness. Plain, pointed, and practical.	4	½
True Temperance. A definition of true temperance, and the true temperance platform. All who are interested in the establishment of temperance reform upon a permanent basis should read and circulate it.	4	½
The whole series, put up in a neat package, ...	250	30

The tracts will be furnished at the rate of 800 pages for $1.00. A liberal discount will be made to tract and temperance societies.

JUVENILE PUBLICATIONS.

	Pages.	Price.
Life of Elder Joseph Bates, with portrait. This is a reprint of his Autobiography, which relates his experience of twenty-five years on shipboard, with incidents of his advancement from cabin-boy up to master and owner. Here will be found the record of fearful dangers and adventures, and wonderful escapes and deliverances. And right here, associated more or less with all that is evil, Captain Bates became a most thorough reformer, and a devoted Christian. Tinted paper, ...	352	1 00
Plain white paper, ...	"	85
Thrilling Incidents in the Political Life of Francesco Urgos, including his Travels in Africa and Syria. This work vividly sets forth the varied trials and sufferings of one of the noble sons of Italy, while a soldier in the army of Garibaldi, and afterward a prisoner of the Holy Inquisition, before which he was tried, condemned, and flogged to insensibility and almost to death. The author relates his perilous escape from the tyrants of Rome, and subsequent travels with an English nobleman.	318	1 25

	Pages.	Price.
Sabbath Readings for the Home Circle. In two volumes, containing moral and religious reading for the household; carefully selected, and compiled for the use of Sabbath-schools and family libraries. These volumes will be found the most forcible teachers of the principles of obedience, kindness, and benevolence, by relating instances of conformity to them and departure from them, in such a manner as to lead to their love and practice. Great care has been taken to exclude anything of a sectarian character.		
Vol. 1 is especially adapted to the wants of the youthful mind.	384	75
Vol. 2 continues the same course of reading, and introduces articles suited to the wants of the whole family circle....	416	75
Golden Grain Series, a choice collection of instructive stories suited to the wants of children from eight to sixteen years and older, illustrated and beautifully bound in two volumes.		
Vol. 1, The Hard Way, ...	160	50
Vol. 2, The School-boy's Dinner, ...	160	50
Other volumes in preparation.		
Golden Grains in Ten Pamphlets. The same reading is put up without pictures, in ten pamphlets of 32 pages each. In this form they are especially suited to Sabbath-school work, being unequaled as prizes for juvenile classes.		

	Pages.	Price.
No. 1. Robin's Judgment Book.		
No. 2. Annie's Savings Box.		
No. 3. Always the Bible.		
No. 4. The Hard Way.		
No. 5. The Sister's Lesson.		
No. 6. The School-boy's Dinner.		
No. 7. Seven Times.		
No. 8. The Wicket Gate.		
No. 9. The Sensitive Plant.		
No. 10. The Two Gardens.		
The Series,	320	50
The Sunshine Series. Stories for little ones, in ten small books, adapted to children from the ages of four to ten years and older, put up in glazed paper covers, each containing 32 pages of choicest moral and religious stories, taken from a mother's scrap-books of twenty years' collection.		
The Series,	320	50
The same reading in twenty plain books, for Sabbath-school prizes and rewards of merit,	320	40
The Child's Poems. Containing Little Will and other stories that will captivate the young reader and teach many lessons of temperance and virtue. Bound in cloth, and richly embossed with gold and black,	128	30
The Game of Life. Three lithographic illustrations, with explanations. These scenes represent Satan playing a game with man for his soul. In the first scene, The Game in Progress, Satan		

	Pages.	Price.
and man are represented as intent upon the game spread before them upon a covered sarcophagus. The second scene, The Game Lost, represents Satan as victor, man in despair. The Game Won reverses this scene. Neatly bound in board, ...		50
The Advent Keepsake. A collection of Bible texts for each day of the year, on the subjects of the Second Advent, the Resurrection, etc. Muslin,	136	25

CHARTS, PICTURES, ETC.

	Price.
The Way of Life; or, the Plan of Redemption from Paradise Lost to Paradise Restored. This is a beautiful and most instructive engraving, 19 x 24 inches, with a key of explanations.	1 00
The Prophetic Chart; illustrating the visions of Daniel and John. This chart is a fine lithograph 33x43 inches, and is much improved over former editions. Cloth, with rollers, the best form for those who carry them from place to place,	1 50
Paper, backed with cloth, a more elegant form for churches and families,	1 75
The Commandment Chart 33x43 inches. Cloth,	1 50
Paper, backed with cloth,	1 75

☞ Charts on rollers cannot be sent by mail. We will furnish them on cloth, without rollers, by mail, post-paid, at $1.50 each.

FOREIGN PUBLICATIONS.

FRENCH.

Les Signes des Temps. A monthly, same size as the *Review.* This is designed to be a pioneer paper, setting forth in a clear and pointed manner the reasons of our faith and hope. Published in French at Bâle, Switzerland, at $1.25 per year.

	Pages.	Price.
L'Objections contre l'Ancien Sabbat. Refutation of Thirty-eight So-called Objections to the Ancient Sabbath....	64	15
Comment le Sabbat a été Changé. How the Sabbath has been Changed; also Historical Facts concerning the Observance of the Seventh Day since the Time of the Apostles, with Remarks upon the Testimony of the Fathers.	32	10
The same in tract form,.........	32	4
La Grande Statue de Dan. 2. The Great Image of Dan. 2, and the Four Symbolical Beasts of Dan. 7......	32	8
Le Sabbat de la Bible. The Bible Sabbath.	32	8
Les Souffrances du Christ. Sufferings of Christ.........................	32	4
Le Second Avènement. The Second Advent; or, the Manner, Object, and Nearness of the Event............	32	4
Les Deux Trones. The Two Thrones, representing the Kingdoms of Grace and of Glory......................	32	4
Le Sanctuaire. The Sanctuary of the Bible.	16	2
Règne Millénaire. The Millennium......	16	2

	Pages.	Price.
Le Jugement. The Judgment; or, Waymarks of Daniel to the Holy City....	16	2
La Tempérance. Temperance...........	16	2
Défense de la Vérité. Defense of the Truth against the Attacks of a Pastor.....	16	2
Quel Jour Observez-vous? et Pourquoi? Which Day do you Keep? and Why?	8	1

GERMAN.

	Pages.	Price.
Das Wesen des Sabbaths. The Nature and Obligation of the Sabbath.........	80	10
Das zweite Kommen Christi. The Second Advent.........................	32	4
Die Leiden Christi. The Sufferings of Christ.	32	4
Die gegenwärtige Wahrheit. Present Truth..	32	4
Die zwei Throne. The Two Thrones.	32	4
Wer hat den Sabbath verändert? Who Changed the Sabbath?.................	24	3
Das Gericht. The Judgment.............	16	2
Das tausendjährige Reich. The Millennium.	16	2
Das Heiligthum. The Sanctuary of the Bible.	16	2
Die zwei Gesetze. The Two Laws.	16	2
Sieben Gründe. Seven Reasons for Sunday-Keeping Examined...............	16	2
Der Sabbath des Herrn. Elihu on the Sabbath....	16	2
Ohne Entschuldigung. Without Excuse.....	8	1
Welchen Tag feierst Du? Which Day do you Keep? and Why?...............	8	1
Betrachtungen über die Unsterblichkeit. Appeal on Immortality.................	8	1

DANISH.

Advent Tidende, a Danish-Norwegian monthly, devoted to practical religion, and treating upon the Prophecies, the Second Advent of Christ, the Millennium, Judgment, etc. Price, $1.00 a ye

	Pages.	Price.
Syvende-Dags Advent Bibliothek. Seventh-day Adventist Library. Vol. I. contains Life and Death, Sabbath Day, Second Advent, Scripture References, Forty Questions on Immortality	336	1 00
Bibelske Salmer og Lovsange. Bible Songs and Hymns	340	1 00
Profetiens Aand, No. 1. Spirit of Prophecy, No. 1. A translation of the first fourteen chapters of the English work by this name	144	25
De Helliges Arv. The Saints' Inheritance	112	20
Liv og Uforkrænkelighed. Life and Immortality	112	20
De Ugudeliges Straf. The Punishment of the Wicked	64	15
Det Nye Testamentes Sabbat. The New Testament Sabbath	64	15
"Efter Døden." After Death: a Review,...	32	10
Kristi andet Komme. Second Advent	32	4
Kristi Lidelser. Sufferings of Christ	32	4
De to Troner. The Two Thrones	32	4
"Efter Døden." After Death: a Review.	32	4
Henvisninger til Skriften. Scripture References	16	2

	Pages.	Price.
Herrens Sabbat. The Sabbath of the Lord.	16	2
Den rige Mand og Lazarus. The Rich Man and Lazarus	16	2
At opløses og være med Kristus. Departing and Being with Christ	16	2
Det tusindaarige Rige. The Millennium	16	2
Begge Sider af Sabbatsspørgsmaalet. Both Sides of the Sabbath Question; a Review	16	2
Dommen. The Judgment; Daniel's Waymarks to the Holy City............	16	2
Helligdommen. The Sanctuary	16	2
Guds Svar. God's Answers to Man's Excuses for not Keeping the Sabbath...	4	½
Et vigtigt Spørgsmaal. Which Day do you Keep? and Why?	4	½
Det himmelske Møde. The Heavenly Meeting.	4	½
Forbuden Grund. Forbidden Ground	4	½
En kort Fremstilling af det profetiske Ord. Bird's Eye View of the Field of Prophecy,		5

SWEDISH.

Svensk Advent Härold is a Swedish monthly of 24 pages, devoted to practical religion, the explanation of the prophecies, the proclamation of the second coming of Christ, etc. It sets forth the Bible truths pertaining to this generation and time. It also contains a health department and a home and school department. Subscription: $1.00 year.

	Pages.	Price.
Andeliga Sånger. Spiritual Songs, a neat little pamphlet containing 88 selected songs......................Cloth,	64	30
Same in paper covers,...........		20

	Pages.	Price.
De twå Tronerna. The Two Thrones......	32	4
Kristi Andra Ankomst. The Second Advent..	32	4
De Dödes Tillstånd. The State of the Dead.	32	4
Hänwisningar till Skriften. Scripture References..............................	24	3
Hwem förändrade Sabbaten? Who Changed the Sabbath?..........................	24	3
Domen. The Judgment....................	16	2
Herrens Sabbat. The Sabbath of the Lord.	16	2
"Sju Grunder" för Söndagens Helighållande. An Examination of Seven Reasons for Sunday-Keeping.............	16	2
Kristi Lidanden. The Sufferings of Christ...	16	2
Det Tusenåriga Riket. The Millennium.....	16	2
Att Skiljas hädan och wara när Kristus. Departing and Being with Christ.....	16	2
Helgedomen. The Sanctuary.............	16	2
De Ogudaktiges Ändalykt. The End of the Wicked............................	16	2
Sabbaten och Söndagen. The Sabbath and Sunday........................	8	1
Budordens Fullkomlighet. Perfection of the Ten Commandments.............	8	1
Sjunde-dags Adventisternas Grundprinciper..... Fundamental Principles of Seventh-day Adventists......................	8	1
Tankar för de Uppriktige. Thoughts for the Candid............................	8	1
Upprop öfwer Odödligheten. Appeal on Immortality..........................	8	1
Kort Framställning af Profetiorna. Bird's Eye View of the Field of Prophecy......		5

PERIODICALS.

The Advent Review and Sabbath Herald.—An eight-page weekly. This is a religious family paper, devoted to an earnest and thorough investigation of all Bible questions. It is an exponent of the solemn truths that pertain to the present time, some of which are set forth by no periodicals in the land except those issued by S. D. Adventists. Terms, $2.00 per year.

The Youth's Instructor.—This is the title of an eight-page, illustrated, monthly sheet for youth and children. It inculcates the highest morality, and seeks to interest the minds of the young in religious things. We confidently offer it as the best paper for youth and children now published. Terms, 50 cts. a year, in advance.

The Health Reformer.—A live monthly journal devoted to physical, mental, and moral improvement. It teaches the true philosophy of life, the only rational method of treating disease, and the best means of preserving health. Practical instructions are given from month to month relative to water, air, light, food, sleep, rest, recreation, etc. Terms, $1.00 a year, in advance.

The Signs of the Times.—A large, eight-page weekly, same size as the *Review*, issued at Oakland, California. This is designed to be a pioneer paper, setting forth in a clear and pointed manner the reasons of our faith and hope. Terms, $2.00 a year.

The Advent Tidende.—This is a monthly issued in the Danish language, advocating the same truths taught by the *Review*. $1.00 per year.

The Svensk Advent Harold.—A monthly in the Swedish language, designed to teach people of that tongue the great truths of the third angel's message. $1.00 per year.

Les Signes Des Temps.—A monthly, same size as the *Review*, published in French, at Bâle, Switzerland, at $1.25 per year.

Any of the publications and periodicals in this Catalogue will be furnished by mail, postage paid, at the prices named. Address, REVIEW AND HERALD, *Battle Creek, Mich.*, or, PACIFIC PRESS, *Oakland, California.*

www.ingramcontent.com/pod-product-compliance
Lightning Source LLC
LaVergne TN
LVHW020125110826
845151LV00001B/280

* 9 7 8 1 4 2 5 5 4 0 7 1 5 *